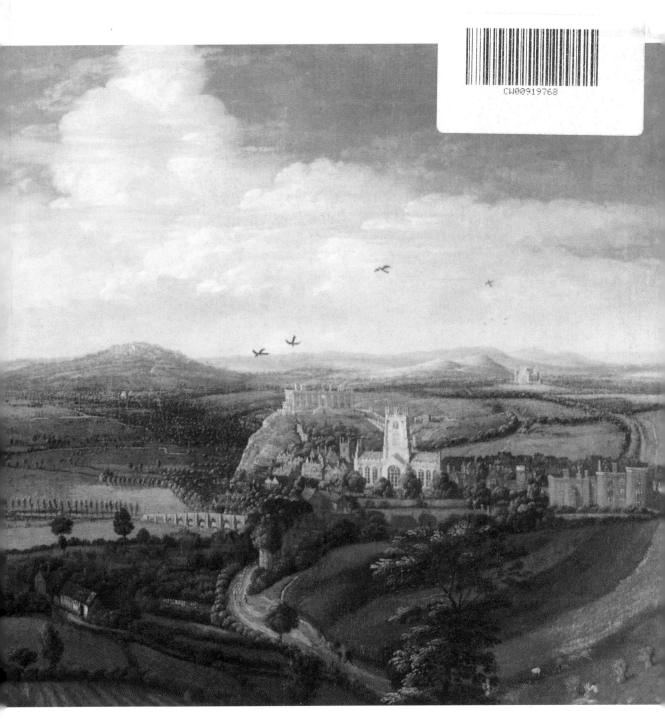

'View of Nottingham from the East', by Jan Sibrechts, c. 1627-1703.

A History of
Nottingham

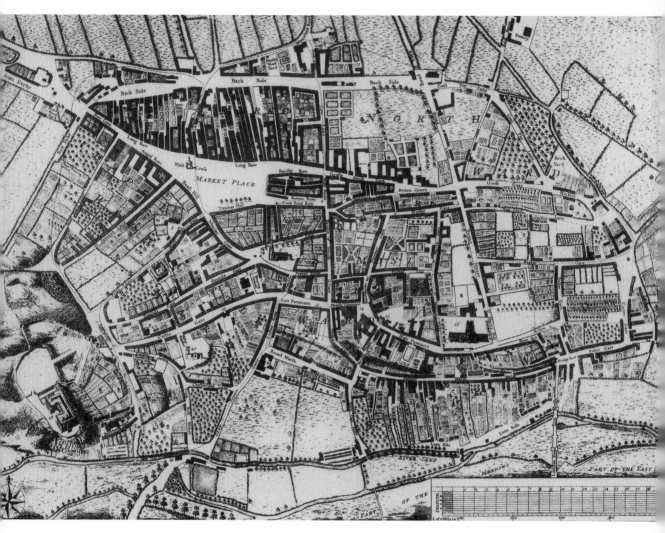

Nottingham, 1744; Badder and Peat's map, drawn for Deering's History.

A HISTORY OF
NOTTINGHAM

Richard Gurnham

PHILLIMORE

2010
Published by
PHILLIMORE & CO. LTD
Andover, Hampshire, England
www.phillimore.co.uk

ISBN 978-1-86077-658-8

Printed and bound in Great Britain
Manufactured by Jellyfish Print Solutions Ltd

CONTENTS

To Jeannie.

LIST OF ILLUSTRATIONS

Frontispiece – Nottingham, 1744; Badder and Peat's map, drawn for Deering's History.

ACKNOWLEDGEMENTS

It is a pleasure to acknowledge and thank those who have helped me in any way in writing this history of Nottingham, and my first thanks must go to those who first sparked off my interest in the history of the city: the late Professor J.D. Chambers and Professor S.D. Chapman. When I first came to Nottingham in 1968, as an 18-year-old student coming to the University of Nottingham to study Economic and Social History, Professor Chambers was an Emeritus Professor and, as my own sixth-form students would say now, already a 'legend'. Professor Chambers' contribution to the study of the history of the city and county of Nottingham, particularly in the 18th and 19th centuries, is immense, and he was already long recognised in 1968 as one of the founding fathers of modern social and economic history. Professor Chapman was one of my lecturers when I first 'went up' to Nottingham, but also later my tutor for my PhD. This was a study of the history of trade unionism in the local hosiery and knitwear industry, and it was in undertaking this research that I first became truly immersed in the history of the city. One of the many pleasures I had in writing this book has been to re-visit some of those aspects of Nottingham's history which I first learnt about all those years ago as a young postgraduate student. As my very select bibliography indicates, I have relied heavily on the researches and writings of both Professors Chambers and Chapman in putting this book together.

Nottingham has been well served by its historians. For any serious student of the city's history the starting point today has to be *A Centenary History of Nottingham*, edited by Professor John Beckett, which was first published in 1997. This is a superb example of collaborative historical writing, to which more than twenty historians and archaeologists have contributed, and from which I have also drawn heavily. A much briefer history, *Nottingham: An Illustrated History* has also been written by Professor Beckett and in 2002 Chris Weir brought out his very readable and relatively brief *Nottingham: A History*, which tells the story of the city's development in the last hundred years. My intention in writing this history is to try to offer the interested general reader a study that charts the main themes of the city's history from its earliest years to the present in rather more detail than these two works but which is (hopefully) equally readable.

In trying to find illustrations for this book I have also incurred many debts and I am most grateful to those who have let me reproduce pictures they hold. The *Nottingham Post* has been most helpful in letting me use pictures from their archives, namely illustrations 19, 31, 33, 41, 75, 80-1, 101-2 and 110. Sarah Skinner, the Keeper of Fine Art for Nottingham City Museums and Galleries, kindly let me use illustrations from the Nottingham Castle Guide and from the permanent Story of Nottingham exhibition in the castle: illustrations 2, 3, 10, 17, 22, 28, 35, 37 and endpapers, and the Nottingham Archives has also been most helpful, allowing me to reproduce illustrations 7, 27, 42, 55, 62, 78, 85, 87-9, 92, 97-100, 103, 106, 108. Two of the great companies which have played such an important role in the history of the city in the last 150 years, Alliance-Boots and Raleigh Cycle Limited, have also been most co-operative. Boots UK Archives let me use illustrations 69-71 and Raleigh gave permission to use illustrations 67-8, 91 and 105. Many pictures have also come from my own collection and I must thank my wife for taking the photographs which appear here of Nottingham today.

I am also very grateful to the staff of Nottinghamshire Local Studies Library, who were invariably very helpful, to Dr Tom Green for his expert advice regarding some aspects of the first chapter, and to Mr Ken Woolley, whose reminiscences of his childhood days in pre-war and wartime Nottingham have helped bring extra colour and human detail to these sections of the last chapter. Finally, and as always, I must thank my family, and especially my wife Jeannie, who has once more had to put up with living with the writing of a book for the last two years, but has also contributed a great deal to it, not only by taking so many photographs but also by reading through the first drafts of the chapters and suggesting numerous improvements. Responsibility for all errors and omissions, however, must be mine.

ONE
Origins

The First Inhabitants

Men and women have been living on the site now occupied by the city of Nottingham for many thousands of years. Long before the arrival of the last ice age, hunter-gatherers passed this way as they followed their migrating prey. Their stone tools have been found at a number of sites across the East Midlands, including Stoney Street and Tottle Brook gravel pits in Beeston, to the west of the city, and excavations on the castle site have revealed the flintwork of communities living here between 10,000 and 4,000 B.C., in the years of the warmer climate that followed the last ice age. The first farmers have also left traces of their presence during the following two millennia, including two axe-hammers, one found in the area of the Victoria Centre and the other at Wollaton Park. Moreover, not far away, near Attenborough and Holme Pierrepoint, gravel extraction has revealed fragments of Neolithic pottery.

Most notable of all has been the abundant evidence of Bronze-Age habitation. Many bronze tools and weapons have been found in the Nottingham area, dating from the second and early first millennia B.C. Most have been found in the River Trent and other local rivers, but important finds have also been made in the city. During building work in Great Freeman Street in 1860 workmen unearthed a hoard of late Bronze-Age metalwork comprising 10 socketed axes, some of which were broken, a palstave, a hollow ring, four spearheads and a spear shaft 'ferule', perhaps collected together by a metalworker for re-casting.

Large numbers of Iron-Age sites have also been found in the Trent valley near Nottingham and in the city. During excavations in 1994, in the area of the former north bailey of the castle, pottery was found that could be tentatively dated to the Iron Age, and Late Iron Age pottery has also been found during excavations at Willoughby House on Low Pavement, at Fisher Gate, at Halifax Place, and in a shallow ditch between Barker Gate and Woolpack Lane. Evidence of Roman occupation, however, is very slight, both in the city itself and in the surrounding area: a little pottery, a Roman brooch of the first century, and at least one coin, a second-century sestertius, probably of Antoninus Pius (A.D. 138-61) found by metal detecting. The most substantial find has been a small horde of coins near the River Trent at Clifton. Nor is there any evidence that the Romans exploited the shallowness of

the Trent at this point to develop north-south communications. The main crossings of
the Trent for Roman travellers lay downriver at Thorpe by East Stoke, known in Roman
times as *Ad Pontem,* and to the west at Sawley near Derby. The Fosse Way ran north, from
Leicester to Lincoln, following for a while the Trent valley, but no road was built to branch
off towards Nottingham.

The Settlement of Snot's People

The archaeological evidence suggests that the first Anglo-Saxon settlement in Nottingham
was to the east of the site of St Mary's church. Saxon pottery, dating from the seventh or
eighth century, has been found near Fisher Gate. Moreover, the pottery was found in what
would seem to have been a ditch that had been part of the defensive system of a small
fortified enclosure. This impression is given further weight by the discovery of what would
appear to be more sections of the same ditch between Woolpack Lane and Barker Gate.
The first Anglo-Saxon settlement was therefore possibly a place of strategic importance: a
fortified enclosure commanding both the crossings of the rivers Trent and Leen and also
the east-west trackway which ran along the north side of the Trent valley. The enclosure was
probably defended by the ditch on the north, west and south sides, and on the east side
by a little river, known as the Beck, which flowed north-south to form a tributary of the
Leen. The cemetery for the little community lay about a mile to the east. An early Anglo-
Saxon cemetery, and one of the very few yet found on the west bank of the Trent, has been
recorded in the Netherfield area, near Carlton. The earliest name of the settlement – which
first appears in the *Anglo-Saxon Chronicle* in A.D. 868 – is *Snotengaham,* meaning the *ham*
or 'settlement' of Snot's people, and names such as this, indicating a territory controlled by
a tribal or family group, are usually associated with Anglo-Saxon settlements of the sixth
and seventh centuries.

On the top of this sandstone hill above the marshy lands bordering the wide Trent, this
was surely a site well chosen for its defensive capabilities. And for the earliest Anglo-Saxon
arrivals in this area this would have been of the utmost importance, for they were a
minority people in a hostile environment. The absence of early Anglo-Saxon cremation
or inhumation cemeteries west of the Trent suggests that the Germanic migrants did not
settle west of the river Trent before about A.D. 600 and place-name evidence suggests that
many settlements to the west of Nottingham long remained in British hands, particularly
in the region of Burton on Trent, where we find place-names beginning in Wal-,
indicating a Welshman, or foreigner, and Bret-, suggesting the settlement of Britons.
Moreover, to the north the archaeological record suggests that this remained a largely
empty, well-forested border area in the seventh century, a battleground for powerful and
ambitious Mercian kings challenging the territorial claims of equally determined and
ambitious kings of Northumbria.

The settlers would also at first have been greatly outnumbered by their British hosts,
among whom they lived but who spoke a different language and shared a different culture
and religion. The relatively small number of immigrants probably meant that the community
could only grow by inter-marriage with the British population. Eventually the Germanic
language would outlive its Celtic forebear, and today very few Celtic place-names survive.
As late as the ninth century the monk Asser (the biographer of King Alfred) referred to the
settlement at Nottingham by an Old Welsh name: *Tig Guocobauc,* which translates literally

1   *Caves in Brewhouse Yard.*

as 'House of caves', but this was very probably not a genuine earlier name for Nottingham. In their translation of Asser's work, Simon Keynes and Michael Lapidge suggest that this was Asser's own invention.

Today, Nottingham is almost as famous for its caves as it is for Robin Hood and its castle, and it is possible that the existence of the caves may also have been one of the reasons for the choice of this site by the first Anglo-Saxon settlers. The caves had long been used as a place of shelter and habitation, and would prove useful as a place of refuge in times of danger. The area had other attractions too. The land immediately below the hill was too marshy for settlement but provided valuable summer pasturage for herds of sheep, and the settlement was close to the fresh water supplies of the river Leen and other rivulets that ran into both the Leen and the Trent. A great variety of fish could be caught in the two rivers and the land of the Trent valley was very suitable for these farmers from the cold plains of North Germany. Food offerings from the cremation cemeteries demonstrate the keeping of sheep and pigs in this area, although cattle are rarely represented and this may suggest that at this early stage the numbers of cattle kept by the settlers were relatively small. Grain impressions on early Anglian pottery indicate that wheat, barley, oats and flax were all grown, and some of the nearby place-names are also evidence of both pastoral and arable farming.

When Snot's people established their settlement, probably in the late sixth or early seventh century, the area to the south and east of the Trent was already being settled by

Germanic immigrants. During the sixth and seventh centuries numerous Anglo-Saxon chieftains attempted to carve out their territories. The eponymous Snot may well have been such a chieftain, and *Snotengaham* the chief centre of the territory of the *Snotingas*. Writing in the early 12th century, Henry of Huntingdon was probably reflecting a long-established oral tradition when he wrote of the Midland counties in the sixth century:

> At that time many came from Germany, and on many occasions, and they occupied East Anglia and Mercia, but they were not yet brought under one king. Many leaders occupied these regions, whence innumerable wars arose. The names of the leaders, since they are so many, are unknown.

During the sixth and seventh centuries many of these territories were brought under the control of more powerful neighbours, and by the middle of the seventh century the leaders of one such powerful group, the kings of Mercia, had established their hegemony over the rest. The first about whom we know more than just his name was Penda, who succeeded Pypba as king of Mercia in A.D. 632. At his death, in 655, he was leading an army composed of 30 subordinate rulers and their contingents, including Welsh kings and the king of Lindsey. If *Snotengaham* existed by this time – and it probably did – its inhabitants would have been subjects of King Penda.

An Administrative Centre for Mercian Kings?

It is generally thought that at the time Nottingham first comes into the historical record, in A.D. 868, when the *Anglo-Saxon Chronicle* records the arrival of the Danish army, it was a fairly small settlement, of little importance to either the Danes or the English. There is some evidence, however, to suggest that in the century before the Viking conquest Nottingham might already have become a high-status Mercian settlement.

Although only a small area may have been fortified at first, the area that came to be placed under the control of *Snotengaham* seems to have been quite substantial. One village that was almost certainly included was Sneinton, whose original name, *Snotinton,* means 'village of Snot's people'. Another was Whiston, now one of the city's northern suburbs, for its church, St Michael's, was part of the parish of St Mary's. We can learn much about early estate boundaries from the lands later held by the parish church, for these boundaries are often very ancient and may have been the same as the original territory of the *Snotingas*. Many of the lands held by St Mary's church were given to Lenton Priory shortly after the Norman Conquest, making it difficult to identify the likely size of the estate, but it could well have been composed of most of the lands in the immediate vicinity of the borough at the time of the Conquest: Lenton, Radford, Basford, Arnold, West Bridgeford, Wilford, Barton and Clifton.

Large estates such as this were common in the eighth and ninth centuries. Mercian kings found this a convenient means of collecting tribute, principally in the form of food rents. These might include vats of honey, bread loaves, ale, cows, sheep, geese, hens, cheeses, butter and fish. Estates were also expected to provide men for military service and help in constructing bridges and fortifications. Moreover, if any of the king's officials, or the king himself, should choose to stay on the estate then the expense had to be met by the inhabitants. A charter of one Mercian king, Ceolwulf I, dated A.D. 822, lists the wide variety of officials who might have to be catered for. They included the king himself, bishops, ealdormen, reeves, tax gatherers, and keepers of dogs, horses or hawks.

The large size of the Nottingham estate means that it was also possibly a centre for administrative purposes. Later, in the 10th century, it would be given responsibility for the administration of the four wapentakes and four half-wapentakes that composed the shire and this suggests it had long been an important royal centre, perhaps as early as the seventh or eighth century. The larger Mercian estates frequently became the permanent bases for royal officials, from which they could operate and where they could collect and store the food rents, and Nottingham's highly defensible position, together with its strategic position controlling the Trent crossing, made it a likely choice. At the time of the Norman Conquest we are informed by Domesday Book that the king and earl owned substantial property in the city and the surrounding district. This is also often an indication of a base for an ealdorman or other royal agent in the period of Mercian rule.

This, of course, has to be speculation, but the archaeological evidence is supportive. An excavation at Halifax Place, just to the west of St Mary's church, has revealed that here, right on top of the hill, there was built in the eighth century a large timber hall, probably surrounded by its own enclosure. This was built in two phases and then later replaced, perhaps in the ninth century, by an even larger bow-sided hall, probably also with its own enclosure. The eighth-century hall has not been fully excavated but it was clearly a very substantial building indeed. It was at least a hundred feet long and therefore as large as any hall known to have been built in England at this time. This building probably stood until the early ninth century, when it was replaced by a series of three similar halls a little to the west, the last of which was taken down in the early 11th century. All these buildings seem to have faced towards the track that would become High Pavement. Throughout this long period, and in the medieval era as well, this would be the main street of the Anglo-Saxon borough. All these buildings were constructed in timber and it is highly likely that the first church on the site, perhaps also dating to the eighth century, would have been built of wood as well, on the site now occupied by St Mary's. The first stone building to be found was a large aisle

2 *Reconstruction drawing of eighth- or ninth-century bow-sided hall building discovered at Halifax Place.*

hall, built probably at the end of the 11th century and, like its timber predecessors, also facing High Pavement. These grand halls would have been fit for the entertainment of a Mercian king, and they have been compared to very similar great halls discovered in excavations at Northampton, next to St Nicholas's church, which are believed to be Mercian royal palaces.

The Viking Invasion and Settlement

The *Anglo-Saxon Chronicle* records that in A.D. 866 a Danish army – 'the great heathen host' – invaded England and established its winter quarters in East Anglia. In the following year it moved north, crossed the Humber, and took York. An attempt by the Northumbrians to re-take the city was defeated 'and great slaughter was made of the Northumbrians there'. That winter the surviving Danes stayed in York but in the following year they struck south again, this time towards Mercia, and in 868 Nottingham consequently appeared for the first time in the *Chronicle*:

> In this year the same host went into Mercia to Nottingham, and there took winter-quarters. And Burghred, king of Mercia, and his councillors begged Æthelred, king of Wessex, and his brother Alfred to help them fight against the host; and then they proceeded with the West Saxon levies into Mercia as far as Nottingham, and came upon the host there in the fortification, and besieged it therein, but there was no serious engagement, and the Mercians made peace with the host.

Archaeological excavations have not yet identified with any certainty the fortifications defended by the Danes in 868, but discoveries so far make it very likely that they were on St Mary's hill. This hill is not quite as high as the one to the west, on which the Normans would later build their castle, but it afforded considerably more level ground and

3   *Reconstruction drawing showing how the defences of the Saxon borough were constructed.*

was highly defensible. The steep slope of the cliff to the south provided a natural defence and the Beck, the little stream to the east, would also have been a useful barrier.

The enclosure thought to have surrounded the great hall at Halifax Place was probably utilised by the Danes, but another possibility is that the Danes built the defences which were later rebuilt and added to by the English king, Edward the Elder, when he re-conquered Mercia in 918. The Chronicler, Æthelweard, states that this was the case and excavations have revealed that the defences associated with Edward the Elder were built in two stages. The difficulty with this theory, however, is that these fortifications were extremely substantial, and it seems unlikely that the Danes would have gone to so much trouble to build such defences in 868. They seemed to have no intention at this stage of remaining in Nottingham for more than the winter, and in the following year they did indeed return to York. Moreover, the fortifications which they are thought to have erected

at Repton and Stamford in this period were much more modest.

The king of Mercia's dependence on West Saxon help and his consequent failure to dislodge the Danes in 868 were probably a consequence of the weakened state of the Mercian monarchy at this time. Many of the Mercian aristocracy did not accept his right to rule, instead favouring an alternative royal line which had strong connections with the Nottingham area, and in 874 King Burghred was replaced by a member of this royal line, Ceowulf II, probably with Danish help. The new king, however, would enjoy little independence, for in 877 Danish warlords took control of a large area of the East Midlands, including Nottingham, and for more than 40 years Nottingham would remain in Danish hands.

Almost nothing is known about the years of Danish control. One expert on this period, Dr Roffe, has suggested that the settlement was probably of relatively little political or military significance in this period and consequently may not have been garrisoned by the Danes for many years. The principal Danish centre was at York and the forces there could be sent quickly to Nottingham if needed. This situation changed, however, when Edward the Elder and his sister Æthelflæda began a highly successful joint campaign to re-conquer Mercia and enjoyed their first major success in 910, with the defeat of a Danish army in Northamptonshire. In 917 Æthelflæda took Derby and the battle for Nottingham seemed imminent. But now a new enemy appeared, threatening both English and Danish interests, in the shape of the powerful Norwegian Viking forces of King Rægnald. Fearful – and rightfully so – that they could not hold even their chief centre, York, against Rægnald's forces, the Danish garrison at Nottingham quickly submitted to Edward, who, the *Chronicle* reports, hurried there from Wales to secure his position:

> Then he went thence to Nottingham and occupied the borough: he had it repaired and garrisoned both by Englishmen and Danes, and all the people settled in Mercia, both Danish and English, submitted to him.

And two years later Edward was back again, but now the strategic importance of the settlement was greater than ever, for in 919 the Norsemen had taken York, and Nottingham was now of vital importance for the defence of Edward's recently expanded realm. The Trent was an obvious highway south for the Norse armies now occupying York and Edward was determined that here their passage would be firmly resisted. As well as strengthening the fortification at Nottingham, he now also ordered the building of a second fort immediately to the south of the river, together with a bridge, as the *Chronicle* again records:

> Before midsummer King Edward went to Nottingham with his levies, and had a fortress built on the south side of the river, opposite to the other, and made a bridge over the Trent to connect the two forts.

All trace of this second fort has disappeared and it would seem that it enjoyed only a brief existence. This is not true, however, of the mighty defences that were probably now erected on Edward's orders at Nottingham itself. A ditch of some 30 feet wide and at least 15 feet deep was cut, surrounding the settlement on three sides: on the north, west and east, with the cliff providing a natural barrier to the south. Behind the ditch a great timber rampart formed a second line of defence. Although it is possible that Edward simply repaired defences already erected by the Danes, the dimensions of the fortifications suggest that this was entirely Edward's work, for they were similar to those of the fortresses that he and his father had long been erecting in Wessex as the chief focus for their defence of Southern England against the Danes.

An Anglo-Danish Borough

The great earthen and timber defences that surrounded Nottingham in the 10th century can be traced today in the street pattern of this part of the modern city (see map of Nottingham today on frontispiece). Warser Gate and Woolpack Lane together run immediately to the south of the northern wall, while just to the north of the line, and almost parallel with it, are Goosegate and Carlton Street; Belward and Bellargate follow the line of the eastern wall and ditch; and the western defences run roughly midway between Fletchergate on their eastern side and Bridlesmithgate on their west. Today there is a drop of about ten feet between Fletchergate and Bridlesmithgate; this may indicate the height of the rampart.

The cost and labour of building and maintaining the defences, and of manning the garrison, fell on both the inhabitants and the surrounding countryside. The task for the fortresses north and south of the river was to defend river and road communications, the latter now greatly improved by the building of a bridge. The degree of taxation was calculated according to the size of the two enclosures and the number of men required to garrison them. This was no doubt an onerous and much resented burden, imposed by a Wessex overlord, but the town was now a royal centre established to administer a wide area.

Nottingham now had the right to mint coins and to administer an area that may have composed not only much of the modern county but also a substantial area of Derbyshire, including the borough of Derby and the town of Ashbourne. Both these towns seem to have been still paying tolls to the burgesses of Nottingham in the late 12th century. The tolls collected at this time suggest that the late Saxon borough of Nottingham had authority over an area stretching from the Trent valley westwards to the valley of the river Dove and northwards to the river Ryton.

The heavy Danish settlement of the area meant that the inhabitants' allegiance to the English Crown was always uncertain. During the reign of Athelstan (924-39) the five boroughs of the area known as the Danelaw (Derby, Leicester, Lincoln, Nottingham and

Stamford) appear to have remained reasonably securely in the king's hands, and coins minted for Athelstan in Nottingham are among the few survivals so far discovered in the city from this period. Following his death, however, the Scandinavian warrior chief Olaf Guthfrithson attempted to regain control of both York and the Midlands and he was soon successful. The existence of a powerful Danish contingent in the town probably explains the swift submission of Nottingham to Guthfrithson. In 940 Athelstan's heir and younger brother, King Edmund, formally recognised the secession of Nottingham and the other Danelaw boroughs to the Anglo-Scandinavian crown of Northumbria.

But Edmund had no intention of leaving matters like this for long, and only two years later he was back in the area with sufficient force to oblige the five boroughs to once again accept English control. The Humber again became the southern border of Northumbria and Nottingham's importance as protector of a vital highway north was undeniable. It was now that the defences of the town were strengthened and the loyalty of the town reinforced by English colonisation. A new fortification was also erected at Newark, whose name means 'new fort', and the town was shortly afterwards placed under the control of Nottingham.

Acceptance of royal authority was further strengthened by dividing the whole of the Danelaw area into wapentakes, each with a royal court with power to administer the collection of taxes, to raise militia armies for the defence of the region, the administration of justice, and the maintenance of the king's peace. Nottingham was given authority over four wapentakes and four half-wapentakes, and later in the century this area became the territory of the shire of Nottingham, administered by a royal agent, the shire reeve, or sheriff. Nottingham's pre-eminence in the East Midlands was further emphasised by placing the newly created shire of Derby also under the authority of the sheriff of Nottingham and the leading men of both shires met together with the sheriff at the Moot Hall, in the street now known as Friar Lane. The English kings wisely made no attempt to undermine Danish customs or culture and in return the Danish landowners appear to have accepted and administered the new system loyally and successfully, guaranteeing English control of the Danelaw until the invasion of King Swein of Denmark, and his son, Cnut, in 1013.

During Cnut's reign (1016-35) the whole of the Danelaw area was placed under the administration of the larger area of the earldom of Mercia, but the wapentake courts had already proved themselves too useful to kings to be tampered with, particularly in the raising of taxes and armies, and sheriffs also continued to be appointed as the king's agent for the shires.

Nottingham in 1066

When Anglo-Saxon rule in England came to an end on Senlac Hill in October 1066, the borough of Nottingham, for all its importance as an administrative centre for two shires, was still a relatively small market town of perhaps a little under a thousand people; a small compact community of craftsmen and traders serving the local rural area. There is evidence, however, of at least modest growth in the late 10th or early 11th century. Excavation of a site between Woolpack Lane and Barker Gate revealed that land had been cleared for development and new structures erected in the late 10th and early 11th centuries. At this stage there was clearly still room for development within the town's great earthen walls and wooden palisade. The new structures – probably modest housing and workshops – were

4   *St Mary's church.*

well spaced but extended up to the intramural road. The walls and their gates necessarily dictated the road pattern, and the pattern of streets found in the later medieval period was probably already almost complete before the Norman Conquest.

The earliest stone buildings to have been found within the walled area date from the late 11th century – in other words from the post-Conquest Norman era. Anglo-Saxon Nottingham was probably an entirely wood-and-earth-built town. It is possible that St Mary's church had been rebuilt in stone before the Conquest but no trace of any Saxon work has survived and we know that the church was rebuilt in stone in the Norman period. Two arches from this era survive today, although unfortunately no longer as part of the church. The church we see today is almost entirely 15th-century but two Norman arches taken from an earlier St Mary's can still be seen in the plain brick wall of a warehouse in Broadway.

Whether of wood or stone, the Saxon church of St Mary was an important early Christian centre. It was probably a minster church, founded by a Mercian king possibly as early as the late seventh century, and able to draw on the renders, taxes and offerings of a large royal estate covering much of the area now part of the city of Nottingham. At the beginning of 1066 it was still a royal church, the property of King Edward the Confessor, and the only church for this royal borough.

In 1066 the shire of Nottingham was part of the diocese and province of York, and had been so for about a hundred years, but the early history of Christianity in the Nottingham area was also intimately related to the history of the Mercian church. Christianity had not been established in this area until relatively late, until the latter half of the seventh century, for King Penda of Mercia (632-55) had lived and died a pagan. However, he had agreed to the conversion of his son, Peada, on his marriage to the daughter of the Christian king of Northumbria, Oswiu, in about 653. Four priests had been allowed to accompany the young couple on their return to Penda's kingdom, and on Penda's death in 655 one of the four, an Irish priest known as Diuma, was consecrated as the first bishop of the Middle Angles and Mercians by Bishop Finan of Lindisfarne. Conversions probably followed soon after this but progress must have been slow for Diuma and his successors were responsible for a vast area, stretching across much of the area of Mercian control, from the Humber to the Thames and from the Severn to the Wash. The first churches established to assist the bishops in their tasks were built either in former Roman cities, such as Lincoln, York and Leicester, or on royal estates, and it is likely that St Mary's church was one of the latter.

If this was the case, then St Mary's would have been the main centre for evangelism for a wide area and this in turn would almost certainly mean that it would have been served by a community of clerks and chaplains, living rather like a monastic community, close to the church. The street pattern of the borough may be evidence for such a community. The absence of an east-west road running through the borough might be explained by the early existence of a large and perhaps enclosed church site stretching north of St Mary's, up to Warser Gate and the northern defences, with St Mary's Gate marking the western boundary and Stoney Street the eastern. It was perhaps this part of the town that the Domesday survey of 1086 describes as 'the priest's croft'. The nature and usage of this property may have changed considerably since it was first established, but its continuing value to the church, and therefore to the king, was spelt out clearly by the survey. We are told that it now contained 65 houses, or about a third of the entire borough.

The great majority of the householders in the town in 1066 were tradesmen and craftsmen. Of the 192 householders in the town at the time of the Conquest, 173 are described as burgesses and only 19 as villeins. The principal occupation for this latter, relatively low status, group would have been farmwork on the town's open fields. The burgesses were townsmen who were free from the obligations of labour services and most probably paid their dues to the king's agents mainly in cash. Most of them would have earned their living by the making and selling of goods for the local community but a minority – 35 to be precise – were also farmers, employing between them 20 smallholders, and farming between them six carucates of the town's fields, or approximately 720 acres of arable and pasture land. They also had rights to graze their animals on the town meadows and, most important for pig keeping, also in the woodlands on the edge of the town, which are described as six furlongs long (three-quarters of a mile) and five furlongs wide. Most of the 19 villeins recorded were probably tenants of the farmer-burgesses.

Nottingham had not grown as quickly in the previous 150 years as some of the other Danelaw towns. Lincoln, in particular, had grown far more rapidly and was by this time a much larger city. Nottingham had probably only become a market town in 920, when the bridge was erected over the Trent, greatly improving its communications, and the mint established in the town at about the same time was much smaller than that at Lincoln. In 1066 there were two moneyers. There is evidence of pottery being made in Nottingham from the late 10th century, for distinctive wares and kilns have been found, and the scale and quality of work was sufficient for the pottery to be traded across the shire. But Nottingham had not yet developed as an important industrial centre, unlike Lincoln and Stamford, and for many years after the Conquest it would remain of primarily military and strategic importance, rather than a commercial centre.

Two

The Medieval Town, 1066-1500

A New Castle and a New Borough

William the Conqueror was not slow to recognise the strategic importance of Nottingham's position as a gateway to the north. During the winter of 1067-8, little more than a year after his victory at Hastings, a serious rebellion threatened to break out in the northern counties, centred on York. One of William's first actions to secure his authority in the north was to order the building of a castle at Nottingham. The *Anglo-Saxon Chronicle* tells us:

> When the king was informed that the people in the north had gathered together, and would oppose him if he came, he marched to Nottingham and built a castle there …

He then proceeded to York, where he built two more castles, and to Lincoln, where some of the surviving Roman walls were utilised to build another. His new castle at Nottingham was therefore part of a network of strongholds required to protect and preserve his fragile hold on the Crown, and to deal swiftly with any challenge either from abroad or from a bitter and resentful population. The castle at Nottingham was built, says William Camden, writing in the 17th century, 'to bridle the English'.

Like most of the other castles built at this time, Nottingham Castle was built of earth and wood: a motte and bailey castle consisting of a number of enclosures each protected by a palisade of wooden stakes on an earth rampart, surrounded by a series of broad ditches. The first phase of the structure would probably have been put up quite quickly, with the unskilled labour force provided by local people, under the supervision of their new Norman masters. The site chose itself: a rocky crag with steep cliffs overlooking the river Leen, immediately to the south, and the Saxon borough only 500 metres away to the east. The highest point, at the southern end of the rock, provided a natural motte. While the cliffs to the south constituted what appeared to be an insuperable barrier, the ground to the north could be soon protected with a ditch and palisade to complete the motte's defences, and this was probably the first part of the castle to be built. This was the heart of the castle and must have enclosed the private accommodation of the constable or his deputy, perhaps a small hall or tower. The castle bailey, similarly defended, was then added on the slightly lower land

5   *A castle under attack, from the Bayeux Tapestry.*

to the north, enclosing an area about 230 to 263 feet wide and 328 feet long, large enough to house a small permanent garrison. Finally, to complete the defences and provide an outer bailey capable of housing a division of cavalry, a large area to the east and north was also enclosed by a third line of ditch and rampart.

The Conqueror gave the castle to one of his most trusted knights, William Peveril, who was rumoured to be William's illegitimate son and who had fought with William at Hastings. Peveril was richly rewarded for his loyalty with lands in Nottinghamshire and Derbyshire, including a second castle at Castleton. He was also made sheriff of the county and few, if any, of those who held the post of sheriff in the first half of the 12th century were not Peveril men.

Peveril could have relied on the existing Saxon town to supply provisions for the castle but he preferred to use the land between the castle and the town to have a new or 'French' borough laid out, peopled with new settlers, and placed under his own separate authority. Three new streets were made, Friar Lane, Hounds Gate and Castle Gate, each radiating out eastwards from the east gate of the outer bailey of the castle, and he probably intended to develop a new market place immediately outside the castle gate. Before the Conquest this area of relatively low land had been the property of Earl Tosti, King Harold's treacherous brother, who had attempted to overthrow Harold but died at Stamford Bridge fighting alongside Hardrada, the king of Norway. Tosti had been appointed Earl of Mercia by Edward the Confessor but the earldom was abolished by William and Tosti's lands in Nottinghamshire were given to Peveril.

The new borough was already established by the time Domesday Book was compiled in 1086, when we are told that the former sheriff, 'Hugh, son of Baldric', had built 13 houses on the land which was now part of 'the new borough'. Most of those who are listed as tenants of William Peveril in 1086 were probably also to be found in the new borough: they included 48 merchants and 12 'horsemen'. Peveril, together with another powerful Norman lord granted estates in the county, Ralph de Buron, held his position and privileges partly on the understanding that he would fight for his king and provide some of the soldiers required to garrison the castle. The 12 'horsemen's houses' were the properties provided by Peveril as accommodation for his soldiers. Ralph de Buron is listed as owning 13 other such houses. No church other than St Mary's is mentioned in 1086, but the church of St Nicholas may have been founded shortly before the Conquest as the estate church for Earl Tosti, and St Peter's was probably built to serve the growing 'new borough' soon afterwards.

The first stone castle was probably built in the early or mid-12th century by one of Peveril's descendents, also a William Peveril, who succeeded to the constableship in 1114. The first stone building was a square tower built on the motte, about 14 yards square. Nothing remains of this today but the plans of the medieval castle, drawn in 1617, have survived and indicate that the tower was of very similar dimensions (although probably one storey taller) to the one probably begun by Peveril at his castle on the Peak at Castleton, which was later completed by Henry II and can still be seen today.

S N O T I N G H̃ S C I R E.

280 a

IN BVRGO SNOTINGEHAM FVER̃ .CLXXIII. T.R.E.

burgenſes.7 xix. uilli. Ad hc̄ Burgū adiacent. vi.

car̄ tre ad glđ regis.7 unū p̄tū.7 ſiluæ minutæ. vi.

q̃z lḡ.7 v. lat̄. H̃ terra partita fuit int̄ xxxviii.

burgenſes.7 de cenſu tre 7 opib burgenſiũ redđ

lxxv. ſot 7 vii. den.7 de duobʒ monetarijs. xl. ſoliđ.

Inibi habuit cõm Toſti. i. car̄ træ. de cuj træ

ſoca habeb̄ rex. ii. denar.7 ipſe comes tciū.

Hugo.f.Baldrici inuenit. cxxxvi. hões man̄. uicecomes

modo ſuʒ. xvi. min. Ipſe tam̄ hugo in terra

comitis|ſtatuit. xiii. dom quæ antea n̄ fuerant. in nouo burgo

apponens eas in cenſu ueteris burgi.

In Snotingehā. ē una æccła in dñio regis. in qua ia

cent. iii. manſiones burgi,7 v. bouatæ træ de ſup̄

dictis|carucatis cū ſaca 7 ſoca.7 ad eanđ æcclam fex

ptiñ. v. acræ træ 7 dimidia. de qua rex hr̄ ſacā 7

ſocā. Burgenſes hñt. vi. caruc̄|ad aranđ.7 xx. fre

borđ.7 xiiii. carucas. In aqua Trente ſoliti eraʒ

piſcari.7 m̃ querelā faciuʒ q̃d piſcari p̄hibent̄. eo

T.R.E. redđ Snotinghā. xviii. lib̄. m̃ redđ. xxx. lib.

7 x. lib̄ de moneta.

6   Part of the Nottingham entry in Domesday Book.

Peveril may have built the stone tower during the civil wars between King Stephen and the Empress Matilda (1135-54), for the strategic importance of the castle became very apparent during this long-drawn-out and very bloody conflict. Peveril saw it as his duty to support Stephen and it was perhaps in revenge for his participation at the 'Battle of the Standard', when Matilda's forces were defeated, that Robert of Gloucester (a leading figure in Matilda's faction) attacked the undefended town in September 1140. Those who could escape the soldiers fled to the churches but during the assault a terrible fire broke out, completely destroying the town, and those who had taken refuge in the churches perished in the flames. The castle remained in Peveril's hands for the time being but five months later he was captured at the battle of Lincoln, together with King Stephen, and the castle had to be surrendered to Matilda as part of the price of his release. Two years later, however, it was back in Peveril's hands, after a small number of his soldiers managed to scale the castle rock and surprise the unsuspecting garrison. But Peveril's hold on the castle would again be short-lived. When Stephen died in 1154 Peveril lost his protector, and with the peaceful, unopposed, succession of Matilda's son, the young Henry II, he faced an implacable and formidable opponent. The final blow came a year later, when the leading men of the town were received by the new king at York and, in return for their pledges of unfailing loyalty,

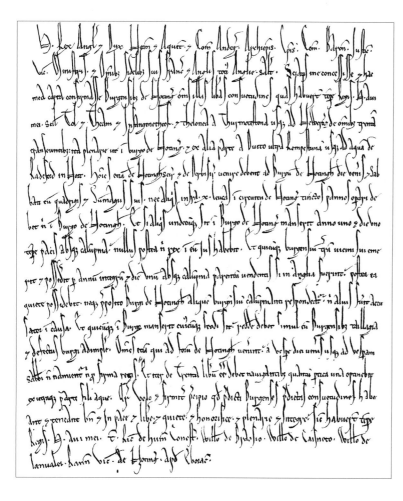

7   *Charter of Henry II, c.1155.*

granted a charter confirming the town's rights and liberties. Now utterly isolated, Peveril fled from his castle to his monastery at Lenton, and from there, in the disguise of a monk, he slipped abroad. Henry, meanwhile, quietly took possession of the castle, the town and all the other estates of the 'honour' of Peveril.

Henry II spent lavishly both in strengthening the castle's defences and in constructing new buildings. During the 1170s the timber walls that still enclosed the area of the motte and inner bailey were taken down and replaced with stone walls, and new buildings included a treasury, the king's chamber, a royal bedchamber, and, in the inner bailey, an almonry and a great hall. Henry and his court particularly enjoyed the opportunities for hunting and falconry afforded by the park, laid out immediately to the south-west of the castle by the first constable a hundred years before, and in the nearby Sherwood Forest. One of Henry's additions to the castle was 'a house for the king's falcons'.

The castle was also a particular favourite of Henry's youngest son, John. Long before John succeeded his brother, Richard I, to the throne it was at the heart of one of the disputes that plagued his relationship with Richard. In 1175, when he was only eight years old, his indulgent father had given both the castle and county of Nottingham to John, as part of a series of gifts given to the boy to punish his two older sons after they had been implicated in a plot to overthrow their father. When Richard succeeded to the throne in 1189 his main concern was to complete his preparations for a crusade to the Holy Land. To achieve this he felt it was necessary to give the county of Nottingham to John, along with numerous other counties in the South West and the Midlands, but he refused to give him control of the castle. Richard's intention was to secure his brother's loyalty in his absence but to restrict his political and military power. This proved impossible, however, and within 18 months the young John had exploited the widespread unpopularity of Richard's regent, William Longchamp, to seize control of Nottingham castle, a stronghold he regarded as being already rightfully his own, the gift of his father 16 years before. Richard's capture by Leopold of Austria, during his journey home from the Third Crusade, and his consequent long absence from England, enabled John to hold the castle for the next two years, but when Richard returned in 1193, landing at Sandwich on 13 March, almost his first action was to march his forces into the Midlands to retake John's castles at Nottingham and Tickhill. He then held a council at Nottingham where he formally stripped his brother and those nobles who had supported him of their estates and castles.

Later in John's reign, the castle became one of the most important royal strongholds in the country. During the summer of 1207 John developed a network of castles in which he was able to deposit large quantities of money to raise armies and pay his financiers as and when needed, to maintain order and wage war on his enemies. Silver pennies were placed in barrels in units of £100 as part of his military stores. Nottingham castle, together with the castle at Northampton, became John's chief depository for taxes raised in the Midlands and North. He chose as his constables ruthless but loyal and efficient administrators. Robert of Vieuxpont was made constable of Nottingham castle in 1207 and in October 1208 he was replaced by the infamous Philip Mark. The defences were further strengthened by reducing the size of the outer bailey, adding another defensive ditch to protect the new earthworks, and building a barbican to protect the gate. During the Welsh wars and the succeeding baronial unrest of John's latter years the castle remained his loyal headquarters. When he crushed the rebellion of Llywelyn ab Iorwerth in 1211, and took as hostages 30 young

Welshmen, it was to Nottingham castle that they were sent as prisoners. When Llywelyn rose in rebellion again the next year, John vented his anger by having many of the hostages hanged from the castle walls, while money was collected in the royal treasury in the castle to finance another punitive expedition against the rebellious Welsh.

John's son, Henry III, was also anxious to strengthen the castle's defences. On a visit to the castle in 1251 Henry gave orders to build a stone wall encircling the outer bailey and twin towers to protect the outer gate. He also shared his father's and grandfather's enthusiasm for the recreational opportunities of the adjacent countryside, and much of his expenditure on the castle was devoted to turning it into a more comfortable domestic residence. Henry visited the castle on more occasions than any other medieval monarch – 13 in all – and he would also seem to have been unusually interested in the finer details of home furnishings. He gave explicit instructions regarding new panelling, wainscoting, plasterwork and glazing. The changes made in this reign set the pattern for many years to come. Until the 16th century the castle would remain both a most formidable and well maintained fortress and a comfortable royal palace.

Among the royal visitors to the castle in the first half of the 14th century were Edward II's widow, Queen Isabella, and her lover, Roger Mortimer, who was widely blamed for the murder of Edward II in 1327. Although Isabella's son, Edward III, had been crowned in 1327, the Queen and her lover effectively ran the country for the first three years of Edward's reign. In 1330, however, the young king decided to take control of the government for himself, and to take revenge for his father's death. In October 1330 Mortimer found himself trapped in Nottingham Castle while Edward's forces occupied the town. Provided his own forces remained loyal to him, Mortimer could expect to remain safe within the castle for a considerable period, but the castle proved rather less impregnable than Mortimer might have hoped. Unbeknown to him, a small group of Edward's soldiers were able to secretly enter the castle by an underground passage and arrested him with almost no resistance. Isabella was sent into comfortable captivity but Mortimer was taken to London and put to death. The passage by which the soldiers entered the castle is probably the one still known today as 'Mortimer's Hole'. This is a tunnel running from Brewhouse Yard, at the foot of the castle rock, up into the Upper Bailey. It is 321 feet long and was probably dug as a short-cut service passage to receive goods into the castle.

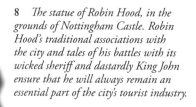

8   *The statue of Robin Hood, in the grounds of Nottingham Castle. Robin Hood's traditional associations with the city and tales of his battles with its wicked sheriff and dastardly King John ensure that he will always remain an essential part of the city's tourist industry.*

9   *The king hunting.*

The Slow Growth of the Town, 1100-1349

Although the castle became a significant royal centre in the first two centuries after the Conquest, the town grew only slowly. Only 204 burgesses were listed for taxation in 1341 and in 1334 the town's wealth for taxable purposes was assessed at £371, putting it in 26th place in a list of 37 towns. Lincoln, by comparison, was assessed at £1,000. What growth there had been was probably largely due to the expansion of the wool-dying and cloth-making trades. Weavers are mentioned in the sheriff's accounts sent to the Exchequer – the Pipe Rolls – in 1155, and dyers are also mentioned in the charter granted to the town's leading citizens by Henry II in the same year. The charter confirms the dyers' right to a local monopoly of the industry; no one was permitted to work in dyed cloth within 15 miles of the town. Such a monopoly may have been first granted in Henry I's reign (1100-35) as the charter claims to be simply confirming the rights enjoyed since that time. The right of local merchants to establish their own guild, however, is not mentioned until the end of the 12th century, when it was granted by Prince John during his brother's absence and then confirmed on his accession in 1200. Although the majority of the population were craftsmen of one sort or another, only the weavers appear to have been numerous enough to have established their own craft guild by the 14th century.

The absence of a powerful and prosperous local family from the castle, after the expulsion of William Peveril in 1155, probably inhibited the growth of the new borough just outside the castle walls. For most of the time after this the castle was almost empty, only occasionally and very briefly visited by its royal owners. Henry II visited the castle seven times during his 30-year reign but never for more than a few days, and Edward II was unique in staying in the castle twice for almost a month. Many years could pass without any royal visits at all. Consequently, the impact of the castle on the economy and growth of the town was slight. The new development was not sufficiently successful to justify the creation of a new market adjacent to the castle, as had probably been planned. Instead, a site for a Saturday Market and an annual fair was eventually chosen much closer to the English borough, midway between the two communities, 328 feet wide and 656 feet long, stretching from the north-eastern edge of the new borough to the north-western corner of the English borough. Although in the 13th and 14th centuries the two boroughs each had their own bailiff, for most purposes they were administered as one, and when the town obtained the right to appoint a mayor in 1284, his responsibilities were for both boroughs, and no distinction was usually made between inhabitants of the two boroughs in the borough court.

The terrible destruction suffered by the town in the fire of September 1140 must also have impeded the town's growth, but it appears not to have prompted any attempt to protect the new borough. The first reference to any work being undertaken to extend the castle defences eastwards, to link with the earth and ditch defences of the English borough, comes only in the first half of the 13th century. A town ditch is mentioned in deeds relating to the north of the town before the mid-13th century and it reached at least as far eastwards as St John's Hospital, on the York Road, by the 1250s. In 1267 Henry III gave the town's governing officials the right to raise a special tax, known as murage, to build and maintain a wall, but progress seems to have been slow. Deeds refer to the wall having been built near St John's property soon after this but the wall east of Chapel Bar is not mentioned until 1336, and some of the town's other gates were also built long before the wall. Although begun in the 13th century, the wall was probably not completed until the 14th century. During demolition work parts of the wall have been frequently uncovered but then reburied, and at present no section of the wall is visible to the public. The line of the wall is today followed by Upper and Lower Parliament Streets and a line indicating its course can be seen marked on the walls of the underpass in front of the Theatre Royal.

In many respects the appearance of the town changed little during the 12th, 13th and 14th centuries. It remained a town of timber cottages and timber-framed houses. Stone houses might be found in wealthier cities, such as Lincoln, but in Nottingham even the richer merchants appear to have built their houses and halls in timber. It was also a very rural town. Although the streets were often very narrow and the houses were packed closely together, there were also plenty of gardens, orchards and other open spaces, some of which were used to keep chickens, sheep and pigs. The plots on which properties stood were often only 17 or 18 feet wide but they could be 80 or even 120 feet long and in the yards and gardens behind could be found stables, barns, granaries and sometimes little cottages rented out to the poorer classes. Many houses were also built over caves, which appear to have been used mainly as cellars for storage purposes, for which their constant temperature and fire-proof qualities made them ideally suited.

The town's richest inhabitants were merchants, who traded in a wide variety of goods and on an international scale. Nottingham's position close to the river Trent gave the town's merchants good communications with important ports such as Boston and Hull. Lincoln and York were also accessible, although the silting up of the Foss Dyke was making access to Lincoln by water increasingly difficult by the 14th century. The wealthiest merchants, such as William Amyas, who was assessed for tax purposes as worth £60 in 1341 (more than twice any other inhabitant) owned or chartered ships and traded abroad, particularly in France and the Low Countries. A lot of money could be made in supplying the royal armies – and sometimes the enemy as well – in time of war. Most of the town's wealthiest inhabitants in the 13th century were dealers in wool, the country's most important export, but two families appear to have owed their wealth to their positions as suppliers of wine to the castle. Both the Brian and Kitte families prospered as royal vintners during the reigns of John and Henry III, importing large quantities of Gascon wine through Bristol and Boston.

Although a relatively small town, Nottingham's trade was sufficiently substantial by the beginning of the 13th century to attract a small community of Jews, able to offer her merchants very valuable money-lending facilities. Nottingham was one of only 17 towns where Jews could live and relations appear to have been unusually free from hostility. The community's synagogue was in Lister Gate and most Jews probably lived in nearby Jew Lane. This was not too far from the castle, and the Jews could flee here for safety should they be attacked. The community remained small throughout the 13th century until, in 1290, Edward I expelled all Jews from England, and the 20 Jewish families then living in the town had to take whatever goods they could carry and try to make a new life as best they could in other countries.

For Nottingham's wealthier merchants their prosperity also meant civic responsibility and power, at least at a local level. William Amyas served as mayor on four occasions in the first half of the 14th century and the majority of the town's wealthier inhabitants served either as mayor or bailiff, and frequently both. The town's bailiffs are first mentioned in 1220 and their main responsibilities seem to have been the collection of the fee farm (a tax paid to the king in recognition of the liberties of the borough), the regulation of markets and the calling and supervision of the borough court. In the 12th century the senior local administrative official was known as the reeve. His responsibilities are not known but he may have worked under the authority of the county sheriff. When the city obtained the right to have a mayor he was 'set over' the bailiffs, and presumably took over some of the functions previously performed by them, but his responsibilities are also unclear and probably developed over time.

Those who served as bailiffs or mayors were the town's social elite. Beneath them in the urban hierarchy – and in many cases far below – were the town's craftsmen. The most numerous, but probably enjoying the lowest status among craftsmen, were the weavers. Their numbers were already large enough before 1155 to establish their own guild, but the guild payment was relatively low at £2 and only one weaver is recorded as being of sufficient wealth and status to be required to witness a charter. The 12th and 13th centuries were the heyday of the town's cloth trade and the term 'Nottingham Cloth', which was common in the 15th century, probably dates from this period. Before the end of the 13th century, however, it was already in decline, unable to compete with the growing rural industry which benefitted from lower wage costs and the increasing use of water-powered fulling mills.

The production of finished cloth required numerous different skills, each of which added to the value of the final product. First, the cloth had to be fulled, that is felted and made smooth either by 'walkers' stamping on it in water, or by hammers driven by a water mill. It was then dried on tenters, and the nap raised by using teazles before the loose fibres were removed by the shearmen. Each stage required specialist workmen. Some of the crafts were reflected in the street names of the town. Walker Gate and Fuller's Street, for instance, were both locations where fullers walked and stamped the cloth or where a fulling mill had been constructed. Similarly, Lister Gate, a later name for Fuller's Street, refers to the work of the dyers. Master dyers tended to be some of the wealthiest craftsmen found in any town because some of the raw materials they used were extremely expensive and only obtainable from the far side of the world. One merchant who is known to have been importing very rare and costly brazil wood from the East Indies for use by Nottingham's dyers early in the 14th century was John Amyas, the son of William Amyas.

Pottery was also a well-established and important industry, and one in which local craftsmen established a reputation for producing high-quality wares in the early 14th century. 'Nottingham reduced green glazed' jugs and kitchen wares dating from this period have been found throughout the East Midlands, much of it coming from a kiln found in Goose Gate, where production of this type of pottery probably began in the mid-13th century. Limited quantities of 'splashed glazed ware' were being produced in the town from the 11th century and kilns have been found at Goose Gate, Glasshouse Street and on the site of the Victoria Centre. By the early 14th century there were probably nine

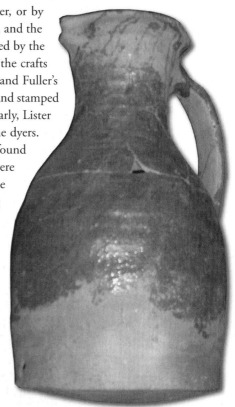

10   *Thirteenth-century splashed glaze jug made in Nottingham.*

potters at work in Nottingham, most living near the ditch on the east side of the town. One or two potters may have grown relatively wealthy from their trade. Roger le Potter's widow, Margery, was assessed for taxation at £5 in 1341, and Richard le Potter at £2.

Also living in the same area in the early 14th century were the tilers. Theirs was a new industry for the town, probably only established in the second half of the 13th century, but Nottingham floor-tiles dating from this period, like green glazed pottery, are found across the East Midlands. Another important group of craftsmen were the metalworkers. Street names such as Bridlesmith Gate, Great Smith Gate and Smithy Row hint at the importance of the varied metalworking crafts found in the town in the 13th and 14th centuries. Not only was a great variety of metal wares for everyday use made in the town but also luxury items affordable only to the wealthiest of customers. Five goldsmiths are recorded in the town in the early 14th century, making, selling and repairing gold and silver ware. One, Henry the Goldsmith, had a stall on the daily market at Weekday Cross in 1311.

The presence of the castle might have given an occasional extra boost to demand for bridles, stirrups and horse shoes and almost certainly explains why craftsmen skilled in producing swords and armour were also to be found in the town. One craftsman who was known as Gilbert the Armourer was killed in 1339 and another, John le Forbur, is recorded as transporting swords from Nottingham to Lincoln in 1316.

One industry which became more important in the 15th and 16th centuries but was certainly established at least on a modest scale in the 13th and 14th centuries was tanning. Tanners are mentioned in Narrow Marsh in the late 13th century, using the waters of the river Leen to wash and soak their raw material, and a little later, early in the 14th century, on Barker Gate, presumably exploiting the water of the Beck on the eastern edge of the town. The term 'barker' is another word for a tanner. The 19th-century Nottingham historian, Holland Walker, believed that the tanners were probably first established here and only subsequently moved to the Narrow Marsh area.

The Religious Life of the Community

Almost nothing is known about the origins of the three parish churches of St Mary's, St Peter's and St Nicholas's. Domesday Book only mentions St Mary's and it has usually been assumed that the others are later foundations, established as part of the development of the 'new borough'. Excavations at St Nicholas's, however, have shown that the first church on the site may have been built before the Conquest, perhaps as the estate church for Earl Tosti. It was a cruciform structure and rather larger than might have been expected for the new borough. Nothing of this first church survives above ground level, however, for the medieval church was razed during the civil war, and the church we see today was built during the Restoration. The last of the three churches to be built was probably St Peter's. This was never a high status church and Pevsner comments that 'it might easily stand in any prosperous Notts village'. Perhaps partly because of this some of the 13th-century features survive, including the piers of the south arcade. St Mary's, by contrast, is an exceptionally fine building, but it is almost entirely 15th-century. It is a fine reflection of the wealth that the city would enjoy in the 15th century. It had always been the principal church of the town, probably founded as an Anglo-Saxon minster and rebuilt in the Norman era. It was also the only church for which a vicarage was built, in 1234, and the only church to hold lands in the open fields.

The income from all three churches, and the power to appoint their priests, was granted early in the 12th century to the Cluniac Priory of Lenton, founded by the first William Peveril in 1103-14. It was probably because of the priory's dominant position in the town that no other churches were built, but in the 13th century the priory was unable to prevent the arrival in the town of two important orders of friars: the Franciscans and the Carmelites.

The Franciscans, or Grey Friars, first arrived in the country in 1224 and within six years they were established in the town, or rather, just outside it, on the common lands just to the south of the new borough, known appropriately as Broad Marsh. In his 'Itinerary of Nottingham' Holland Walker described the area as 'low, swampy and foul land by the marshy banks of the river Leen'. They at first built a timber chapel but by 1256 their growing numbers and wealth, together with royal patronage, enabled them to build a new church in stone. Henry III allowed them to take stone from his quarry in Nottingham, and his daughter, Margaret, Queen of Scotland, persuaded him to also grant the Franciscans timber for their chapter house and dormitory. The Carmelites, or White Friars, seem to have arrived a little later, for they are not mentioned until 1271, when their church already stood in the new borough between Moothall Gate and St James's Street, close to the Saturday Market.

Both friaries appear to have prospered. Soon after their arrival the Franciscans were building a wharf on the Trent, and later in the century they had two conduits built to carry spring water to their house. The building of their new church seems to have continued for many years and was not completed until 1310. The Carmelites' growing numbers and wealth prompted them to extend their establishment early in the 14th century, and further expansion followed later in the century. Both communities had a reputation for piety, learning and charitable works among the poor, the sick and the dying. This naturally endeared them to the poor, but their willingness to preach in the streets meant that the ordinary parish priest tended to regard them with suspicion, seeing them as a threat. The necessity to appoint able priests who could match the preaching abilities of the newly arrived friars might explain the decision to build a vicarage for the priest of St Mary's in 1234.

11   *St Peter's church.*

12 *St Mary's church, south transept window.*

Other religious foundations included the hospital of St John the Baptist on the corner of the modern Glasshouse Street and Lower Parliament Street, which in 1208 took over responsibility for maintaining the bridge over the river Trent, and the hospital of the Holy Sepulchre, which is first mentioned in 1267. The precise location of this hospital is not known but, as was the case with most English towns, all Nottingham's hospitals were to be found outside the town's defences. An 'alms house' is mentioned in a papal document of 1181-5, and there would appear to have been a number of leper hospitals established. St Leonard's is mentioned early in the 13th century, when the lepers were permitted to collect wood in Bestwood, and two others are mentioned in the 1330s: St Mary's, just outside Chapel Bar, the town's west gate, and St Michael's, whose location is not known.

The Black Death

A series of appalling harvests in the first two decades of the 14th century almost certainly brought a sharp check to the modest growth that the town had enjoyed in the 12th and 13th centuries. An even greater blow came when the Black Death approached the town in May 1349. The collection of the pontage tax (to raise money for the repairing of the bridges over the Leen and Trent) had to be cancelled that month owing to 'pestilence threatening'. The plague had first arrived in the south-west of the country the previous summer and by early spring it was still largely confined to the southern counties. It is likely that by March the people of Nottingham had begun to hope that they had been spared. However, it would seem that before the end of the month the pestilence had reached the county, even if the county town itself was still not affected. Every citizen would have known that they had little more than a 50/50 chance of surviving the year. On 23 March a bull of Pope Clement VI referred to the plague having reached the diocese of York. Nottinghamshire was the southernmost part of the diocese and therefore probably the first to be affected.

Just how badly the town and the surrounding district were affected is not known. The county seems to have been rather less badly affected than many other areas. The mortality rate among the beneficed clergy in the archdeaconry was 36½ per cent, which was well below the national average (about forty-five per cent), and it is reasonable to assume that the death rate among the rest of the population of the county was also lower. There were, however, considerable variations across the county. In Newark almost half the clergy were wiped out but in the Retford area only about a third died. But even if Nottingham escaped relatively lightly it is still very likely that at least a quarter of the population died in the course of the summer of 1349.

One consistent feature was the tendency for the mortality rates to be highest of all in the months of May, June, July and August. This was the case right across the Midlands and northern counties. It is also fairly certain that the principal type of plague suffered across this area was the bubonic variety. It was the black swellings, or 'buboes', which appeared in the armpits and groin of the sufferer, causing excruciating pain, that gave rise to the term 'Black Death'.

It was widely believed that the plague had been sent by God as a punishment for the sins of mankind. As early as July 1348, at about the same time as the first outbreak was being reported in the country, at Melcombe in Dorset, the Archbishop of York wrote to his parish priests to give them the benefit of his views on the plague then sweeping across the Continent:

> Everybody knows, since the news is now widely spread, what great pestilence, mortality and infection of the air there are in divers parts of the world and which, at this moment, are threatening in particular the land of England. This, surely, must be caused by the sins of men who, made complacent by their prosperity, forget the bounty of the Most High Giver.

When the plague did reach the Midlands and North in the following year, however, it was among the poorest classes – whose lives were so frequently wracked by hunger and disease – and not among those made complacent by prosperity, that the death rates were highest. As in virtually all medieval towns, the conditions to be found in Nottingham in the middle of the 14th century were in many respects ideal for the spread of the plague. Although the town was not large, even by medieval standards, some of the streets were extremely narrow and the houses closely packed together. The flimsy hovels of the poor were especially overcrowded as all the children, and often all members of the family, would usually sleep together on the floor in the same room. In such circumstances plague-carrying fleas and rats had little difficulty in infecting entire families. Moreover, those whose bodies were already weakened by hunger and malnutrition were also the ones most likely to succumb to the plague.

The impact of the sudden loss of so large a proportion of the population may be seen to some extent more than two hundred years later, when the first detailed maps of the town were drawn, early in the 17th century. Large sections of the town, and especially the eastern parts of the old English borough, are shown as empty spaces, quite devoid of any housing whatsoever. Given the years of famine and probable economic decline in the first half of the 14th century, it is quite likely that the maps reveal a process of urban shrinkage already begun before the Black Death struck the town, but then greatly accelerated by the horrors of the summer in 1349.

Economic Recovery and Prosperity

Today, the handsome perpendicular church of St Mary is striking evidence of the wealth of Nottingham's merchants in the 15th century, in spite of recurrent outbreaks of the plague. A complete rebuilding of the church seems to have begun early in the new century. The first phase of the work was the building of the south porch and south transept, but the rest

13   *St Mary's church, south porch.*

soon followed, and today there is barely a fragment of the earlier church surviving. The slim pillars of the nave and the enormous windows, creating (to quote Pevsner) the impression of a glasshouse, represented the very latest and finest in architectural fashion in the first half of the 15th century.

It is not known just how quickly the town recovered from the Black Death. Figures for the numbers of tax payers recorded may suggest continuing population decline, at least among those wealthy enough to be taxable, for some years after the disaster of 1349. The taxable population in 1377 has been estimated as 1,447 but in 1381 the figure is only 1,266. However, it may have been that Nottingham's inhabitants were simply becoming more adept at avoiding taxation and there are also some more positive signs of growth and prosperity long before 1400. The north arcade of St Peter's church, for instance, was rebuilt in about 1360, the Carmelite friars were undertaking building works and extensions in 1356, and the first evidence of a new and growing industry – the manufacture of alabaster panels and figures – appears in the 1360s. It is also probable that work on the town's defences continued in the second half of the 14th century, although the evidence for dating the building of the wall is confusing and incomplete.

14   *St Mary's church, north transept.*

The first mention of alabaster manufacture in the town comes in 1367, but it was clearly a trade in which the local craftsmen had already established a national reputation for producing work of the highest standards. In that year Edward III commissioned a huge alabaster altarpiece for St George's Chapel, Windsor, from Peter the Mason. The transport costs alone totalled £200, a huge sum in those days. It took 17 days for 10 carts, each pulled by eight horses, to make the journey by road from Nottingham. The stone used was cut into manageable pieces at the quarries at Chellaston near Derby and brought the short distance down the Trent. St Mary's church contains a number of alabaster monuments dating from the 14th and 15th centuries. The earliest, from the second half of the 14th century, is a badly battered effigy to be found in the north aisle. Much better preserved are two monuments from the early 15th century. One is a monument to John Samon, a wealthy wool merchant who served as mayor on three occasions and died in 1413. This is to be found in the recess in the south wall of the

15   *Alabaster reredos portraying scenes of the Passion, made in Nottingham, c.1400, now in the chapel of Haddon Hall, Derbyshire.*

16   *The three central panels of Haddon Hall reredos.*

south transept. Another is an alabaster tomb-chest in the north transept thought to have been made for John Tannesley and his wife. John died in 1414. Also from approximately the same period is a small alabaster monument to a bishop.

Fine Nottingham-made alabaster monuments were sold throughout England and even abroad but alabasterers are only rarely mentioned in local records in the 15th century, and the numbers employed in this highly specialist craft were probably always small. The town's prosperity in the 15th century, as in the 12th and 13th, was built mainly on the wool and cloth trades. Good communications meant that the town's wool merchants were well

17   *Alabaster carving, 'The Annunciation', made in Nottingham, c.1400.*

18   *'Severns'; a late medieval timber-framed house.*

19   *The late 15th-century Guildhall which stood at Weekday Cross, close to the site now occupied by a new art gallery, Nottingham Contemporary.*

placed to exploit the growing demand from the Continent for English wool and English woollen cloth, and the necessary skills for the weaving and finishing of cloth – the fullers, shearers, dyers – were already long established in the town. It may be significant that the earliest reference to a fulling mill – an expensive piece of capital investment – appears in the local records only in 1403. Merchants from Italy and Brabant were regularly to be found at the Nottingham fairs, buying huge quantities of cloth manufactured both in the town and in the surrounding villages and smaller towns. A small group of wealthy Nottingham merchants bought wool from a wide area and controlled the various stages of manufacture. One was John Plumptre, who is mentioned in the borough records

20   *Nottingham Castle gateway; one of the few remnants of the medieval castle that still stand today.*

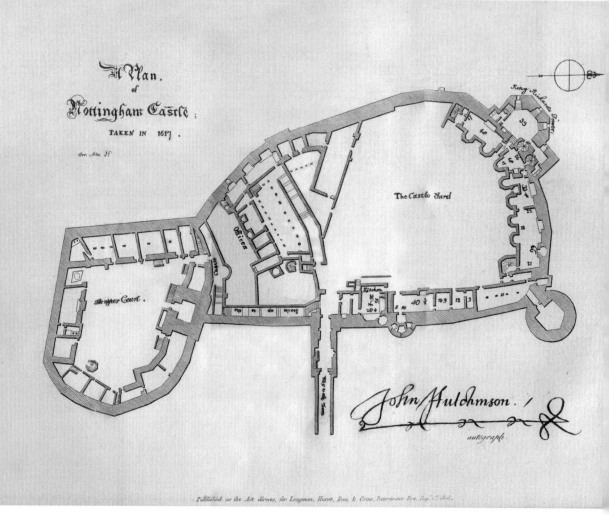

21   *Plan of Nottingham Castle, made in 1617 and signed by Colonel John Hutchinson, the Governor of the Castle during the English Civil War who later ordered the castle's demolition.*

in 1420 as supplying to the town's weavers 'gode Nottyngham shire woll' and 'northern woll'. Another was Thomas Thurland, who built for himself the finest house in the town in 1458, Thurland Hall. This was rebuilt early in the 17th century and demolished in 1831, but the name survives in the road which now passes through the site of the house. Like other members of the town's elite, he is buried in St Mary's. The fine canopy for his tomb can be found in the north transept but the alabaster tomb-chest beneath it is the one mentioned above, thought to have been made a generation earlier for fellow wool merchant John Tannesley.

Other industries which also appear to have flourished in the 15th century include the long-established pottery industry – although this may have been in decline from the mid-century – and the leather trade, which became an even more important business in the 16th century. And with the growth of trade and manufactures, and a flourishing fair, the number of alehouses and brothels also grew. In 1463 the corporation was sufficiently alarmed by this development to issue orders against prostitutes, brothels and disorderly alehouses, but to little effect, as the numbers of houses of ill-repute continued to grow.

The men who dominated the wool and cloth trades also ensured that their wealth brought them political power. This had always been the case, but in 1449 the town's elite managed to secure a new charter from Henry VI which strengthened their position further. The town was given county borough status and instead of a governing body consisting of a mayor and two bailiffs there would now be a corporation consisting of seven aldermen, all of whom would enjoy the power and status of JPs, and from whom the mayor would be chosen. The aldermen would be elected by the burgesses but elections would be few for they would hold their office for life, and they alone could appoint the mayor. Three other officials would also be appointed to serve the corporation, a chamberlain and two sheriffs, but they too would be chosen by the aldermen. The town's government had for long been mainly in the hands of the town's wealthier merchants and tradesmen, but the charter of 1449 entrenched their position considerably and accelerated a tendency to focus power in fewer hands, reducing the power of the rest of the burgesses even further. The separation and distinction of the town's ruling body from the rest of the community was underlined by the fine robes of office they gave themselves, scarlet with fur trims, which they alone were allowed to wear, by numerous grand processions, when the scarlet robes would be much in evidence, and by the building of a new guildhall at Weekday Cross.

In spite of Henry VI's generosity in granting so favourable a charter, the town fathers generally supported the Yorkist cause during the Wars of the Roses and were richly rewarded after Edward IV's decisive victory over the Lancastrians at Towton in March 1461. In recognition of their support Edward agreed in 1462 to cut the town's annual fee farm by £20 for the next 20 years. He also made the castle his chief base during the campaigns of 1464 and 1471, and between 1476 and 1480 he spent the enormous sum of £3,000 on the castle, building a new three-storey stone tower and adjoining royal apartments, earning the poet John Skelton's famous description of the castle as 'a place full royall'. The castle would also be a favourite residence of Edward's younger brother, Richard III,

22 *Model of Nottingham Castle as it would have appeared in about 1500.*

and it was from here that the last Yorkist king set out with his army in August 1485 to do battle with an obscure 28-year-old Welshman, Henry Tudor, Earl of Richmond, who had recently landed at Milford Haven with a small army of French mercenaries.

THREE
The Tudor Century

The Pre-Reformation Town

The town's governing body fully appreciated the need for extreme flexibility when dealing with questions of loyalty to the Crown. The victory of Henry Tudor at Bosworth in August 1485 demanded a rapid change in allegiance. Very shortly after the battle a deputation was despatched to obtain a copy of the new king's proclamation and to assure Henry of the same loyalty so recently and so enthusiastically shown to his Yorkist predecessors.

The town did not have to wait for long to receive the first indication of a cordial relationship with their monarch. In March 1486 Henry made his first visit to the town. What feasts and entertainments were provided to please the royal guest is not known, but there can be no doubt that the town's ruling elite were anxious to impress upon the new king their undying affection. As the royal procession made its way north towards the town the mayor and all the aldermen, decked in all their splendid scarlet finery, trimmed with expensive furs, awaited the royal visitor and his retinue a mile south of the river Trent and, after all due obeisance had been performed, conducted Henry the last two miles into the town.

The town that Henry saw was still very small: able to boast probably only about two thousand inhabitants and probably little larger than it had been a hundred years before. But it was a bustling, confident little town that came alive on market days, and still boasted two market places and two annual fairs. A new guildhall, or town hall, had been recently built near the ancient market place at Weekday Cross, on the corner of Middle Hill and High Pavement. The town's premier church, the recently re-built St Mary's, was a splendid tribute to civic pride, and the figures for the number of tradesmen and craftsmen purchasing their burgess rights, so that they might work and trade in the town, had never been higher. The researches of Dr Trevor Foulds have revealed that between 1480 and 1490 there were more than 200 admissions of burgesses, significantly more than in either of the two previous decades.

The wealth that had been lavished on the rebuilding of St Mary's was primarily an indication of a profoundly religious and pious community, for whom access to the next life was at least as important as any concerns about secular welfare in this one. All three of the town's churches received numerous and generous gifts and bequests from wealthy townsmen anxious to win favour with God, and to shorten their passage through the pains

35

of purgatory, and those who could not afford such conspicuous giving might still purchase the prospect of salvation through their membership of one of the local religious guilds. At the end of the 15th century there were at least two guilds in the town, those of St George and St Mary. For a small annual fee both men and women could enjoy the reassurance that at their death their fellow members would organise a vigil and ensure that their funeral was well attended and, above all, ensure that prayers for their immortal soul would be regularly said by a chantry priest paid for by the guild.

In the late 15th century traditional Catholic teaching would appear to have been unquestioned and there is no evidence of any Lollard influence in the town. Indeed, we have seen that by this time one of the town's best-known crafts had long been the manufacture of very high-quality alabaster religious monuments. Thus traditional religion and economic interest coincided happily. Moreover, as in most towns, the religious guilds were also at the centre of civic events and popular entertainment. Some of the most anticipated events of the year were the Corpus Christi Day and St George's Day processions, in which not only the mayor and aldermen would deck themselves in their expensive robes, but also every member of the guilds could put on his or her special guild livery. For many the highlight of the day's festivities for Corpus Christi was the special Corpus Christi play, in which large numbers of local people, representing almost every craft in the town, would play their part. Favourite Bible stories would be retold and re-enacted yet again and as many people as possible would be participants as well as spectators. For the St George's Day procession local craftsmen in the guild ensured that every year the chief participant was a splendidly ferocious canvas dragon – and probably a very large one too.

Corpus Christi Day and St George's Day were holidays to be enjoyed by all. Drinking, dancing, feasting and merry-making were, of course, essential elements, and the alehouses would do a roaring trade. After the Reformation, many Protestants, especially those of the Puritan variety, expressed their horror at such events and eventually managed to ban them altogether. But in the 15th and early 16th centuries they were at the heart of the town's communal life and helped bind the people together and to bind them to their church.

The guilds were also charitable institutions. They distributed alms to the poor and to travelling pilgrims, and to some extent augmented the work of the town's hospitals. Charitable giving was widely seen to be at the heart of good Christian behaviour and essential if one was to achieve salvation. It is possible that the town's guilds had once supported the local grammar school, as was the case in many other towns, and it is known that a school existed in the town in 1380 and was still there in 1430. Soon after this, however, it would seem to have closed down, but its re-establishment in 1512 owed everything to the piety, as well as determination and organising skill, of one very remarkable, well-connected and reasonably wealthy local widow, Agnes Mellers.

Agnes was the widow of a Nottingham bell-founder, Richard Mellers, a former alderman and a member of one of the town's leading families. On his death in 1507 his widow pledged herself to pious causes, one of which, she decided, should be the revival of the grammar school, and in 1512 she managed to use her excellent network of powerful friends – most notably Sir Thomas Lovell, the constable of the castle – to gain from Henry VIII a licence to establish the school. For Agnes, the object of the school was not simply to provide a classical education for the town's more able boys, although this was indeed achieved. Just as important were the prayers that had to be regularly said for the souls of the founders; that is, herself, Sir Thomas Lovell, and others whom she had persuaded to support the scheme, which included the entire corporation.

However, although in 1512 there was as yet no hint of discontent with traditional Catholic doctrine, there were good reasons to criticise some of the local religious institutions, or, more precisely, the behaviour of some of their personnel. In 1500, for instance, there were allegations that the wardens of the Greyfriars were procuring women for sexual favours, and the allegations were repeated again in 1522. Relations between the town and the priory at Lenton had long been strained by economic rivalry, with Nottingham's tradesmen particularly resentful of the annual Lenton fair, which caused all business in Nottingham to be suspended for eight days, but relations became markedly worse in June 1516 when one of the prior's retainers attempted to murder the mayor, Thomas Mellers. There were also complaints by the 1530s that the hospitals – St Leonard's, St John's, and Plumptre Hospital – were no longer providing care for the poor, and indeed that the master and chaplains of St John's had in 1529 abandoned their hospital altogether. And then yet another scandal shook the town: in 1532 it was reported that the prior of the Carmelite house, Richard Sherwood, got into a drunken brawl with one of his friars and in the fracas had killed him.

Scandals such as this were damaging enough for the church but their impact in weakening traditional loyalties was probably all the greater because now, in the 1530s, they coincided both with the king's developing disagreement with the papacy over his desire to annul his marriage to Catherine of Aragon, and with the arrival of new Protestant ideas that challenged traditional Catholic beliefs. By this time the radical criticisms and alternative theology of the German ex-monk Martin Luther had been circulating in some educated circles in England for more than a decade. Now, in Nottingham, doubts were beginning to be expressed for the first time about the value of saying prayers for the dead, a practice Luther had particularly condemned. It was said of the Plumptre Hospital, for instance, that the money given to the hospital was being used purely to pay a chantry priest and there was nothing left for the relief of the poor. When, later in the same decade, the full impact of the Henrician Reformation came to be felt in the town, local opinion might best be described as divided and confused, but there was little opposition of any sort to the closure of either the friaries or the hospitals.

The Impact of the Reformation

Today, the once important medieval friaries and hospitals of Nottingham have completely disappeared, and the great Cluniac Priory at nearby Lenton – once the richest and most powerful priory in the whole county – has also all but vanished. The Nottinghamshire volume of Pevsner's 'Buildings of England' series succinctly lists all that can be seen above ground today:

> In a patch of grass at the corner of Old Church Street and Priory Street lies the lower part of an easterly pier of the ambulatory. Buildings in Priory Street occupy the site of the nave, and up to seven feet of the north and west walls are incorporated in the south boundary of the churchyard together with nine feet of the west buttress.

The so-called Priory Church that stands nearby was built in 1883 but it incorporates as its chancel a chapel which once stood in the Priory courtyard.

The dissolution of the two friaries in Nottingham was carried out with little fuss in 1539, with their 15 inmates quietly pensioned off, and the hospitals were closed a few years

23 *The remains of Lenton Priory today: the lower part of a pier of the ambulatory.*

later, when Edward VI's government completed the process of secularisation of church property (although Plumptre Hospital was allowed to survive as an almshouse for poor widows, but without the prayers for the dead). But the reformation in Nottingham would not be a quiet or bloodless affair. The Prior of Lenton and two of his monks would pay with their lives for their opposition to the dissolution.

In February 1538 Prior Nicholas Heath, seven of his fellow monks and one secular priest were put on trial in the town, accused of treason. According to a monk who gave evidence for the prosecution, both Heath and some of the other monks were guilty of making treasonable statements in 1536, at the time of the rebellions in Yorkshire and Lincolnshire against Henry VIII's religious changes, known as the Pilgrimage of Grace. The judges did their duty by the Crown and duly found all the accused guilty, for which they received the handsome reward of two gallons of wine. But only Heath and two others were condemned to death, perhaps as a sign of clemency, and the executions were carried out soon afterwards in front of a large crowd in Cow Lane (now Clumber Street).

Such harsh punishments were always intended, of course, as a warning to others and to intimidate opponents. Heath and his fellow victims, however, were perhaps particularly

24 *The chapel which was once part of Lenton Priory.*

unfortunate. At the time of the Pilgrimage of Grace, Nottingham and its royal castle was seen as in the front line, facing a dangerous and rebellious enemy from the north. To make matters worse, the Crown had sadly neglected the upkeep of the castle for more than 40 years. In 1536 there was virtually no garrison and no artillery, and it was only due to the energetic efforts now made by the Earl of Rutland that it was once more swiftly re-enforced to become a viable military base. Any hint, therefore, of disloyalty or rebellion in this strategically important town at such a time was for King Henry very dangerous. The evidence against Heath and the other monks was slight indeed, but the king's suspicions could only have been encouraged when it was learnt that the leaders of the Pilgrimage of Grace had called for a Parliament to be called either at York or Nottingham to hear their grievances. To the king's mind this would indicate that the rebels really did believe they had strong support in the town, and any such support would have to be quickly crushed.

During the next two decades or so the country experienced a bewildering series of changes in both religious practice and belief, in the internal appearance and decoration of churches, and in social values. The religious guilds, which had played such an important part in so many townsmen's lives, disappeared altogether in 1547, together with the chantry priests and the altars they had supported, prayers and vigils for the dead, the old Corpus Christi plays and the merriment and feasts that had always accompanied them. Nottingham produced no more martyrs after the executions of 1538, and remained a conforming community. To be anything else was extremely dangerous. The clergy who accepted and implemented the Protestant changes demanded during the reign of Edward VI, with varying degrees of enthusiasm, reconciled themselves both to the brief return to Catholicism under Mary Tudor and then again to the moderate Anglicanism imposed eventually by Elizabeth.

The Elizabethan Town

Careful analysis of baptisms, marriages and burials in the town's three parishes from about 1575 has enabled historians to gain a fairly good idea of the changing size of the town's population from this time onwards, and the population was about 2,100 at the time of Elizabeth's accession in 1558. During the next 30 years the population grew faster than it had done for a very long time. This was partly owing to immigration but it was also because for many years births consistently outstripped burials, until the latter was suddenly pushed up sharply by two serious outbreaks of plague, in 1588 and 1593-4. Analysis of the parish registers suggests that by 1590 the population had risen to about 3,440, and although punishingly high death rates caused the population to shrink in the 1590s, to about 3,080 in 1600, Nottingham at the end of the 16th century was still a significantly larger town that it had been in 1500.

The appearance of the town, however, changed little during the century, except for the disappearance by 1600 of much of the town wall. Little effort had been made to maintain the walls in the 15th century and as early as the 1540s John Leland could report that 'much of the waul is now down' when he visited the town. At the end of the century the housing of the town was still almost exclusively timber-framed and most houses were still thatched. A few high-status houses, however, had been roofed with locally made tiles, and just before the turn of the century the first examples of glazed windows appeared. However, the town would have to wait until the new century, until 1615 to be precise, for the appearance of the first brick-built house.

It was also still a very rural town. Many of the burgesses kept cattle, sheep and pigs on the town fields, so many indeed that the corporation still had to employ as town officers a neatherd and a swineherd and frequently attempted (with apparently little success) to limit the 'stints' each burgess was allowed. When a ruling was made limiting the number of sheep that could be kept to 60 it was reported that some of the town's burgesses had flocks of more than 300 sheep in the fields. Not surprisingly, complaints were frequently made about the obstruction to traffic and the filth and stench caused when large numbers of animals were being driven through the streets – many of which were very narrow – to graze on the common fields. For many decades to come the streets would remain open sewers and piles of muck and manure a common sight in all streets. The burgesses who sat on the ancient Mickleton Jury (an institution first mentioned in 1308 but probably dating to the 11th century or earlier) frequently suggested that the corporation should appoint paid street cleaners – 'scavengers' – but this seems to have had little effect.

But there was nothing exceptional about this. What most impressed 16th-century visitors to the town was its geographical position and the spaciousness of the Saturday market. John Leland said, 'Nottingham is booth a large town and welle buildid for tymber and plaster, and standith stately on a clyminge hille', and described its market place as 'the most fairest without exception of al Inglande'. He was especially struck by its size, the surrounding buildings and (rather more surprisingly) by the cleanliness of its paving. Writing at the end of the century, in 1598, William Camden made similar comments. He described the town as 'seated most pleasant and delicate upon a high hill, for buildings stately and number of faire streets surpassing and surmounting many other cities, and for a spacious and most faire Market Place doth compare with the best'.

It was because of its success as a market and trading centre, and as a centre for processing the products of its agricultural hinterland, that the little town grew steadily in the latter half of the 16th century and attracted many migrants. A study of the town's parish registers, undertaken by Adrian Henstock, Sandra Dunster and Stephen Wallwork, has shown that between 1570 and 1593 approximately 1,050 people migrated into the town, an average of about 46 per year. This, they found, was far higher than in any period during the 17th century and not overtaken until the rapid growth of the town in the first half of the 18th century. 'Nottingham', they note, 'offered the promise of opportunity, or at least an escape from rural poverty, to many men and women from small towns and villages throughout the East Midlands.' An analysis of the origins of Nottingham apprentices between 1567 and 1579 gives us some idea as to the range of the town's catchment area. The majority (62 per cent) came either from the town itself (40 per cent) or from elsewhere in the county (22 per cent) and most of the latter had travelled only from nearby villages, such as Lenton, Beeston, Radford, Sneinton and Clifton. But a sizeable minority had come from the neighbouring counties of Derbyshire, Leicestershire, Lincolnshire and Yorkshire, and one lad had migrated from Staffordshire and another from as far away as Cumberland – a tailor's son from Keswick who in 1578 was apprenticed to a Nottingham baker.

The latter half of the 16th century was, however, also a period of considerable readjustment for the economy of the town. Some of the crafts which were important in medieval times had disappeared altogether, including both alabaster manufacture and pottery, and woollen cloth making was now of only minor importance. Wool was still spun into yarn in many households, as was some linen – spun from locally grown flax – but there were now only a few weavers in the town and the numbers involved in the cloth finishing trades had declined correspondingly. What cloth was produced in the town at the end of the century was mainly for domestic consumption. The town still boasted its own bell foundry, however, and was manufacturing bells for churches throughout Nottinghamshire, Lincolnshire and beyond, and other metalworking trades were also still important. A generation later, in 1625, 44 of the burgesses listed are described as metalworkers of some sort. There were 22 blacksmiths, three cutlers, three locksmiths and six spurriers. By this time, by contrast, there were only six weavers listed and only one fuller and one dyer.

Among the town's commonest occupations, and the ones which were probably growing fastest, were those involved in the food and drink industries. Precise figures for this period do not exist but there can be little doubt that many people found work as butchers and bakers, brewers and maltsters, inn-keepers and alehouse keepers. The latter would seem to have been a particularly fast-growing sector. Early in the next century there would be many complaints in the borough records about the cheap alehouses which by then lined the northern edge of the town and many of the poorer migrants to the town were said to have set up unlicensed alehouses in this area if they were unable to find other work. Similarly there were complaints in 1603 that the malting industry needed better control. This was a new and highly lucrative trade. The researches of Henstock, Dunster and Wallwork have revealed the existence of three malt mills in the town early in Elizabeth's reign, in Narrow Marsh, Goose Gate End and the Backside (Upper Parliament Street today). All were owned by the corporation and by the end of the century it had acquired one more, but in 1603 the tenants of the mills complained that other people had also set up rival mills and were threatening their trade and profits.

Another major occupational group were the leather trades. Nottingham's rich agricultural hinterland, together with its well-established livestock markets, meant that it was well placed

25 *Jollity outside an inn.*

to develop a large and flourishing butchery industry, and the various leather trades were a by-product of this. Moreover, the town's tanning industry was long established and still to be found concentrated in the low-lying area of Narrow Marsh, close to the River Leen. The prosperity it enjoyed in this period may be indicated by the number of the town's mayors who were tanners, and it was probably also in this period that the trade first established a particularly high reputation for producing the best upper leathers for boots, shoes, harnesses and coach leathers, all of which were important trades in the town during Elizabeth's reign.

Many of the town's tradesmen and craftsmen rented stalls in the markets. Most foodstuffs required day-to-day, including meat, fish, poultry and dairy produce, could be bought from the daily market at Weekday Cross, but a much wider range of commodities was to be found in the Saturday market. The earliest maps of the town, made in 1609 and 1610, show that the west side of this great market place was divided down the middle by a low wall. To the north of this, along Long Row, were pitches for corn, malt, oatmeal and salt and nearby were tented stalls for milliners, chandlers, white leather workers, coopers, and herb and seedsmen. On the other side of the low wall were the pens for cattle, horses, sheep and pigs. At the east end of the market place (including the area where the Council House now stands) were the permanent and roofed stalls of the butchers and fishmongers, the shoemakers, tanners, glovers and leather sellers, haberdashers, mercers and grocers, and ropemakers and cloth merchants selling linen as well as woollen cloth.

Nottingham's corn and malt merchants played an especially important role in the economy of the region. Nottingham's Saturday market acted as the exchange point for huge quantities of wheat and barley, brought by boat and cart from the rich arable lands of the Trent flood plain and the Vale of Belvoir, which were then sold throughout the region to provide bread and ale for a large population. Little is known about trade on the river Trent in Elizabeth's reign but some indication of the importance of waterborne trade between Nottingham and Newark in the late 16th century was provided when Sir Philip Stanhope erected a series of fish weirs on this stretch of the river in 1592. Civil disturbances were reported because of the interference he had caused to trade on the river, and altogether complaints were made by 39 villages.

An essential and expanding service for all who travelled far to Nottingham's markets was provided by the town's inns. The earliest list of inns and innkeepers appears only in 1615, when there were 13, but some of these were certainly established in the 16th century. The earliest known inn operating in this period was *The Swan*, which was in existence in 1549 and was to be found on High Pavement, one of the first streets a traveller coming from the south would reach, after crossing the Leen Bridge. Other early inns included the *White Hart* (1558) and the *Bullhead* (1577), both of which were to be found on Long Row and therefore very conveniently situated for the Saturday market. Not far away, and dating from at least 1563, was the *Lion*. This inn was located just to the east of the Saturday market, on Chandlers' Row (now Bottle Lane). As well as providing refreshment and lodgings for visitors the inns were also used by both short- and long-distance carriers, and on market days their carts could be found lining up in the inn yards. The latter included a weekly service to and from London before 1600, but the great majority served a wide network of Nottinghamshire villages and provided an early form of rural bus and postal service. Perhaps no other service could better illustrate and encapsulate Nottingham's importance by this time to its surrounding region.

One other function often provided by the larger inns of the country at this time was to put on plays performed by troupes of travelling actors, and this may well have been the case in Nottingham. In 1571, the borough records tell us that the Queen's Players came to the town and the corporation enjoyed a special performance in the Guildhall, with a special stage being erected for the purpose. They also show that visits to the town by travelling musicians and actors were by no means unusual. In 1547, indeed, we learn of the visit of no less than six different troupes of minstrels, and payments were made from the corporation accounts to travelling players in 1569 and again in 1573, when the performers were from Italy and were paid five shillings 'for certain pastimes that they showed before Mr Mayor and his brethren'. The corporation also paid a small group of musicians, the 'Town Waits', to perform at civic occasions and during official processions, and occasionally also paid to be entertained by visiting waits from other towns.

The 1590s: Plague, Poverty and the Elizabethan Poor Law

Life for the poor, in Thomas Hobbes' famous words, had always been 'nasty, brutish and short', but the 1590s was a particularly appalling decade, and this was as true in Nottingham as anywhere else. An outbreak of plague in 1588 – the first for many decades – would later be seen as the harbinger for something much worse. The 1588 outbreak pushed the burial rate up above that of baptisms for the first time since the local clergy began keeping regular records (1575) and in 1593 it returned, with the most devastating consequences since the Black Death of 1349. It has been estimated that during the 1590s as many as one in seven of the population died. There has to be some guesswork here as only the records of St Peter's are complete for this period. There are no burial records for St Mary's from June 1591 to March 1600 and there are gaps in the records for St Nicholas's in some months in both 1593 and 1594, which may well have been due to the disruption caused by the plague. What is clear, however, as has already been noted, is that the long spell of population growth in the town was now halted and reversed. Moreover, because of recurrent outbreaks of plague during the next half-century, the town would grow only slowly, with numerous checks and reverses, until the middle of the century.

High food prices, the consequence of a series of bad harvests, also added considerably to the misery of the poor in the 1590s. In some parts of the country it was reported that the poor were dying of starvation, and food riots broke out in London. There are no reports of deaths in Nottingham being directly attributable to famine, but there can be no doubt that many of those who succumbed to the plague and other diseases in the 1590s did so because their bodies were already so weakened by hunger.

The normal response of the corporation to an outbreak of plague, both in the 1590s and in later outbreaks, was to try to isolate the victims, either in their own homes or in plague huts and cabins set up outside the town. Some preventive measures were also taken. If plague was reported to have 'visited' a neighbouring town then watchmen would be paid to ensure that no visitors from the affected town came into Nottingham nor any local residents travel there. Although the causes of the plague were not understood, there was some recognition that very low standards of hygiene and overcrowding might be contributory factors. Consequently, when plague was again feared in 1603, the corporation ordered the closure for two weeks of all the alehouses on Backside, an area then notorious for its number of unlicensed alehouses, brothels, prostitution, filth, disease and crime.

An inevitable consequence of high food prices and plague was an increased number of paupers, and a growing concern on the part of both burgesses and corporation regarding the

26   *The rich man and the poor man; a contemporary print.*

costs this might entail. In 1556 an appeal had been addressed to the mayor by a number of burgesses calling on him to expel from the town all poor people who 'daily came in and tarried in the town'. What action was taken is not known but in the 1570s the burgesses who sat on the ancient 'Mickleton Jury' twice called upon the town's aldermen to 'weed out idle persons that be come into this town of late'. There was particular concern in the 1570s – although this was a relatively prosperous period – because it was known, in the words of the burgesses, that 'the plague is sparkled abroad in the country' and it was generally believed that vagabonds and poor people coming into the town might bring the plague with them. Those townsmen who made money by renting out cheap housing on the edge of the town to poor incomers, or put up new hovels for them, were also criticised. The jury recommended that:

> all such as make any buildings in any lane or back side of this town and take in any tenants to them, that then the landlord shall be bound to Mr Mayor and the town in a good round sum of money to discharge the town if they leave any children behind them.

When, in 1601, news reached the town that Parliament had agreed new poor law legislation, allowing parishes to levy a rate to meet the costs of poor relief, the corporation acted extremely quickly to take advantage of the new opportunity. In the same year the former hospital of St John, on the York road, was converted into a workhouse and John Cooper was appointed overseer. He was told by the corporation that he must 'walk the town to take up rogues and such like and punish such as shall be committed to him' but he also had to provide care for such 'poor infants' as were lodged with him. Although the workhouse was situated in St Mary's parish all three parishes were soon contributing towards meeting its costs, and it was effectively the workhouse for the whole town.

FOUR

The Jacobean Town and the Civil War, 1603-60

The Early Seventeenth Century

The first half of the 17th century was for Nottingham, as for many other English towns, a period of continuing economic stagnation, recurrent 'visitations' of the plague, and an almost desperate determination to keep down the costs of poor relief. Concerns amongst the burgesses regarding what many saw as the unwarranted degree of power exerted in the town by a few wealthy inhabitants, through their monopoly of seats on the corporation, also came to a head in these years. Also, with hindsight, we can see that a much greater national crisis was slowly developing from the 1620s, namely a growing discontent among many people, including some of the most wealthy and powerful families of the region, with the political and religious decisions of the government. Such discontent would end in the complete collapse in trust between king and Parliament, and in a Civil War announced by Charles I when he raised the royal standard at Nottingham in August 1642. These developments, the Civil War itself, and the so-called 'Interregnum' that followed are the subject of this chapter.

The twin problems of poverty and plague, which we have seen were such an important feature of the last years of Elizabeth's reign, continued to play a major role in the social history of the town throughout the first few decades of the new century. For the corporation and most townspeople the chief concern became the need to prevent a constantly threatening influx of extremely poor and possibly plague-carrying country folk. We saw in the last chapter that even in the 'good' years of economic growth of the 1560s and 1570s there had been concern that too many 'foreigners' were being allowed to settle in the town, but now the issue became more pressing than ever. The workhouse, which opened in 1601 in the former premises of the medieval St John's hospital, quickly became also the town's House of Correction, where 'foreign rogues and beggars' could be lodged and set to work after a whipping from the beadle.

Further measures soon followed. In 1606 it was ordered that the 'holes' (presumably the caves) in Hollow Stone should be filled in to prevent them from becoming homes for beggars. In 1612 attempts were made to stop poor migrants building hovels for themselves on the underdeveloped east end of the town and in the already notorious Backside, and in 1619 another order was made allowing the mayor to prosecute and fine landlords who took in lodgers from outside the town, unless they paid a surety of £20 to cover any expenses incurred if the lodgers become a burden on the poor rates. Since the middle of the 16th century the town had been divided into seven wards, with each alderman assigned certain responsibilities for each. It was now felt that the aldermen also needed the assistance of constables and beadles to control the poor. In December 1615 the borough accounts therefore included payments made for 'keepinge out the cuntrie poor on Christmas even.'

A number of attempts were also made during the century to set the town's own poor children to do some form of work in the workhouse, such as wool spinning and carding, in the hope that the costs of poor relief could be offset and the children might learn useful habits and skills. Such attempts, however, were hardly ever successful. In 1615 £20 was set aside by the corporation to pay for the necessary equipment and raw materials. Nothing more is then heard about the scheme but in 1623 there were complaints from the Mickleton Jury that pauper children from the workhouse were being sent out to beg in the town streets, licensed to do so by the overseer. In 1627 new, more ambitious, plans were drawn up to ensure that the children were gainfully employed but again the scheme seems to have failed. Three years later the governor of the workhouse, Martin Hill, was in debt to the corporation for £100 and had to be replaced 'with all convenient speed'. Licensed begging continued and in 1647 the borough records refer to a Beadle of the Beggars, charged with ensuring that only the town's own beggars, wearing their appropriate beggar's licence, were on the streets, and that any outsiders were rounded up, whipped at the pillory at the Saturday market, and driven out of the town. Further attempts to employ the poor continued to be made, however, involving flax spinning and candlewick making. If possible, efforts were also made to apprentice pauper children to local tradesmen, with the corporation meeting the costs of the indentures. In 1630-1 the corporation paid for 11 pauper children to be apprenticed.

The winter of 1630-1 was an especially miserable time for the poor as high bread prices and high levels of unemployment threatened famine conditions. In the face of this the corporation felt obliged to buy up basic foodstuffs and sell them at a subsidised price to those in the most desperate condition. In November 1630 it was therefore agreed to appoint five overseers:

> to buy for the use of the poor of this town … twenty quarters of barley and five quarters of pease, and weekly to deliver by pecks and half-pecks to the poor according to the greatness or number of their families, and at some reasonable prices, under the market, and the loss to be borne from time to time by the town.

For the parish constables, responsible for maintaining law and order, large numbers of desperately poor people on the streets begging for bread or money were a serious cause for concern. In the winter of 1630-1 the situation was particularly worrying in the west side of the town, and especially in the Hounds Gate and Castle Gate area. The food subsidies begun two months before were clearly insufficient. In January 1631 the constables for this area asked the Corporation to do more for the poor:

> either to set them on work to cloth making, or else that every man may be cessed according to his ability, that so they may be kept at home, and restrained from swarming in our streets as they do, both young and old.

There are also many examples during the century of the better-off leaving money in their wills to help the 'deserving poor' or setting up charitable trusts for this purpose. In

1617, for instance, William Gregory paid for 11 almshouses to be built in Hounds Gate, known as the White Rents almshouses, for 'poor aged people' to live rent-free, and in 1630 Alderman Staples established a fund to provide interest-free loans to help young burgesses set themselves up in business.

Another issue of considerable concern to many of the town's burgesses at the beginning of the 17th century was the oligarchical nature of the corporation. This had been a major cause of contention and frustration since at least 1449 when the charter granted in that year had given the town a new and more powerful governing body consisting of a mayor and six aldermen who, once elected by the rest of the burgesses, would serve for life. Pressure from disgruntled burgesses had led the corporation to agree in 1577 to enlarge the corporation by admitting six burgesses who had previously held office as chamberlains (treasurers), but this was hardly calculated to satisfy many. Anger and discontent rumbled on, fuelled frequently by allegations that some members of the corporation neglected their duties, were guilty of 'lewd' and immoral behaviour or, worse still, were corrupt and profited from their positions by leasing to themselves corporation property or tithe-collection rights at below market rates. Disappointment over the 1577 decision had prompted a number of burgesses to particularly target the mayor for that year, Henry Newton, whose private life made him vulnerable to allegations of inappropriate conduct. Later that same year they managed to have him driven from office after accusing him of being 'not worthy … to be an alderman for divers causes, as abusing himself with a naughty quean (prostitute) in his Mayoralty, being taken there withal'.

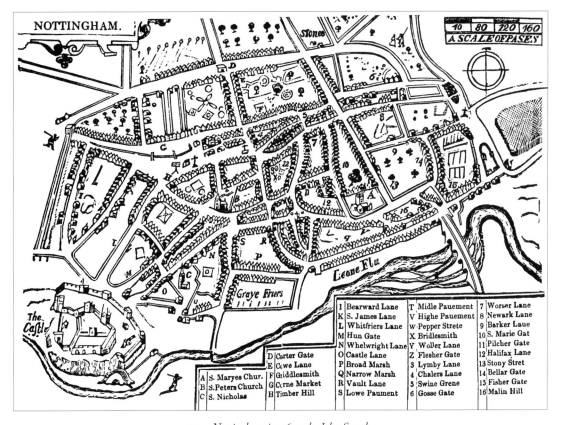

27   *Nottingham in 1610, by John Speed.*

The burgesses' ancient right to form the Mickleton Jury, and make regular reports to the corporation on matters of general concern, was particularly used as a means of highlighting their grievances. Early in the 17th century matters came to a head again when the long-standing demand that the corporation should be substantially enlarged, by creating a 'lower house' of 48 burgesses, was again pressed. In 1602 the arguments for a larger, more representative, corporation were put to the Quarter Sessions but attempts to agree a compromise failed again. In 1605, however, the dispute was referred to an assize judge who finally imposed a settlement. The corporation would in future be composed of the mayor, six other aldermen, 18 senior councillors who had at one time held office as chamberlains or sheriffs (and had therefore already been chosen by the mayor and aldermen) plus six commoners who had never held any office before elected by their fellow burgesses. Dissension in the town was for the time being much diminished but little really had changed. Effectively, the oligarchy had been simply enlarged a little and there remained plenty of scope for self-seeking councillors. The senior and junior councillors all held their positions for life so elections were few and irregular. The aldermen were appointed by the corporation, and the burgesses usually had very little choice in the election of senior councillors as the numbers eligible for election were strictly controlled by limiting the numbers of those chosen to act as sheriffs or chamberlains. Those admitted to this select group were known as the Clothing or Livery. The addition of six junior councillors was to make very little difference as the aldermen could only be chosen from either the senior councillors or from the Clothing; besides the six junior councillors could always be outvoted and their presence was not required to have a *quorum*.

The Approach of Civil War

It is not difficult to see why a number of the decisions taken by Charles I alienated large sections of English society, including at least some of the leading figures who either served on the town's corporation or represented their town or county in Parliament. Charles had been on the throne barely a year when, in June 1626, he quarrelled with his second Parliament over the Duke of Buckingham's policy of war against France, promptly dissolved it and resolved to raise the money for Buckingham's extremely unpopular foreign venture by imposing forced loans. To make matters worse it was announced that any gentleman who refused to pay would be thrown into prison without right of *habeas corpus*. The anger felt by many in Nottingham was made very clear when the king's commissioners collecting the forced loan passed through the town. The streets were strewn with leaflets denouncing the king's actions, and among the county gentlemen who refused to pay and suffered arrest and imprisonment was Sir Thomas Hutchinson, a county MP and one of the town's richest inhabitants with a house on High Pavement.

Further developments that were also likely to stir up resentment included the king's insistence on his right to collect customs duties on wine and wool, known as tunnage and poundage, without parliamentary authority, and the aggressive church reforms initiated by Charles' religious advisor and confidante, William Laud, Bishop of Bath and Wells. Most damaging of all, however, was probably the king's decision in 1635 to impose a Ship Money tax on the entire country. Not only was this not authorised by Parliament, which had not been called since 1629, but it was unprecedented to levy such a tax in peacetime. Moreover, in the past it had only ever been imposed on coastal towns, to raise money for coastal defences. Now, however, the county was being ordered to pay £3,509, of which Nottingham had to raise £200. For two years the great majority of both country folk and townspeople paid their assessment, albeit grudgingly, but in 1637 it was reported that growing numbers were refusing to pay and being summoned before the courts, and in 1638 and 1639 the revolt grew steadily so that by 1640 the new high sheriff, Thomas Williamson, had to report that he could raise no money at all in either Nottingham or Newark.

By this time anti-government feeling was also being exacerbated by the demands being made on the town by the war against Scotland, where Charles and Laud were attempting to impose the Anglican prayer book on an unwilling Calvinistic kirk. In 1639, and again in 1640, Nottingham had to contribute its trained band soldiers and provide them with money and food, and in the latter year the troops also had to be billeted in the town. Charles' army then suffered a humiliating defeat at the hands of the Scots and the townsmen had to contribute to the costs of maintaining and disbanding not only the English army in 1641 but the Scots' army as well.

After Charles left London in January 1642, having failed to arrest Pym and four other parliamentary opponents, it soon became apparent that there was now a struggle for power between King and Parliament that could end in civil war. Both sides were now busy taking measures to secure fortresses and arsenals. Nottingham, like most other towns, was deeply divided but the mayor at this time, John James, was already known for his parliamentary sympathies. The corporation was too divided to act together but in June James 'and other prominent citizens' sent an urgent message to the parliamentary leaders at Westminster asking for their permission to raise a local force of volunteers which could be trained and equipped to defend the town if necessary. This action had been prompted by an attempt by some of Charles' supporters, led by Lord Newark, to seize the town magazine. This had only been prevented by a group of townspeople led by John Hutchinson, the son of Sir Thomas. Parliament readily agreed to the mayor's request but on 21 July, before any serious measures could be taken, the king himself arrived in the town accompanied by a force of 800 soldiers, and the mayor was obliged to kneel before his sovereign, kiss the king's ring, and perform all other usual obsequies.

The corporation also felt obliged to present the king with a purse containing £50 in gold and for the time being it was agreed that the town's magazine would remain under the corporation's control. Charles and his retinue then left to try to secure control of the arsenals kept at Leicester and Coventry, but on 19 August the high sheriff, John Digby, acting on Charles's orders, broke into the Nottingham magazine and seized the weapons and ammunition stored there. Three days later, on 22 August, Charles himself, with his court and his accompanying forces, was back in the town and ready to declare war on his enemies, and that evening he had the royal standard raised on an exceptionally tall flag pole just to the north of the castle, on a site known ever afterwards as Standard Hill.

The Civil War and the Interregnum

Charles remained in Nottingham for three weeks, rapidly gathering support throughout the Midlands. The story that few rallied to his cause, so often repeated by historians, is false and dates from the often unreliable account of the Civil War written by the Royalist Edward Hyde, Earl of Clarendon, in his *True Historical Narrative of the Rebellion and Civil Wars in England,* which he completed in 1674. As soon as the royal party had

28   *Nottingham Castle – 'King Charles I raising his standard – 22 August 1642', painting by Henry Dawson, 1811-78.*

arrived in the town, the Parliamentary faction had fled into hiding, among them the mayor, John James, the deputy recorder, James Chadwick, and John Hutchinson and his brother George. A number of the local gentry were quick to pledge their support and raise forces for the king's cause, including the Clifton family, Sir William Staunton and Gervase Holles, and even after the king's party had left the town in September it was not at first safe for the Parliamentary faction to return. Although the town was clearly of some considerable strategic value, controlling as it did an important river crossing, the Royalists both within and without the town failed to take the necessary initiative. Charles and his advisors were apparently at this stage focussed almost entirely on assembling an army capable of marching on London and retaking the city, and on 23 October the two sides met at Edgehill. The battle proved indecisive, however, and it was now that the Parliamentary group in the town seized their opportunity to put together a force to support their cause and take control of both the castle and the town. A cavalry regiment was raised by one of the local gentry, Sir Francis Thornhagh, commanded by his son, and a regiment of foot soldiers was raised by Colonel Francis

Pierrepont, commanded by himself but with the assistance of John Hutchinson, who was now made a lieutenant colonel, and George Hutchinson, his younger brother, who became a major. A Nottinghamshire Defence Committee was also established, including Francis Thornhagh Jnr, Colonel Pierrepont and the Hutchinson brothers, charged with taking all necessary measures for the defence of both castle and town. Relations with the corporation might have been expected to be a source of friction but instead the two bodies seem to have worked well together. There were few determined Royalists on the corporation and they now found themselves isolated and out-manoeuvred. Only a few townsmen are known to have left the town to join the Royalist forces, among them the town clerk, Robert Greaves, and Alderman Robert Burton. Fear that their property would be confiscated in their absence was no doubt an important disincentive to Royalists thinking of leaving the town. As a warning to others, Robert Greaves' malt mill was confiscated by the corporation.

In December 1642 the defence committee had the corporation's full support in raising a special tax to pay the wages of the soldiers who now formed the Parliamentary garrison, and a month later defences began to be erected at key positions, particularly on the main roads into the town. A small fortress was also built to protect the bridge over the Trent. In April it was agreed that new defence works were particularly needed at Chapel Bar and Cow Lane Bar and that a drawbridge should be erected over the river Leen. To meet the costs of these works the defence committee insisted on another tax assessment of the townsfolk in June, and yet another followed only two months after this. The fear of an attack from the Royalist forces controlling Newark ensured co-operation, and there was also concern that those in the town who secretly hoped for a Royalist victory would betray the town if a serious assault was launched. Both fears were well justified. In September a Royalist force of about six hundred soldiers entered the town, helped, it was alleged, by the negligence or treachery of one of the town's aldermen, Francis Toplady, who was known for his royalist sympathies. Not all members of the 30-strong nightwatch appear to have been at their posts and the Royalists were able to slip in to the town under cover of darkness, unseen by the soldiers in the castle. Numerous prisoners were taken, including the mayor. They were tied up and placed in the sheep pens in the market place, while their shops and houses were looted. Lucy Hutchinson, the very loyal wife of John Hutchinson, who was now the castle governor, tells us in her *Memoirs of Colonel Hutchinson* that 'the cavalliers … fell to ransack and plunder all the honest men's houses in the towne, and the cavalliers of the towne, who had call'd them in, helpt them in this worke'. They also set up their muskets on the tower of St Nicholas's church and were able to fire into the castle yard, killing one man. John Hutchinson managed to send messengers to Derby and Leicester to ask for assistance and within five days the castle garrison had been reinforced by about 400 men and was large enough to be able to force the Royalists to withdraw to Newark, taking with them their prisoners and plunder. Toplady's house was now plundered by the garrison troops and 'he himselfe, with severall other townsmen and countriemen, who had been very active against the well-affected, at this time were brought up prisoners to the castle'.

At the time of the first Royalist attack Lucy Hutchinson was only 23, five years younger than her husband. She was a well-educated, very intelligent and resourceful young woman who enjoyed writing poetry and translating the Classical authors, particularly the Roman poet Lucretius. She stayed with her husband in the castle garrison throughout the Civil War and used her medical skills, acquired from her mother, to nurse the wounded and dying on both sides of the conflict. Her *Memoirs of Colonel Hutchinson*, written after her husband's death, is one of the best contemporary accounts of the Civil Wars and the events leading to them. She was a committed Republican and remained absolutely loyal to her husband. At times her account reads as a eulogy to John Hutchinson and is never an entirely impartial or dispassionate history of events. It remains, however, wonderfully vivid and very readable.

A good example of this comes with Lucy Hutchinson's description of the next Royalist attack on the town, four months after the first. She tells us that it was a bitterly cold January day and estimated that about three thousand Royalists were involved in the action. Once again, the town could not be defended and a small Parliamentary cavalry force which engaged the Royalists was forced to withdraw to the safety of the castle, much to the fury of her husband. This time John Hutchinson was determined to drive the Royalists out of the town before they could establish a foothold. Lucy Hutchinson gives us a graphic description of what happened next:

29   *Colonel John Hutchinson.*

> [He] stirred them up to such a … shame, that they dismounted, and all tooke musketts to serve as foote, with which they did so very good service, that they exceeding well regain'd their reputations … Betweene thirty and forty of [the enemy] were killed in the streetes, fourscore were taken prisoners, and abundance of armes were gather'd up, which the men flung away in haste, as they ran … towards evening they all withdrew … Many of them died in their returne [to Newark] and were found dead in the woods and in the townes they past through … Many of their horses were quite spoyl'd: for two miles they left a greate track of blood which froze as it fell upon the snow, for it was such bitter weather that the foote had waded almost to the middle in snow …

Colonel Hutchinson had been appointed governor of the castle in the previous August, shortly before the previous attack on the town. His appointment was extremely controversial and very much resented by those who were his senior in rank, and particularly by Colonel Pierrepont, his immediate superior, who had been passed over for this promotion. Hutchinson was a man of action, a very strong-willed character capable of inspiring great loyalty from his troops, who admired his personal bravery. He was also inspired in his devotion to the Parliamentary cause by his experiences as a child. As an 11-year-old boy he had seen his father arrested, humiliated and taken to prison for refusing to pay what he regarded as an illegal forced loan, and without trial or any certainty as to when he would be released. But at 28 he was also much younger than most of the other members of the Nottingham Defence Committee; he was no diplomat, he had strong views on religious matters, and he did not hesitate to tell those who crossed him precisely what he thought of them. In consequence, the defence of Nottingham was conducted for much of the duration of the Civil Wars by a castle governor who was completely at odds with both his own defence committee and the town's corporation.

On two occasions the defence committee and corporation attempted to have him removed from his position, but on both occasions the Parliamentary leadership at Westminster supported him, no doubt suspecting at least some element of petty jealousy, but also mindful of Hutchinson's considerable abilities and his dedication to the cause. One of his more controversial decisions, and one of the reasons for the first attempt to have him removed, was his instruction to have the city's cannons removed to the castle. His reasoning was sound. The town could not be defended against a determined assault with or without its guns and when it fell the guns could be then used against the castle. The castle, on the other hand, could be made defensible, especially if given sufficient firepower, and the townsfolk could take shelter in the castle when an assault came. This was not, however, a message calculated to win him friends in the town, particularly as the townsfolk and corporation already resented the imposition of martial law and their consequent loss of independence.

Only a little less controversial was his order to pull down St Nicholas's church after the Royalists had withdrawn following their first assault. As the Royalists had used the church as a high point from which to attack the castle this was not an unreasonable decision, but his known antipathy towards the town's Presbyterian clergy may have made his motives suspect to his enemies. In one of the petitions presented to the Parliamentary leadership it was alleged that he had maligned the local ministers of religion, describing them as 'proud', 'factious' and 'peevish'. His opinion of his own defence committee was also highly critical. The petitioners claimed that he had told one of their number that he was 'a base lying cheating fellow' and he was alleged to have declared at one point, 'Let me die and perish, rot and starve before I will comply with such knaves as are in the Committee at Nottingham.'

30   *Lucy Hutchinson.*

Hutchinson was obliged to go to Westminster to defend himself against the accusations and the case dragged on well into 1645. While he was away a Royalist raiding party again managed to capture the bridge over the Trent and its fort. On hearing this, the case was speedily concluded, the governor's authority was once more confirmed and Hutchinson hurried back to Nottingham to take charge again.

A regular guard continued to be kept and the town's defences were maintained, but the town was not attacked again. Relations between the governor and his critics also improved. There had always been a minority on both the defence committee and the corporation who had refused to support the petitions against him, and in November 1645 a majority of the corporation were willing to support a motion that the governor be offered the freedom of the town, in recognition that he 'hath done faithful and good service in his place to the State and garrison'. We can only speculate about what had brought about such a remarkable change. The young colonel may have learnt to be a little more diplomatic in his dealings with his colleagues and a second endorsement by the Parliamentary leadership in the Commons may also have convinced even his most bitter opponents that continued opposition was futile.

By this time it was becoming clear to many that the end of the war could not be long delayed, and that the Parliamentary forces would be triumphant. The Battle of Naseby, fought on the Leicestershire-Northamptonshire border in June 1645, had been a crushing victory for the New Model Army under Fairfax and Cromwell. The king's principal army had been defeated and large numbers of veterans had been killed or captured. The Royalist armies attempted to regroup but then suffered a second catastrophe in September when the New Model Army stormed Bristol and Prince Rupert, finding his forces trapped, surrendered ignominiously. No longer fearing an assault on the town, the Nottingham garrison was able to take part in the final siege of Newark in the winter and spring of 1646. When Newark fell on 6 May 1646, the Royalists had lost almost their last stronghold; only Oxford still held out, but only for two more months.

The Civil Wars did not end, however, with the surrender and imprisonment of King Charles, although this was not at first apparent. In Nottingham, as elsewhere, it was believed in 1646 that the fighting was over. The garrison was reduced to 100 men on orders from the Commons, although this was still too many for the townsmen as the soldiers were billeted in the town. The town's defence works on the bridges were taken down in October 1646, and in March 1647 a start was made on the removal of the town's other defences, beginning with the bar on Cow Lane. This had not been completed, however, when news came in the early summer of 1648 that the wars had begun again. Although a prisoner on the Isle of Wight, kept under close guard, Charles had been able to contact the Scots and persuade them to march on England. As they marched south new hope was given to the Royalists and once again Royalist forces were being mustered in the county. This time, however, the war would be short-lived. An attempt was made by a Royalist force under Gilbert Byron (ironically a cousin of John Hutchinson) to seize the town. In July, a Royalist force of 400 horse dragoons and 200 musketeers over-ran the small Parliamentary garrison at Lincoln, burnt down the Bishop's Palace and looted much of the upper town before retreating and crossing the Trent at Gainsborough, pursued by a much larger Parliamentary force. They headed towards Nottingham but the Parliamentary army caught up with them a few miles to the south-east of the town, near the village of Willoughby-on-the-Wolds. The battle quickly became a massacre and the few Royalists who did survive were brought as prisoners into the town. A little later, in August, the town learnt that the main Scottish and Royalist army had been defeated by Cromwell's New Model Army at Preston.

At the end of the year Charles was brought to London from the Isle of Wight and early in January 1649 he was put on trial in Westminster Hall. One of those who sat in judgement on the King was Nottingham's Colonel Hutchinson. The colonel had been elected to represent the town in the so-called Long Parliament in 1646. At the end of the trial he was one of those who signed the King's death warrant.

The castle was repaired in 1648-9 and then kept in good order for the next two years. The removal of the town's defences, however, was only temporarily halted and in 1651 Colonel Hutchinson applied for permission to have the castle destroyed. While serving as a member of the Council of State he had come to fear the ambition of Cromwell, and he now feared that he might use the castle, as he believed he had used the army, as an instrument to advance his own position. Permission for demolition was granted in May and during the next two months the ancient castle was reduced to rubble. The removal of the town's defences was also now completed. By this time the wars were truly over. Charles II's forces had been defeated at the battle of Worcester on 3 September and Charles had fled into hiding before escaping to France in disguise.

During Cromwell's Protectorate the town's loyalty to the new regime was underlined by the election to Parliament in 1654 of two men who had served as officers in Nottingham's Parliamentary forces during the war: Colonel James Chadwick, who was also the deputy recorder for the town, and Captain John Mason, who had been in charge of the town volunteers and had been made an honorary freeman of the borough in recognition of his services in 1645. Men of a similar stamp were also elected in the next two elections (1656 and 1658). Interference in local affairs by Cromwell's major-generals, including the elections of 1656, was – as in the rest of the country – much resented, but the corporation nevertheless felt it a diplomatic necessity to offer Major-General Edward Whalley the freedom of the town, which he graciously accepted.

The corporation continued to reflect a range of views, however, with even the Royalist Alderman Toplady managing to survive in place. Many in the town still held him responsible for the damage done in the first Royalist attack on the town but he would appear to have had sufficient friends on the corporation to prevent any attempt to have him removed. Ironically, it was Toplady who, as mayor, had to lead the corporation in proclaiming, on 21 December 1653, 'My Lord General Cromwell' as 'Lord Protector of the three nations of England, Scotland and Ireland'. Moreover, in August of the same year, the former Royalist town clerk, Robert Greaves, was given his old job back even though he had left the town to join the Newark garrison in 1642. And then to complete this policy of putting the past behind them and forgiving and forgetting, Greaves was also elected onto the corporation as well – and on the same day that Mayor Toplady had to make his declaration of loyalty to the new Lord Protector.

Francis Toplady was mayor again in 1660-1 when (and this time to his genuine delight) he was able to proclaim the restoration of the monarchy and hail the return to England of King Charles II. Cromwell had died two years before and the intervening years had been a period of considerable anxiety and uncertainty as it quickly became clear that Cromwell's son, the gentle Richard Cromwell, had inherited none of his father's gifts for leadership, and was quite incapable of controlling the myriad of religious and political factions that until now his father had kept in check. Consequently, the mayor was probably reflecting a widespread feeling of relief and genuine happiness. He ordered a troop of soldiers in the town to beat their drums and fire their muskets in the air to mark the event, but most of the townspeople also happily joined in and shouted their approval. The corporation minutes record there was 'such shouting of people as was to the wonderment of all' and those few in the town who did not welcome the return of the Stuarts were clearly taken completely by surprise to witness such enthusiasm. The minutes add that the people's evident joy was to the 'astonishment of those few Phanaticks in town'.

For many, a major reason for their delight was the prospect that the days of Puritanism were now surely over. During the previous decade children had been forbidden from playing in the streets on the Sabbath and even Christmas celebrations had been stopped. Music had also been frowned upon. A request to the corporation to reinstate the town waits was turned down in 1647, and in 1656 Lucy Hutchinson was strongly criticised for allowing music to be played in her house on the Sabbath. For many townspeople the establishment of new and radical religious sects in the town was another most unwelcome and worrying development. The arrival of garrison troops in the town at the beginning of the war had led to the establishment of a small Baptist community, which soon won support and encouragement from Lucy Hutchinson. Even more alarming to many was the success of the Quakers in establishing themselves in the town in the 1650s. Their willingness to interrupt church services and publicly denounce all other Christian denominations in strong language was especially resented. When their founder, George Fox, came to the town in 1649 he noisily interrupted Sunday worship in St Mary's church and had himself arrested and placed in the custody of one of the town's sheriffs, John Reckless, whom he then proceeded to convert. For the majority of townspeople the return of the king meant hope for both a more stable and freer society, and the minority who dissented from this view could be dismissed as 'Phanaticks'.

Some, however, had every reason to fear the restoration of the monarchy, and particularly those who had signed the death warrant of Charles I, including Nottingham's former governor, Colonel John Hutchinson. At first it seemed that after the Restoration the colonel might be allowed to remain in retirement and obscurity on his estate at Owthorpe, where he had rebuilt his family home, following its destruction during the Civil Wars. However, he had many powerful enemies and was constantly under suspicion, and in 1663 he was arrested and accused – without any evidence – of involvement in a plot against the king. Lucy Hutchinson made every effort to secure his release and managed to obtain an interview with the Secretary of State, Henry Bennet, but to no avail. He was already in poor health and did not long survive his imprisonment in Sandown Castle in Kent, dying there just a year later, in October 1664.

FIVE

Restoration, 'Glorious Revolution' and Economic Revival, 1660-1714

Population Growth and Economic Revival

The half-century between the restoration of Charles II in 1660 and the death of the last of the Stuarts, Queen Anne, in 1714, was a period of considerable political and religious turmoil in Nottinghan in which it remained almost as deeply divided as it had been during the Civil Wars. But it was also a period of economic growth and expansion in which two industries, malting and framework knitting, grew particularly rapidly, making sizeable fortunes for a number of the town's more successful entrepreneurs and drawing in new immigrants from the surrounding countryside. Moreover, with economic prosperity came also a rapid growth in the number of new, high-quality, fashionable houses being built in the town.

Analysis of parish registers has enabled historians to estimate that the town's population increased by approximately three-quarters between 1660 and 1720, from about 4,300 to approximately 7,700 people. This was partly due to the disappearance of plague after the 1660s. The last serious outbreak appears to have occurred in 1667 and in consequence the parish registers suggest that the population in 1670 was probably no larger than it had been 10 years before. During the 1670s, the town's population grew by almost a thousand and, after a sharp check in the 1680s, continued to expand to reach about six thousand by the turn of the century. Growth would have been more marked had it not been for a series of serious outbreaks of smallpox, which caused particularly high death rates among infants and young children. During the first half of the 18th century there was not a single decade without at least one serious outbreak of the disease.

One reason for the growth in population was immigration. Although the corporation continued to do its best to keep out of the town any impoverished incomers who might prove a burden on the poor rates, the number of immigrants settling in the town increased considerably after the ending of the Civil Wars. Some traditional crafts were in decline, most notably perhaps the tanning and ironworking trades, but employment opportunities generally were expanding, and the town was again becoming an attractive prospect for the would-be immigrant.

No industry in Nottingham grew more rapidly in these years than framework knitting, and in particular the production of high-quality silk hosiery. The stocking frame had been invented in about 1589 by a Nottinghamshire clergyman, the Revd William Lee, in the village of

31   *Prospect of Nottingham from the west, 1677.*

Calverton, about eight miles north-east of Nottingham. Lee was unable to gain a patent for his invention and emigrated to France in about 1610, but not before he had developed his machine to knit fine silk stockings as well as worsted, and had taught a small number of local craftsmen how to build and operate his machine. By 1620 Lee was dead and his brother James and most of his associates had returned to England. Most settled in the Old Street district of London and this would become the principal centre of the industry during the rest of the century. James, however, returned to the Calverton district of Nottinghamshire, where he was able to help ensure that the industry begun by his brother continued to grow steadily, and this forest area of the county became the industry's first local centre. But this would not remain the case for long, and in 1641 we hear of the first two stockingers' shops in Nottingham, employing at most perhaps 20 knitters. By 1660 there were probably about 200, according to the industry's first historian, Gravener Henson, and from the evidence of marriage licences we can deduce that by this time there were probably as many framework knitters in Nottingham as in the rest of the county put together.

Professor Chapman's work using Nottinghamshire marriage licences also shows that the industry grew steadily in each decade from 1660 to 1700 in both Nottingham and the county parishes. Just 16 framework knitters are mentioned in Nottingham marriage licences in the 1660s but in the 1670s there are 24, in the 1680s 34, and in the 1690s 40. Other evidence suggests that recruitment into the industry was particularly rapid during the 1690s, both in the town and in the surrounding area. An apprenticeship register kept by the Nottingham Deputies of the London Company of Framework Knitters shows 104 apprentices registered in 1695, 122 in 1696 and 54 in 1697, and 300 masters are mentioned, including some women.

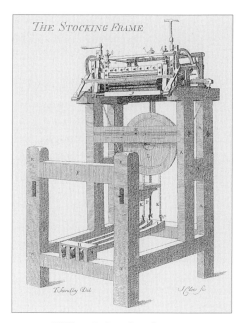

32   *William Lee's stocking frame, c.1750.*

In the late 17th century the Nottingham framework knitters, like their London rivals, still specialised mainly in producing high quality silk hose, for much higher prices could be demanded for silk stockings than for wool or worsted. The best quality men's black, scarlet and blue silk hose bought for the court of Charles II in the 1670s cost from 10s. to 18s. a pair. The earliest evidence for the price of woollen and worsted stockings comes from Leicester in 1690. At this date woollen and worsted stockings were worth no more than 1s. 6d. to 2s. 6d. a pair.

Nottingham's links with London were of the utmost importance. London was by far the largest market for silk hosiery and the silk used by the town's knitters was imported through London. London merchants had for many years attended the annual Lenton Fair, just a mile to the west of Nottingham, and until the 1680s it would seem that the initiative remained with them, rather than with the Nottingham hosiers. The local historian, Dr Charles Deering, writing in the 1740s, tells us:

> Our Nottingham shopkeepers till within these sixty years last past did not venture to go long journies, but depended upon the great annual Martinmass Fair at Lenton, a village about a mile distant from Nottingham, where they used to buy their mercers, drapers, grocers, and all sorts of goods they wanted, brought thither by the Londoners, and others; and when first they attempted to travel to London they would take leave of their relations and friends (as I am informed) in as much form as if they were never to see them more … but now they are no more concerned at going to the metropolis and other distant trading and manufactury towns, than they were formerly to go a journey of twelve or twenty miles.

From the earliest days of the Nottingham industry a number of framework knitters had close family and business links with London merchants. Thomas Selby of Nottingham, who is described in his will of 1659 as a 'silk stocking maker', appointed John Groson, 'citizen and merchant of London', as one of the supervisors for the administration of his estate. In 1664 Groson became the first master of the London Company of Framework Knitters. It was also common practice for youths to be sent from Nottingham and surrounding villages to London to serve their apprenticeships as framework knitters. The Foster brothers of Gedling, for instance, were sent to Shoreditch in the 1650s. When John Foster of St Leonard's, Shoreditch, 'citizen and framework knitter', died in 1674 his first bequest was to his cousin in Nottingham, the hosier William Cooper.

The first framework knitters in the town seem to have been men of some substance. The first for which we have any biographical details is John Hoe (c.1640-97), who was mayor of the town in 1695. His father, John Hough, described himself as 'gentleman' in 1652 and was probably comfortably off, and well able to give his son a good start in life. In 1663 John Hoe is described as a silk stocking worker but when he became mayor in 1695 he is described as a hosier, and at his death he possessed five stocking frames and left assets worth about £1,000. His transition from manufacturing to merchanting was not at all unusual among the merchant hosiers of the late 17th and early 18th centuries. The renting out of stocking frames was also a practice established very early, for Thomas Selby charged his son-in-law 1s. 6d. weekly for his frame in the 1650s, and a little later 1s. per week became the standard charge. Many of the knitters in the villages around Nottingham owned their own frames at the end of the century, but many others were renting their equipment from Nottingham hosiers, who also supplied the raw material and purchased the finished products.

A number of factors helped boost the industry's expansion in the late 17th century. The trade was helped in the 1670s by a change in fashion. The flamboyant fashions of the previous hundred years required stockings to be embroidered but now the demand was for plain colours and the bottleneck of the embroidering stage was broken. Also, the success of the trade in the 1680s and 1690s owed much to the banking facilities now being offered by Thomas Smith (1631-99), one of the leading tradesmen in the town at this period. Moreover, by the end of the century the industry had come to be seen as a highly profitable and safe investment by the town's merchant elite, well worthy of investment. One well-documented example is the merchant Joseph Reckless. His inventory of 1708 reveals a wealthy tradesman with assets amounting to £1,214, which included 25 stocking frames valued at £150. Also, by this time the Nottingham stocking-making trade was beginning to benefit from the migration of London hosiers into the region, hoping to escape some of the limitations imposed upon them by the London Company, although this would become of much greater importance in later decades, as we will see in the next chapter.

The town's other major employer in this period was the malting trade. In 1641 there were 60 maltsters in the town, equalling the number of butchers as the largest occupational group. Most, however, were operating on a very small scale and many were probably also tipplers, providing cheap accommodation and refreshment in unlicensed alehouses. Sixty such tippling houses were said to be in the town by 1615. 'When all trades feaylle, [men] turne tiplers', a petition to the corporation complained in 1619. None of the tradesmen who left a will before 1640 is described as a maltster. The town's first historian, an anonymous writer of 1641, reckoned that a major reason for the expansion of the trade up to this time was the many manmade caves and cellars cut into the sandstone bedrock. These were used to keep the ale and beer cool in summer, to store the bracken used to dry the malt in winter, and:

> some that have floors that are large and level use them for making malt, having in them wells and cisterns for steeping of barley. In these they will make malt as kindly in the heat of summer as above ground in the best time of winter by reason whereof there is great abundance made in this town.

As well as the local alehouses selling Nottingham beer there were also 14 inns in the town by 1641 and the larger producers were also exporting their products to other counties. The anonymous writer of 1641 specifically lists 'Lancashire, Cheshire, Shropshire, Staffordshire and the Peak of Derbyshire [where the malt was transported] by badgers, carriers, or hucksters of those counties which fetch it … dayly'.

After the Restoration the number of inns and the number of larger-scale malting houses increased considerably, and malting became a recognised occupation in its own right. Seventeen maltsters left wills between 1660 and 1700, and some were among the wealthiest men to be found in the town. William Coppock, for instance, owned goods worth £355 when he died in 1689. This included 180 quarters of malt in store, his own malt mill, and the 'screen in the malt chamber'. Robert Linley, who was also an ironmonger and roper, possessed £140 worth of malt when he died in 1696.

The quality and taste of Nottingham ale enjoyed a wide reputation. When Celia Fiennes visited the town in 1697 and stayed at the *Blackmoor's Head*, she was, she wrote, 'very well entertained'. This remarkable lady, who was then in her early 30s, travelled throughout the country, riding side-saddle. She had been advised to visit the seaside and spa towns to improve her health, but soon found that she greatly enjoyed the adventure of travel for its own sake, and reporting on the interesting things she learnt about her native country. She noted, for instance, that 'Nottingham is famous for good ale' and attributed this largely to the cool rock-cut cellars where the ale was stored. 'Att the *Crown* is a cellar of 60 stepps down all in the rock like arch worke over your head; in the cellar I dranke good ale.'

While visiting the town she also made sure that she visited one of the town's other relatively new and expanding industries, the glassworks. A glasshouse had been established on a site near Glasshouse Street in 1675, specialising in making clear lead glass drinking ware. A second glassworks was opened in 1700 by Robert Brentnall at the east end of Barker Gate and proved so successful that when Brentnall died in 1713 his possessions were valued at £766, including large quantities of bottles, drinking glasses, decanters and apothecaries' glasses. Another glassmaker in the town, Nicholas Strelley, specialised in producing glass trinkets and novelties, and it was almost certainly Strelley whom Celia Fiennes met in 1697:

> There was a man that spunn glass and made severall things in glass, birds and beasts; I spunn some of the glass and saw him make a swan presently; with divers coloured glass he makes buttons which are very strong and will not breake.

The success of industries after the Restoration such as fine glass manufacturing and mechanised silk stocking production has been seen as evidence of a consumer revolution in these years, driven by rising living standards among the growing middle and upper classes. Further evidence for this development was the opening in Nottingham of a new pottery in about 1692-3, also at the east end of Barker Gate, devoted to the production of high-quality orange-brown stoneware, using clay from Crich in Derbyshire. Nottingham-made stoneware jugs, mugs, tea and coffee cups and garden urns soon found a ready market both across the Midlands, to which they were carried by pack horses or by carriers' wagons, and even in London, to which they were transported by water.

By 1641 wharves had been built on both sides of the Trent and during these years Nottingham remained a small port, from which coal from the nearby mines at Wollaton and Nottingham pottery were exported, along with cheeses from Cheshire, Warwickshire and Staffordshire, corn from the fertile soils of the Trent valley, and lead from Derbyshire. Nottingham malt was transported mainly by carriers' wagons. The chief imports brought

33 *Nottingham Castle as rebuilt for the Duke of Newcastle, 1674-9.*

down the Trent to Nottingham included barrels of herring and other salt fish from Hull, iron, also from Hull, and Scandinavian timber, especially pine planks and boards for use as panelling, floorboards and stairs. For many commodities Nottingham was the effective head of navigation and consequently also an entrepôt for the distribution of goods by road transport to other market towns, including Leicester, Loughborough and Derby.

The growing wealth of many of the town's 'middling sort' of hosiers, maltsters and other merchants, lawyers and doctors and urban gentry, meant that following the ending of the Civil Wars the town enjoyed a building boom, and hence the large imports of timber. Dr Robert Thoroton, in his *Antiquities of Nottinghamshire*, which appeared in 1677, tells us that: 'many people of good quality from several parts, make choice of habitations here, where they find good accommodation'. Fine new houses, built in the latest fashion

34   *Newdigate House in Castle Gate, built* c. 1675-80.

with elegant façades, were being built by the new urban gentry, who vied with one another, as Thororton wryly remarks, to lead 'the fashionable dance of building new Fronts in this Town'.

In the latter years of the century Nottingham became a fashionable residential centre. The Duke of Newcastle gave considerable encouragement to this development when, in 1674, he bought the site of the old castle, had the last remains of the Norman tower removed, and began the building of a large ducal palace, built in what Pevsner called the 'Continental Baroque' style. The work was completed by his son, the 2nd Duke, in 1679. Others, far beneath the duke in social status but enjoying substantial incomes, were keen to build their own fine houses in the town. Few, unfortunately, now survive from this period. One that does, however, is Newdigate House in Castle Gate, built between 1675 and 1680. Its most striking features are the stately alternating window pediments. A three-storey terrace also survives from about 1700 in Brewhouse Yard and is now occupied by the Museum of Nottingham Life.

Religious and Political Controversies

Although the new king seems to have been genuinely in favour of maintaining a high degree of religious toleration in 1660, his first Parliament – known appropriately as 'the Cavalier Parliament' – was determined to enforce High Church Anglicanism, and drive out from public office all those who felt unable to support so radical a move. The Test and Corporation Acts passed in 1661 required all mayors, aldermen and common councillors not only to take an oath of loyalty to the Crown but also to promise to take the sacrament according to the rites of the Church of England within 12 months of their election. Those who could not comply had to resign their positions or face removal. During the previous two decades the principles of Presbyterianism had established a particularly strong hold among the merchant elite of the town, which they had no intention of abandoning. Such was the strength of the movement also among the local clergy that it was possible for a presbytery of 23 ministers to be formed for the town and surrounding district in 1656, including John Barrett of St Peter's, and John Whitlock and William Reynolds of St Mary's. This also included some of the town's merchants, who were appointed elders and met with the ministers every month to settle disputes and problems in the different congregations, approve new elders and test the 'gifts and graces' of applicants for ordination, of whom there were eight appointed in the next four years. Consequently, when the corporation met in August 1662 six of the seven aldermen, including the mayor, resigned their posts, and new aldermen had to be elected. Only Alderman Francis Toplady, who had welcomed the king's return so enthusiastically, felt able to keep his position and he was chosen to serve again as mayor.

Also in 1662, a new Act of Uniformity was passed, which required all incumbents to make a declaration that from now onwards they would use the Book of Common Prayer in their churches. In Nottinghamshire 38 ministers were consequently ejected that year, including Nottingham's three Presbyterian ministers. Further persecution followed with the Five Mile Act of 1665. This forced all deprived ministers to leave the town they had been living in when they had been incumbents and to live at least five miles away. Barrett chose to move to Sandiacre and Whitlock and Reynolds both moved to Mansfield.

Such was the strength of dissent in Nottingham, however, that the magistrates, including the Royalist-Anglican Toplady, were unwilling to enforce the penal laws against unlicensed preachers too rigorously. The episcopal returns of 1669 show that at that time there were 37 conventicles in the county as a whole, mainly meeting in private houses and attended by about two thousand worshippers, but in Nottingham alone there were thought to be more than 800 dissenters. The largest group in the town, and the wealthiest and best connected, were the Presbyterians, who numbered between 400 and 500, but there were also about 200 Congregationalists, 100 Quakers, 20 to 30 Baptists and a small number of Roman Catholics and Jews. The Lincoln Presbyterian, Gervase Disney, found in Nottingham 'a congenial atmosphere' and chose to settle in the town in 1672. He remained undisturbed until 1682, when a wave of anti-dissenting sentiment forced him to go into hiding. Similarly, the former Puritan rector of Screveton, Thomas Bosworth, managed to settle in the town – although forbidden to do so by the Five Mile Act – and preach in his own house.

The religious divisions in the town tended to coalesce from the late 1670s with political divisions. In 1705 Defoe described Nottingham as 'a violently divided town' but this description was also just as valid two or three decades earlier. One of the first indications of this came with the elections for a new Parliament in 1678, the first general election since the overwhelmingly Royalist Parliament had been elected 17 years earlier. Now the town returned both a Tory (as Royalist-Anglicans were commonly known by now), Robert Pierrepont, whose family had a long history of service to the town, and a Whig (as the king's opponents in Parliament were now known), Richard Slater of Nuthall. The new Parliament was soon dissolved by the king, however, owing to his determination to thwart the Earl of Shaftesbury's attempt to pass an Exclusion Bill, which would have prevented Charles' Roman Catholic brother James, the Duke of York, from succeeding to the throne. By this time, however, Whig-Tory conflict in the town had already been further exacerbated by the

35   *Part of 'View of Nottingham from the East', by Jan Sibrechts, c.1627-1703. The newly built Nottingham Castle can be clearly seen, with St Mary's Church in the foreground, the recently rebuilt St Nicholas' Church just to the left, and the large brick mansion, Pierrepont House, built by Colonel Francis Pierrepont, c.1650, to the right.*

behaviour of the town's Tory mayor, Ralph Edge. On 10 December 1678 a riot broke out when Edge refused to accept the burgess's nominee for a vacancy on the Junior Council of the corporation. He gave as his reasons that the nominee, William Drury, was ineligible as he had not served as either a chamberlain or a sheriff, but this was not accepted by the burgesses and they refused to nominate anyone else. Edge then made his own nomination, the Tory Robert Whortley, prompting a mini-riot, with an extremely angry crowd venting their disgust and fury by pelting Edge and the other aldermen with cheese and bread.

A second parliamentary election was then held in 1679, and again the town's burgesses demonstrated their divisions by returning both Pierrepont and Slater. An Exclusion Bill was again introduced and once more passed in both Houses before Charles blocked it again by dissolving Parliament, triggering yet another election which, both nationally and locally, had much the same result as the previous two. In Nottingham both Pierrepont and Slater were re-elected and the country once again elected a Whig majority which was still determined to try to exclude the Catholic Duke of York from succeeding Charles. When a third Bill was duly passed, however, Charles on this occasion not only refused the royal assent and dissolved Parliament; he was also determined not to call another Parliament, if he could possibly avoid it, until he could ensure a favourable result.

The towns were the strongholds of Whig power and Charles and his advisors were well aware that in many cases the town corporations had a decisive influence over the elections of their Members of Parliament. Charles therefore decided to 'request' the charters of 119 incorporated boroughs and then replace them with new ones which would give him the power to nominate the mayor, aldermen, councillors and officers, and therefore hopefully bring about an end to the Whig majority in Parliament. Even before this was attempted, however, Charles began to interfere in corporation elections, including those in Nottingham. In June 1681 the king wrote to the Nottingham corporation recommending the election of William Petty as alderman to fill a vacancy caused by the death of John Parker.

A green light was also given to Tory mayors to do all they could to block the election of any Whiggish candidates to town councils. Consequently, Nottingham's Tory mayor in 1681, Gervase Rippon, refused to accept the election to the corporation of John Sherwin, although he had won twice as many votes as the runner-up, the Tory William Toplady, whom Rippon insisted on swearing in. Nottingham's magistrates had previously turned a blind eye to Sherwin's Presbyterianism but now he was denounced by Rippon's successor as mayor, another Tory, Gervase Wild, as a frequenter of illegal conventicles and 'a very busy fractious turbulent man leading dissenters in all elections to oppose the interests of His Majesty and the magistracy of the town'.

The election of Wild as Rippon's successor also probably owed something to government interference. Shortly before the election the Secretary of State, Sir Leoline Jenkins, wrote in October 1681 to the Lord Lieutenant of the County, the Duke of Newcastle, who was known to be a staunch Tory, to advise him to attend the crucial meeting to encourage the 'loyal party' on the corporation to do their duty. He wrote, rather ambiguously: 'As for the corporation of Nottingham, I make no doubt you will settle it when you appear among them, but if I can do anything here I shall do it with all cheerfulness imaginable.'

By this time there were persistent rumours in the town that the king's real intention was to pack corporations with enough Tories to ensure that their charters would be willingly surrendered, ready for making the necessary alterations. Fearing that this might be the case, the opposition group on the corporation took the precaution of entering caveats to Nottingham's charter with the lord chancellor and attorney general. These forbade any surrender of the charter without the prior knowledge and approval of the burgesses. Their fears were well founded but their measures proved unavailing. On 25 July 1682, during an ordinary meeting of the corporation, the mayor suddenly announced a resolution to surrender the charter. To the mayor's surprise the vote was tied, 14 all, including the mayor's own vote in favour, but he nevertheless pressed ahead with the surrender, using his casting vote. Sir Leoline Jenkins had sent him the instrument of surrender a month before and plans had already been drawn up for one of the Tory aldermen to take the charter to London. In spite of the fury of those who had opposed the surrender, the mayor despatched the charter and the instrument of surrender to the king. A petition against the surrender of the charter was drawn up and signed by more than 300 burgesses and sent to the mayor and to the lord chancellor, but all to no avail. And to make matters worse, it was later learnt that when the deed of surrender was examined by the court lawyers it was found to be inadequate. A new document was then secretly drawn up and, anxious to avoid another stormy meeting, the mayor also secretly broke into the trunk in which the town seal was kept and affixed it to the new document.

The 'loyal party', as they saw themselves, could hardly have handled things less competently but they were resolved to face down their opponents. Matters came to a head on 29 September when the new charter was due to be delivered to the town and a new mayor and new council officers were to be elected. The opposition group, led by Alderman Greaves, the only alderman to vote against the surrender, met together in St Mary's church in the morning and resolved

36   *Three-storey terrace in Brewhouse Yard, built* c.1700; *now the Museum of Nottingham Life.*

to ignore the new charter, which they no doubt suspected would remove them from office, and to elect Greaves as mayor for the coming year. The councillors and burgesses supporting Greaves were encouraged in taking this position by a number of the local Whig gentry, including the MP Richard Slater and Charles Hutchinson of Owthorpe, who joined them in the church. Meanwhile, the out-going mayor, Gervase Wild, had received the new charter and was proposing to have it read out at the Guildhall. The Greaves faction, together with a considerable crowd of very angry and noisy supporters, now crowded into and around the Guildhall, shouting out their support for Greaves and 'No new charter!'. In spite of the hubbub the charter was read but few could have heard very much of it, and Wild and his fellow Tories rightly believed that it was impossible, and probably dangerous, to try to elect a mayor under the terms of the new charter. One of the aldermen later reported: 'I dared stay no longer; the Rabble [were] buoyed up to that Height, and I [was] afraid we shall be knock'd on the head.' In fact, no one seems to have suffered any injury, although Alderman Rippon later claimed that his coat had been damaged, and Wild and his faction were able to leave the Guildhall and go to Wild's house to elect William Toplady as mayor and make the other necessary appointments. Both sides now tried to have their rival mayors proclaimed, as was customary, at the Weekday Cross, just outside the Guildhall. This, however, sparked off more loud protests and chants against the new charter.

To restore order and put an end to the protests, the Duke of Newcastle was ordered to take up residence in the mansion he had recently had built for himself on the site of the old castle. For some months, however, the town had two mayors and two corporations, and prolonged disorder, until Greaves finally surrendered his 'ensigns of honour'. The charter removed all the Whigs from the corporation and the positions of town clerk and recorder were made offices 'to be held at the royal pleasure', and it was the king's pleasure that the new recorder should be the Duke of Newcastle.

The final triumph for the Nottingham Tories, however, came in March 1684, when 29 leading members of the Greaves faction – including Greaves himself and the Whig gentry who had supported him – were charged at the Court of Kings' bench before Lord Chief Justice Jeffries with 'having riotously, unlawfully and seditiously assembled, with many other evil-disposed persons, to disturb the public peace'. Jeffries already had a reputation for irascibility and he would become notorious in the following year for 'the Bloody Assizes' and his brutal suppression of the Monmouth Rebellion, but on this occasion the sentences were not harsh. The defendants were bound over to keep the peace and various fines were imposed, which were then used to pay the court costs and repair Trent Bridge, which had been damaged by recent frosts.

But the Tories' triumph was extremely short-lived, for within a year of the trial Charles II was dead, and his successor, his brother James, was keen to win the support of the Whigs for his plan to establish religious and political equality for his fellow Roman Catholics. To achieve this he would have to call a fresh Parliament and persuade it to repeal the Test and Corporation Acts. Like his brother before him, he believed that the path to a compliant House of Commons lay through achieving compliant municipal corporations, willing to nominate the 'right' candidates, and this in turn meant further royal interference in municipal affairs and town charters. As the laws that James wished to have repealed were introduced and passed by Tories, and because Whigs and dissenters, as well as Roman Catholics, had been their victims, James reasoned, not altogether surprisingly, that his targets on the corporations must be Tories, and Whigs must be restored to power.

In 1687 the Nottingham corporation was therefore ordered to surrender its charter and receive a new one, which gave to the Crown even more powers than the existing one. The monarch, it declared, could remove from office at will the mayor, recorder, town clerk and any of the aldermen and councillors, and by issuing a royal mandate could replace them with men of his own choosing. On 13 January the Tory mayor, Gervase Rippon, was removed together with two aldermen and eight chief councillors, and two further mandates issued in February and March removed the rest of the corporation. The Duke of Newcastle remained in office as the town's recorder, but his loyalty to his monarch was strained almost to breaking point when he had to oversee the removal of political allies such as Rippon, Toplady and Wild. Most galling of all must have been the royal commissioners' choice of replacement for Rippon as mayor: the turbulent dissenter John Sherwin.

A hint of troubles to come appeared very soon, however, when some of those appointed as new aldermen and councillors refused to accept their positions. The legality of the appointments was highly questionable as the final and completed copy of the new charter had not yet been sealed and sent to the town. Moreover, the town's dissenters and Whigs had no more liking for royal interference in their affairs now than they had had six years earlier, and they were extremely suspicious of James's motives and had no wish to see Roman Catholics enjoying either religious or political equality. Indeed, most of them had voted repeatedly for the pro-Exclusion Bill candidate, Richard Slater, in the elections of 1678, 1679 and 1680. Both in Nottingham and in much of the country at large, James had succeeded only in alienating both Whigs and Tories, dissenters and Anglicans. When rumours began to circulate that summer that a number of powerful noblemen were gathering forces to oppose the king, and had invited the king's daughter, Mary, and her husband, the Prince of Orange, to replace him, there was considerable support for this in the town, although also much fear of a further outbreak of civil war.

Nottingham soon found itself at the very centre of the plot for the leaders of the planned coup, the Tory Earl of Danby and the Whig Earl of Devonshire, proposed as one of their first steps to seize control of Nottingham and York, once Mary and Orange had arrived in the country. On 5 November William of Orange landed at Torbay and began a long slow march on London, and on 22 November the two earls finally made their move. Danby successfully seized York, and the Earl of Devonshire and his forces marched unopposed into Nottingham. Any lingering support for James in the town had been largely erased a few weeks earlier, when a Scottish regiment loyal to James had passed through the town and was briefly billeted on the townspeople. Among those said to have been treated 'rudely' by the soldiers was the town's mayor, George Langford. Moreover, approval in the town for the coup consolidated considerably a few days after the arrival of Devonshire, when he was joined in the town by the king's younger and long-estranged daughter, Anne, who was happy to make her support for her elder sister and brother-in-law very clear. Anne only stayed in the town for about a week, but her presence was of great value to the rebellion, for it gave it considerable respectability, and aristocrats who might have hesitated to be associated with it now joined the movement, keen to present themselves as loyal protectors of the princess. By the time Anne left the town, early in December, she was accompanied by more than a dozen nobles, and by the end of the month James had fled to France and the crown was shortly afterwards offered jointly to Prince William and Princess Mary.

The accession of William and Mary finally ended the so-called 'battle of the charters', and with it the era of monarchical interference. In 1692 the charters of both Charles II and James II were declared annulled and the earlier charter of James I was restored. Moreover, the Toleration Act, passed by the new Whig Parliament in 1689, also brought an end to an era of persecution for the town's many dissenters. No longer were their conventicles illegal; provided a license was obtained, new purpose-built chapels could be built and worship conducted openly. Within a year or so of the passing of the Act the Presbyterians (later known as the Unitarians) had built their first chapel on High Pavement and at about the same time the Congregationalists (also known as the Independents) opened their first chapel in Castle Gate. The dissenting ministers who had been driven from the town under the Five Mile Act could also now return and, happily, Nottingham's three Presbyterian ministers of 1662 – Barrett, Reynolds and Whitlock – were all still alive and able to benefit from their new freedom. Indeed, John Barrett was to live until 1713, by which time he was probably the last survivor of the 'Ejection' of 1662. Roman Catholics, however, remained excluded from the terms of the Toleration Act and it by no means offered complete equality to dissenters. Full civil liberty was still denied. The sons of dissenters could attend neither the town's ancient grammar school nor either of the universities of Oxford or Cambridge.

Six
The Eighteenth Century

The Growth of the Town

At the beginning of the 18th century there were probably about six thousand people living in Nottingham, about double the number to have been found a hundred years before. During the first half of the century, however, the rapid growth of the town's hosiery industry brought in much greater numbers of migrants and consequently the pace of population growth quickened considerably, and this in spite of recurrent outbreaks of smallpox. By 1720 there were nearly 8,000 inhabitants, a decade later almost 9,000, and by 1750 almost 11,000. During the second half of the century, however, as the hosiery industry continued to prosper and stimulated expansion in other industries too, the town grew even faster, and when the first national census was conducted in 1801 Nottingham's population stood at

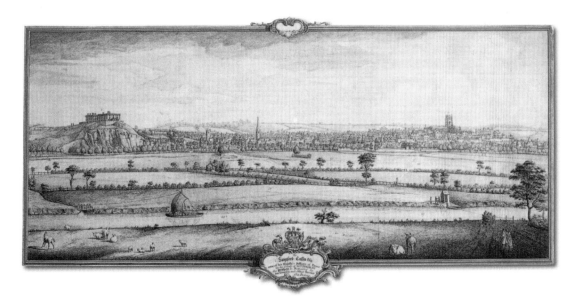

37 'Nottingham from the South, 1742', *Thomas Sandby, 1723-98.*

28,861, between two and three times as large as it had been 50 years earlier. Other towns, such as Manchester and Leeds, had grown more rapidly still and were by this time much larger, but overcrowding in Nottingham at the beginning of the 19th century was probably as bad as anywhere in the country because the enlarged population was still contained within its medieval boundaries. There had as yet been no agreement to enclose the town's surrounding open fields to release land for new housing development, and until this could be agreed the horrors of grossly overcrowded living conditions could only grow worse. During the century the appearance and character of the town had been completely transformed; by 1800 it was rapidly becoming an industrial slum. Moreover, the growth of the hosiery industry had made only a relatively small number of the town's inhabitants wealthy. The majority of the town's population by the end of the 18th century were very poor indeed, and Nottingham was by now no longer famed for its attractive appearance and fine houses – as it was in 1700 – but rather for its radicalism, the seething discontent of much of its population, and for riots so numerous and sometimes so violent that by the 1790s it was felt necessary to build a barracks on the edge of the town to house a regiment of soldiers, making Nottingham the first provincial town in the country to have this distinction.

The Town at the Beginning of the Eighteenth Century

There can be little doubt that Nottingham was a very attractive town in the early years of the 18th century. By this time it had been for many years making a most favourable impression on visitors. In 1675 Thomas Baskerville had visited the town and found it 'as a man might say, Paradise restored; for here you find large streets, fair built houses, fine women, and many coaches rattling about, and their shops full of merchantable riches'. When Celia Fiennes visited the town in the 1690s she called it 'the neatest town I have seen, built of stone and delicate, large and long streetes much like London, and the houses lofty and well built … All the streets are of a good size, all about the town, and well patch'd.' When Daniel Defoe described his visit to the town in about 1725 he, like Baskerville before him and many others since, was struck by the beauty and charm of the local ladies, the excellent taste of the local beers (something Celia Fiennes had also particularly noted), and the size of the market place 'with a vast plenty of provisions'. The town was, he believed, 'one of the most pleasant and beautiful towns in England'.

Such tributes partly reflect the town's success in becoming a fashionable centre for the well-to-do from the late 17th century with many fine houses consequently being built in the town by Nottingham's merchant elite and urban gentry. This development, which is to be found in many towns in this period and is sometimes referred to as an 'urban renaissance', continued well into the 18th century. Two fine houses which have survived from the 1730s are to be found at the upper end of Low Pavement. One, Vault Hall, was erected in 1733 as two semi-detached houses by Francis Gawthern, a white lead manufacturer; the other, Willoughby House, was built by Rothwell Willoughby, the son of Lord Middleton. It is now the premises of a firm of solicitors but looks little different from when it was described by Deering, not long after it had been built, as 'beautiful and well fashioned'. Had he lived a little longer he might also have said the same of Bromley House, another superb example of Georgian architecture, but not completed until 1752, three years after Deering's death. This can still be seen today, in Angel Row, virtually in the market place. In the 18th century the area between the Castle and the Angel Row-Wheelergate-Listergate line was the town's

39   *Willoughby House, built* c.1735.

38   *Vault Hall, built 1733.*

40   *Bromley House, completed 1752.*

41   *The Shire Hall, 1730.*

most fashionable quarter, where many of the town's wealthiest inhabitants chose to live. And few were wealthier than Sir George Smith, the banker, who had Bromley House built. Pevsner described the house as 'very civilised and not at all provincial, as indeed all these best Nottingham houses are, with an elegant, very restrained doorway, Palladian alternating pediments to the main windows and interiors with charming Rococo plaster work. The staircase hall is especially rewarding.'

When Celia Fiennes visited the town she was also particularly struck by the covered walkway on one side of Long Row: 'there is a pyaza all along one side … with stone pillars for walking that runs the length of the streete'. This had probably developed fortuitously

42   *The New Exchange, 1726.*

but by the 1690s the corporation was encouraging property owners to build pillars around the market place in a conscious attempt to imitate London's Covent Garden. Thirty years later, between 1724 and 1726, the appearance of the market place was further improved by the building at its east end of the New Exchange. This concealed the butchers' shambles, stalls and the medieval Spice Chamber and was, as can be seen from illustration 42, a handsome building. By this time both sides of the market place were largely colonnaded and therefore, to achieve architectural unity, the ground floor of the New Exchange was also given a row of pillars. The designer and builder was probably Alderman Marmaduke Pennell, who was mayor for 1724-5, and the driving force behind the development of a number of the town's amenities, including a theatre in St Mary's Gate and the Assembly Rooms in Low Pavement, both of which were calculated to appeal to the town's more prosperous inhabitants and visitors.

The Growth of the Hosiery Industry

One of the main reasons for the town's rapid growth in the 18th century was undoubtedly the success of the hosiery industry. At the beginning of the century Nottingham had already established itself as the largest centre for the industry in the Midland counties, but during the next few decades it would also completely outstrip the London hosiery industry and its entrepreneurs would break the restrictive powers of the London Company. And as the town attracted men of enterprise and capital, willing and able to establish large-scale production, so also did the population of the town swell with migrants seeking employment. But, for all this, Nottingham in 1750 was still a relatively small and attractive town. Badder and Peat's map of Nottingham, published in 1744, shows the impact of the growth of the hosiery industry on the town in the previous half-century. The first concentration of workers' housing can be seen to the north of the market place, in some cases filling up the former yards and gardens of the houses and shops lining Long Row. But the rest of the town is still very open, with many large and formal gardens, open spaces and quite sizeable orchards. During the next half-century, however, as the hosiery industry grew even more rapidly, all this would change. What had so recently been 'one of the most pleasant and beautiful towns in England' became an overcrowded slum, and in the first half of the 19th century the situation would become even worse.

It has been estimated that the number of merchant hosiers in the town rose from something over 50 in 1740 to about a hundred in 1770-5, and then doubled again by the end of the century. They not only controlled the rapidly expanding industry in the town but also much of the industry in the surrounding countryside. In 1812, when the local historian and former framework knitter John Blackner conducted the first census of hosiery frames, there were approximately 2,600 in Nottingham and a further 6,285 in 73 Nottinghamshire villages, and only a small proportion of either town or country frames were in the hands of independent framework knitters; the great majority were owned by Nottingham hosiers and rented out. The second largest centre of the industry in the country by this time was Leicester, with about 1,650 frames.

The success of the industry in Nottingham in the first half of the century was explained partly by the cost advantages enjoyed by Nottingham hosiers over their London rivals. Wages and rents in Nottingham were considerably lower than those in London. Another factor was the greater freedom most Nottingham hosiers enjoyed from the restraints which the London Framework Knitters' Company still imposed in London and which it was

43 *Nottingham, 1744; Badder and Peat's map, drawn for Deering's* History.

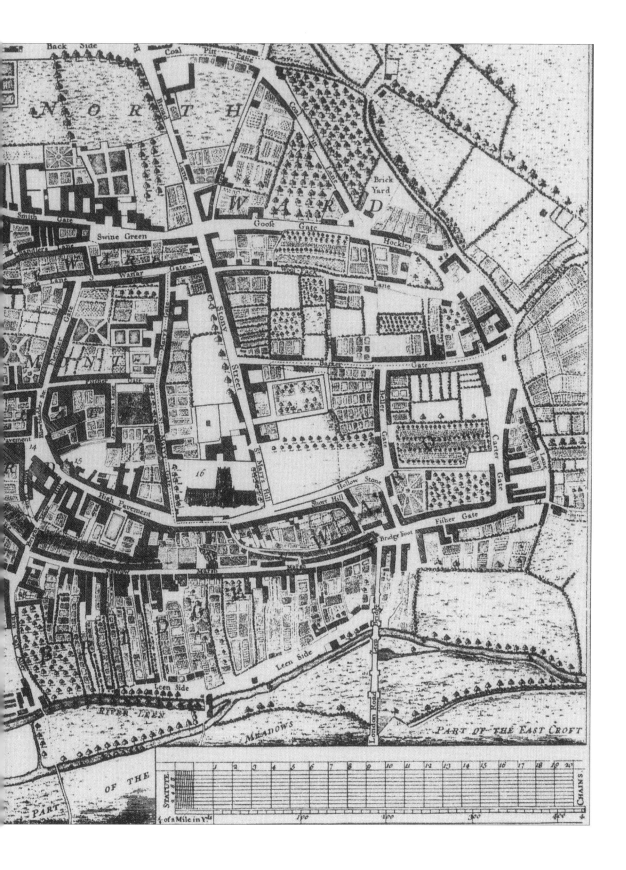

TO THE
WORSHIPFUL COMPANY
OF
FRAME-WORK-KNITTERS

STRENGTH AND TRUTH UNITED

In the Year 1589, the Ingenious WILLIAM LEE, Master
of Arts, of St JOHN's COLLEGE, CAMBRIDGE, devis'd this
profitable Art of Knitting STOCKINGS: But his Invention
being despis'd, he went to FRANCE, Yet of IRON to him-
-self, but to us and others of GOLD. In Memory of so
great a GENIUS this is here depicted.

44   *The arms of the London Framework Knitters' Company.*

trying – but with little success – to impose in the Midlands. Since its establishment in
the mid-17th century the Company had sought to regulate the industry wherever it was
practised, demanding the right to control the indenturing of apprentices and imposing
strict limits on the number of apprentices any master was able to employ. It had probably
never been able to exert as much control in the Midlands, however, as it did in London.
We have seen already that in the 1690s there were women stockingers in the town and
it was said that as many as 200 women were working in stocking frames in the 1720s,
although this was completely against the rules of the Company. In Leicester the Company
abandoned holding its courts in 1726, owing to the impossibility of enforcing its will on
the hosiers there, and by this time there were already a number of hosiers in Nottingham
who had moved their business from London principally to escape from the limitations
imposed by the Company. One of the most important was Samuel Fellows (1687-1765),
who had moved to Nottingham earlier in the century after he had quarrelled with the
London Company over his wish to employ more than the two apprentices allowed by the
Company. The turning point in the decline of the Company's control in Nottingham came
in 1730 when Fellows and another hosier, John Wood, who were both the town's sheriffs for
that year, organised a challenge in the courts to the Company's authority. They persuaded
a group of two dozen Nottingham hosiers to support fellow hosier Joseph Cartwright in
forcing the Company to bring a test-case by denying the right of the Company to charge
eight shillings at the indenturing of an apprentice, and they won their case. This was a
shattering blow to the authority of the Company from which it never recovered.

Nottingham hosiers now felt free to take increasing numbers of apprentices, at considerable profit to themselves. At least 800 frames were moved from London to Nottingham between 1730 and the middle of the century. By the late 1740s, according to Deering, what remained in London 'does hardly deserve the name of trade'. The London hosiers had found that 'they could be fitted from the country with as good work at a cheaper rate than the London framework knitters could afford' and had simply changed their sources of supply.

Samuel Fellows was probably the first hosier in Nottingham to build framework knitting workshops and he also employed large numbers of parish apprentices. The fortunate survival of his insurance policy with the Sun Fire Office, dated 25 March 1730, shows that at this time he already had two workshops in the town, one in High Pavement, in the yard behind his house, and another in Narrow Marsh, containing about 20 knitting frames. He also possessed two warehouses and a number of cottages, which he presumably let out to his journeymen. His Nottingham properties were valued at £800 in 1730 but it is likely that he also possessed other frames in knitters' cottages about the district.

Like many other hosiers, framework knitters and framesmiths, Fellowfs was a member of High Pavement Chapel. The first High Pavement register, which runs from 1690 to 1724, includes many of the town's leading hosiers and gives the impression that a majority of the members were hosiers, framesmiths or framework knitters at the beginning of the century. There could hardly have been more than about a dozen framesmiths in the town at this time but eight were members of the chapel. The importance of Presbyterianism and chapel membership among the manufacturing and merchant classes of the town in the 18th century was remarkable, and it is likely that membership of the chapel was helpful to some of the hosiers in establishing close alliances and business contacts.

The outstanding merchant hosier in Nottingham in the middle of the century was Samuel Need (1718-81) and he, too, was a member of High Pavement Chapel. His father was a baker in the town but he was apprenticed as a framework knitter, probably to his uncle, John Need, who was also a member of the chapel and had inherited freehold land at Arnold. In the 1730s stocking frames could be bought for as little as £4 and it was therefore not difficult for an enterprising young man with some financial support from his family to set up in business on his own account. He completed his apprenticeship and was admitted as a burgess in 1739/40. Within seven years he had made enough money to acquire a row of three houses with attached malthouses on Low Pavement. Shortly afterwards he added a silk mill nearby, and by 1754 he owned 13 tenements, which he let to framework knitters, and his property was valued at £1,200. His partnership with Jedediah Strutt of Derby brought further wealth and by the time of his death in 1781 he owned about 240 frames and also employed many other framework knitters who owned their own frames.

Samuel Need's origins and career pattern was not at all unusual. The hosier Francis Beardsley, who bought a large house on Houndsgate in 1740, came from a family who had lived in Lenton from the early 17th century. In 1758, when he and his brother went bankrupt, he owned 112 frames, 48 in Nottingham and the rest scattered through 25 villages, almost all within 10 miles of the town. One of the most important Nottingham hosiers in the 1720s, and one of the local deputies for the London Company, Samuel Spray, came from a Beeston family of small farmers. A more modest example was Jonas Bettinson, the son of a yeoman farmer from Radcliffe, who at his death in 1747 owned six silk and cotton frames and had total assets valued at £550. Throughout the century most of the men who established themselves in Nottingham as merchant hosiers came from families whose wealth was gradually accumulated over two or three generations. Most of the capital came from the profits of the business but when needed money could be raised from family connections or on the security of land. This can be glimpsed in the fragmentary evidence of the earlier hosiers but the picture becomes clearer in the second half of the century. One particularly notable example was that of Thomas James, who mortgaged family land in Hockley to finance his partnership with James Hargreaves, who was then looking for financial support to develop his new invention to improve cotton spinning, the 'spinning jenny'.

Another major reason for the success of Nottingham's hosiers in developing the trade and maintaining their leadership of the industry was their long-established but continually developing links with the city of London. Hosiery was a fashion trade and accurate up-to-date information on changes in fashion was vital for survival. During the first half of the century the coaching inns in and around Wood Street, in the heart of the city, were at the centre of the trade, but by the early 1770s the more prosperous hosiers had their own warehouses built around the Wood Street inn yards and in the surrounding neighbourhood. Those hosiers who operated on a smaller scale generally sold through London agents or visited the wholesalers themselves, carrying their samples, and in the provinces they sold their goods at markets and fairs, direct to shops, or through pedlars and hawkers, who tramped from village to village.

Innovation and invention, in response to the demands of the market, were key reasons for the industry's continuing growth and development throughout the century. Developments in bleaching and dyeing were among the first important innovations. In about 1736-7 a Scots bleacher, George Robinson, came to Nottingham and in 1738 built the first textile mill on the river Leen at Bulwell to introduce Dutch techniques of bleaching linen. The expense of spun cotton, imported by the East India Company, made linen stockings a very popular line at this time. At about the same time a Nottingham man, William Elliott, developed an improved black dye. Black stockings were highly fashionable for men at this period but traditional black dyes always had a tinge of blue in them. Elliott's methods proved extremely successful and he was quickly able to establish a monopoly of the dyeing and trimming trades in and around both Nottingham and Leicester, and became one of the wealthiest property owners in the town, with a very substantial business on Beastmarket Hill.

Before the middle of the century new knitted meshes were also being developed. In about 1740 an unknown knitter discovered a simple means of making ribbed stockings which was then widely used by other framework knitters throughout the trade. The first patented improvement on this, Jedediah Strutt's 'Derby Ribs', patented in 1758, made a fortune for both Strutt and his partner, the Nottingham hosier Samuel Need. Their success encouraged them to also invest heavily in Arkwright's roller-spinning machinery when he arrived in the town ten years later looking for financial backers. Moreover, the ribbing attachment for the stocking frame Strutt had invented also soon proved capable of adaptation to produce the first machine-made lace fabrics, and before the end of the century the foundations for a new textile industry had been created in the town, but a description of this will have to wait until the next chapter.

Other Industries

When Defoe visited Nottingham in about 1725 he noted that, while the hosiery industry was thriving and had become the principal industry of the town, some of the town's more traditional industries were in a state of decline. One was the tanning trade, which had been in decline since the Restoration. In 1707 there were said to be only 21 tanners still working in the town, whereas in 1667 there had been nearly 50, and by the 1740s the number had dwindled to only three. Also, by the middle of the 18th century, fewer craftsmen were working in the metal trades, although some had found new employment as framesmiths and the demand for ornamental iron railings and gates had created a new specialist industry. Two industries which were flourishing at the beginning of the 18th century, glassmaking and pottery, did not survive the growing competition from other centres, and both had disappeared from the town before the end of the century. For the pottery industry the competition from fine Staffordshire wares and from imported porcelain proved particularly difficult to cope with, and competition from other Midlands towns was also beginning to undermine the profits and market share of the town's malting industry by the 1750s.

The expansion of the hosiery industry, however, stimulated the growth of other related trades. Large numbers of women found work as embroiderers, the dyeing and trimming trades grew considerably in the second half of the century, and, for a few years, it seemed likely that Nottingham would become the leading centre for a new mechanised cotton-spinning industry. When the Preston barber Richard Arkwright arrived in the town in 1768 looking for capital to establish his new roller-spinning machinery, he found willing backers in the partnership of Strutt and Need, who set him up in a house in Hockley, complete with a horse-driven capstan. Just a year later another pioneer, James Hargreaves of Blackburn, also came to the town in need of capital to build large numbers of his recently invented 'spinning jenny', which, like Arkwright's roller-spinning method, also promised to supply the hosiers with relatively inexpensive spun cotton. Not surprisingly he also found willing backers and his first factory, filled with hand-operated jennies, also opened in Hockley, just across the road from Arkwright's.

Arkwright's experiments with horse-driven machinery persuaded him to adapt his method to water-power instead, but rather than set up a mill on the Leen – as a number of textile entrepreneurs had already done – he chose to move out to Cromford, in Derbyshire, and he subsequently built a series of mills in Derbyshire and Lancashire and made a substantial fortune for himself, becoming one of the first 'rags-to-riches' success stories of Britain's Industrial Revolution.

Where Arkwright and Hargreaves led, others soon followed, and during the 1770s and 1780s 11 firms built spinning mills either in the town or on small streams nearby. Further growth, however, was hampered by the lack of suitable fast-flowing streams, for the Leen was soon overcrowded with mills. Moreover, Boulton & Watt steam engines were still in a pioneer stage and consequently very expensive. The largest mill in the town, Denison and Oates' factory on Pennyfoot Street, cost £15,000 to build and equip and employed about 300 workers in 1794. Moreover, Nottingham's cotton spinners would soon find themselves unable to compete with their rivals in Lancashire, where abundant water power, the introduction of Crompton's 'mule', and access to Liverpool (soon to be the chief port for American raw cotton imports) would all prove decisive advantages in the first decades of the next century. By 1833 there would be only four small cotton mills still at work in the town.

Transport Improvements

Nottingham's development as an industrial town in the 18th century owed much to the improvements made at this time in both road and water transport. Deering tells us that at the beginning of the century the main road south to London via Loughborough was 'very bad, not to say dangerous', but that after the passing of Nottingham's first Turnpike Act, in 1738, the road was greatly improved. The trustees undertook to build a new road south to Cotes Bridge, just outside Loughborough (now the A60) and according to Deering it was 'as firm and good as any turnpike road in England'. No further road improvements followed, however, until a second Act, passed in 1753, also improved links with London by securing the building of a turnpike road as far as Kettering. The success of these initiatives now prompted further investment and more Turnpike Acts soon followed. During 1758-9 the roads to Derby and Alfreton were both turnpiked and five years later also the road to Ilkeston. In most cases the corporation played little or no role in the attempt to improve communications but in March 1764 the mayor and a number of other wealthy townsmen petitioned the Duke of Newcastle to support the Ilkeston turnpike. Their principal concern was to reduce the price of coal in Nottingham, especially in the winter months, 'which will be of prodigious advantage to the trade and poor of this town and the country adjacent'. During the next 20 years further turnpikes to Grantham (1767), Sawley (1780) and Mansfield (1787) completed a network of road improvements into the town, but one further improvement was still very badly needed. Until almost the end of the century the road across the area known as the Meadows from the town to Trent Bridge remained perilously liable to flooding and was often impassable. Not until 1796 was a much improved 'Flood Road' built, again by a turnpike trust, and to meet popular demand the corporation felt obliged to pay some of the costs of obtaining the necessary legislation and to contribute towards the cost of repairs. The issue had come to a head in the previous winter, when a sudden thaw after two months of frost caused severe flooding, completely destroying the existing road, drowning cattle, sheep and pigs, and leaving the inhabitants of Narrow Marsh marooned in their upstairs rooms, reachable only by boat.

Although the tolls charged caused much resentment, the turnpikes certainly improved the town's communications considerably. A regular London stagecoach service began in 1770 and by 1793 there were also daily coaches to Birmingham and Leeds. The number of heavy goods wagons on the roads also greatly increased and by 1793 wagons were travelling regularly to and from London, Birmingham, Manchester and Leeds, as well as to more local centres like Derby, Leicester, Mansfield and Lincoln.

Improvements in water transport, for the carriage of heavy and bulky goods, was also hampered by the corporation's unwillingness to take a lead. The appalling state of the road across the Meadows for much of the century necessitated the building of a canal to link the town to the river Trent, as well as an improved road, but local initiative and capital were lacking and the first stage of the Nottingham Canal was not completed until 1793, and the second stage, to Langley Mill and Beeston, only in 1796. The route of the canal as it passed through the town was very quickly lined with warehouses and wharves. Coal was the main item carried but a wide variety of heavy goods were soon being shipped along the new waterway, including timber, corn, iron and stone. One wharf, known as the Sanitary Wharf, specialised in handling night soil, which was collected from the numerous privies and cesspits of the town and carried by barge to fertilise the rich soils of the Vale of Belvoir.

45 *Collin's almshouses, 1709.*

Pauperism and Poor Relief

For the Overseers of the Poor the continuing growth of the hosiery industry during the century proved a blessing indeed. Countless young paupers were found apprenticeships with the local hosiers and the costs of poor relief were generally reasonably manageable. Charitable foundations also played a significant role. Abel Collin's almshouses, built in 1709, stood for almost 250 years between Friar Lane and Hounds Gate, until demolished in 1958 to make way for a new road, Maid Marian Way. Abel Collin was a wealthy Nottingham merchant who left money in his will to build the almshouses for a few of the town's elderly poor, provided they were deemed truly blameless for their poverty and utterly respectable. For most of the town's poor, however, relief could only come from the parish workhouse. At the beginning of the century the town's three parishes shared the rather limited facilities of the St John's workhouse, but as the town grew this was soon found to be inadequate, and from the 1720s each of the parishes built their own workhouse. Also, in particularly desperate years, when recession caused unemployment, or when the harvest failed and food prices shot up, the mayor made appeals for public subscriptions to raise extra money to help relieve the poor.

The distinction made between the respectable and deserving poor on the one hand and those deemed to have brought their sufferings on themselves by idleness or irresponsible behaviour was sharp indeed. Unmarried women who gave birth to illegitimate children who then became chargeable to one of the town's parishes could expect no sympathy, only the harshest of punishments. In 1729 three women found guilty of this offence were sentenced at the Quarter Sessions to be whipped at the House of Correction, tied to the ducking stool and paraded through the streets, and then taken to St Mary's workhouse to be ducked. This was no doubt thought to be an effective deterrent for other young women to bear in mind. It was not poor women such as these whom the founders of the St Mary's Vestry Society had in mind when it was established in 1713, with a declared intention to promote charity and piety.

Food Riots, Framework Knitters' Riots and Radical Politics

One of the major concerns for the corporation, and for the town's more prosperous inhabitants, during times of acute food shortage, was that desperate men and women might take the law into their own hands. In the winter of 1700-1 it was said that food riots had only been prevented by the prompt action of Alderman Trigge in purchasing emergency grain supplies for distribution to the poor, but in the second half of the century riots in the town prompted by severe hunger became commonplace, and by the end of the century Nottingham had a reputation as being one of the most turbulent and riotous towns in the country.

In 1756 colliers employed at the nearby Wollaton and Cossall pits marched into the town to protest about food prices, which were then extraordinarily high and provoking riots across the country. The leaders were arrested but released on condition that they left the town peacefully, and the protest might have passed off without incident if local women had not intervened as the men were leaving and urged them to attack certain local windmills, whose owners were believed to be profiteering from the crisis. As a result a number of mills were badly damaged.

Ten years later food prices were again very high and again an angry crowd of hungry men and women decided to take the law into their own hands. A large crowd which had gathered in the market place for the Goose Fair were particularly incensed by an increase in the price of cheese and vented their anger on the unfortunate cheese merchants by overthrowing their stalls and stealing the cheeses. The barrel-shaped cheeses were also effective weapons which could be used against anyone who tried to stop the riot, as the mayor found as he rushed to the market place up Peck Lane, only to be laid flat by fast-rolling cheeses hurtling down towards him. Troops were called out and one man was killed in the disturbance.

Numerous food-related riots also broke out in the 1780s and 1790s, when the high price of meat meant that the butchers' shambles became a particular target. In 1795 soaring grain prices also provoked an attack on the local bakers' shops. In April that year it was reported that 'a large mob, consisting principally of women, went from one baker's shop to another, set their own prices on the stock therein, and putting down the money, took it away'. Troops were called out but it took nearly 12 hours to restore order. The corporation attempted to ease the tense situation in the next few months by buying grain to sell cheaply but found it impossible to acquire sufficient supplies.

The anger of the poor, however, was not only aimed at those who sold food at prices they could not afford. In the 1770s and 1780s desperately poor framework knitters also resorted to violence in response to wage cuts, and in retaliation for the hosiers' success in thwarting their efforts to gain parliamentary control of their wages. By the 1770s there can be little doubt that although many hosiers had grown rich from the profits of the trade, most of Nottingham's framework knitters and their families endured a life of grinding poverty, involving long hours of work to earn only starvation wages. The ominous phrase 'as poor as a stockinger' was said to have been first heard as early as 1740, but during the next 30 years the situation for the framework knitters grew worse still. A few workmen who were fortunate enough to acquire the necessary skills to manufacture the highly profitable 'eyelet-hole' fabric (an early precursor of lace) could earn as much as 50s. per week, but the great majority of framework knitters could not expect to earn more than 10s. or 15s. for a week's work. The extensive use of pauper apprentices from the local workhouses, together

46 *The stocking weaver; an 18th-century print.*

with the constant influx of cheap labour from the countryside, had long served to depress wages, while the growing popularity of machine-made cheap, coarse, woollen stockings had reduced the skills required of many framework knitters. Conditions were worst of all, however, in the villages around Nottingham, where the knitters were particularly oppressed by not only low wages but also by extra deductions from their pay imposed by the middlemen who collected their work and brought them their raw materials, the village 'bag hosiers'. It is notable that while the majority of the town's knitters attempted to use peaceful, constitutional, means to improve their lot, when they failed and violence broke out in the town a number of eyewitnesses tended to place the blame for the violence on the country knitters.

In 1776 the Nottingham framework knitters took the lead in organising an association of fellow hosiery workers across the Midlands and in London, pledged to petition Parliament for a restoration of the regulation of their industry, as they believed they had once enjoyed under the old London Company. A petition was presented in 1778 in which they called for the regulation of their wages and also complained of the practice of having to pay rent to the hosier for the use of the stocking frames they worked on, together with many other deductions. They claimed that 'notwithstanding their utmost industry, they were incapable of providing the common necessaries of life'. In evidence submitted to the Commons' committee considering the petition it was stated that their wages had been in decline for more than 20 years. It was said that men who 20 years earlier earned 2s. 1d. a day could now make no more than 1s. 7d., out of which they had to pay frame rent and charges for winding, seaming, needles and candles. In Nottingham it was claimed that a good man could not make more than 4s. 6d. a week on coarse worsted. The hosiers employed many women and children in this branch of the trade and they were paid even less. To obtain even these pathetically low earnings the framework knitter had to work 13 to 15 hours a day and, if he lived in one of the villages outside Nottingham, half a day would be lost in taking his work to the warehouse. After the Commons' committee had considered the evidence a motion was put that a Bill should be presented to Parliament, but this was lost following the opposition of a number of hosiers, who had submitted a counter petition claiming that any regulation or improvement in wages would damage the trade.

When the news of this disappointment reached Nottingham many must have expected violence to erupt, but the town's workmen remained calm and determined not to give up their peaceful struggle, and an opportunity soon came to renew it with a by-election in the town in 1779. As burgesses of the town, many of Nottingham's framework knitters had the vote and they now determined to use it to help secure the election of the banker Abel Smith, who promised to bring in a second Bill. Smith died shortly afterwards but his brother, Robert, who succeeded him as MP, was also sympathetic to the cause and a second Bill was presented. This time the Bill reached its third reading before being defeated. On this occasion when the news reached Nottingham large crowds of framework knitters and their wives gathered in the market place intent on taking their revenge on the hosiers who had opposed the bill and whom they blamed for its defeat. According to Gravener Henson, who would later come to know personally some of the knitters' leaders of 1778-9, 'the rude and enraged country people … came into the town in large numbers' and precipitated the disturbances that now followed. The houses, workshops and warehouses of the hosiers who had led the opposition to the Bill were attacked with stones, and in some cases every window was smashed. The hosiers' stocking frames were also a target and it was said that many frames were smashed and the broken remains flung into the streets. Three hundred special constables had to be quickly enrolled but order was not restored until cavalry were sent to the town.

Perhaps fearful of further violence, the magistrates dealt leniently with those identified as the leaders of the riot, but further attacks on the property of local hosiers who had cut wage rates, or who were particularly notorious for their treatment of their employees, followed in 1783 and 1787. Although only one stocking frame may have been smashed in the 1787 disturbances it was after this third framework knitters' riot in less than ten years that Parliament agreed to pass a Bill that made frame-smashing a specific felony. The penalty was fixed at transportation for between seven and 14 years. Even this, however, could not prevent more disturbances in 1791, and it was as a result of this series of riots (plus political violence in 1790) that the government agreed to build a barracks in Nottingham Park to house a regiment of cavalry, which was completed in 1793. For the previous 20 years cavalry had been a regular presence in the town, usually lodged in the town's inns, either as a response to a riot or in an attempt to deter one from erupting. Nottingham was the first large town in the country to be given its own barracks. By this time the town had gained an unenviable reputation as one of the most riotous in the country, and as the century drew to a close that reputation was further consolidated, but now the violent and dramatic events occurring across the Channel were the main cause.

The French Revolution and the Revolutionary and Napoleonic Wars (from 1793) deeply divided the town and sparked further violent disturbances. An election in 1790 was marked by extensive window-smashing, with the house of the Whig candidate, Robert Smith, a particular target, perhaps owing to the support he had recently shown for the Tory government. As in 1779, the account of the riots given in the *Nottingham Journal* again places most of the blame for the violence on country workers coming into the market place. It was said that every window in Smith's house was smashed and when the result was declared, with Smith re-elected, the windows of the Exchange – a symbol of corporation power in the town – were also smashed. When special constables were sworn in to try to restore order they were driven from the market place by the stone-throwing crowd and many were injured. Peace was only restored by the arrival of troops, who were obliged to open fire, killing one man who, it was later claimed, was an innocent spectator.

For many poor people in the town the principles of liberty, equality and brotherhood, enunciated by the revolutionaries in France, were an inspiration, and before the end of 1792 a Nottingham Constitutional Society had been established in the town dedicated to advancing these principles in England. Thomas Hardy, the leader of the London Corresponding Society, visited the town in November to give his support, and membership grew during the following months. On 1 February 1793, however, the government declared war on France and a wave of patriotic sentiment swept through the town. Nottingham was now deeply divided between self-styled 'aristocrats', who deplored the events in France, and the 'democrats' who had welcomed them, but patriotism ensured that for at least a short while the 'aristocrats' would be in the majority. In March 1793 a conservative mob burnt an effigy of the radical hero and author of *The Rights of Man,* Tom Paine, in the market place, and attacked the houses of those known to share Paine's radical sentiments, including the former Whig mayor, Alderman Samuel Oldknow, who the year before had angered a group of Tory gentlemen by refusing to call a public meeting to endorse the Royal Proclamation against seditious writings.

This was now a dangerous time for radicals in Nottingham but this did not prevent the Revd George Walker, a passionately committed radical and minister of High Pavement Chapel, from publishing an outspoken petition for parliamentary reform, which was presented to the House of Commons by the independent MP, Daniel Parker Coke, in the same year. Walker was an immensely talented man and a superb orator. He had opposed the war against America and this was the third petition calling for a radical extension of the franchise which he had written and had presented to the Commons since 1780. In this latest version he denounced the laws recently passed against sedition as 'the grossest abuses' which 'insult the common sense of the nation', and later, recalling this period in Nottingham in his *Essays,* he wrote: 'it came to be in a considerable degree unsafe to express a difference of opinion from those who were attached to the measures of ministers'. One local man who was overheard to express a wish that England might also have a revolution was arrested and imprisoned for three months. Walker himself was careful to avoid breaking the new laws but there was no slackening in his radicalism for in the same year he followed his reform petition by drafting another, but this time calling for an end to the war with France. To many of the 'aristocratic' faction in the town this was little less than treason.

Just how unpopular radicalism was at this time was dramatically illustrated the following summer. In June a large patriotic crowd roamed the streets for a week, seizing any radicals they found and dragging them off either to the river Leen or the nearest water pump for a very rough and uncomfortable 'baptism'. Shortly after this the mob marched to Robert Denison's mill and set fire to the knitters' workshops attached to it. Denison was known to have opposed the outbreak of the war with France, but principally for commercial reasons. Shocked by the attack, he closed the mill and did not open it again until 1801, but a year later it was burnt to the ground and arson was suspected.

Enthusiasm for the war soon petered out, however, in the winter of 1794-5, when rising food prices once again encouraged political discontent and opposition to the repressive measures introduced by Pitt's Tory government. The corporation sent petitions to the Commons protesting against these measures and supported calls for an end to the war. The town's radicals were also keen to remove Robert Smith as MP for the town and replace him with someone likely to be more critical of the Tory government. Dr Peter Crompton of Derby was persuaded to stand against him on a popular radical platform. Smith managed to be re-elected, together with the other sitting member, Daniel Parker Coke, but Crompton won a very respectable 560 votes. During the campaign there was again much window smashing and fights broke out between supporters of the different candidates. Perhaps partly to provoke their opponents, Crompton's radical supporters paraded through the town with a 'tree of liberty' and then tried to plant it in the market place.

A downturn in the hosiery trade in 1797 further boosted support for radicalism in the town and the corporation agreed to support a petition to the king calling for the dismissal of the government and an end to the war. The local radicals' association, now known as the Nottingham Corresponding Society, also called a public meeting in the market place to call for parliamentary reform. The magistrates had the power to ban the meeting but instead allowed it to go ahead, and among those on the platform were the mayor and several aldermen. A majority on the corporation continued to oppose the war and in the elections in 1802 intervened to put forward an anti-war candidate to challenge Coke, who – like Smith before him – was now also regarded by many councillors as too supportive of the government. In London ministers considered Nottingham a centre of radical activity and disaffection. In 1800 the Home Office sent Bow Street Runners to the town to infiltrate radical groups in the town and report back, and their reports were sufficiently alarming to prompt the despatch of extra troops to the Nottingham barracks. The *Mason's Arms*, they reported, was the favourite meeting place for about 200 'disaffected persons'. Here the conversation was 'always of the most seditious nature, and held without any reserve or restraint such as damning the King & praising the French … declaring themselves highly in favour of a Revolution in England, and wishing for it immediately'.

Violence did break out in the town again that year but it had nothing to do with local radical feeling. The harvest of 1799 had been disastrous and grain prices were already soaring the following January. To relieve distress it was necessary to open soup kitchens in the town in February but riots were reported in the market place in April 'on account of the high price of provisions', and when prices rose again in late August there was further violence, lasting intermittently for more than three weeks. The property of millers and bakers were particular targets and grain barges on the River Trent were also attacked. The corporation tried to buy grain and sell it at a subsidised price, but to little effect, and a soup kitchen had to be opened again on Christmas Day. So many were starving, however, that the soup kitchen quickly ran out of supplies, more rioting followed and additional troops had to be brought in from Birmingham to help restore order.

Church, Chapel and School

The dominance enjoyed by the Whigs on the corporation at the end of the 18th century owed much to the continuing strength of Presbyterianism throughout the century, or rather Unitarianism, as it was coming to be known by this time. The movement had established itself very strongly in the town during the Civil War and in the years of the Commonwealth and Protectorate that followed, and if Nottingham's Anglicans had hoped that the Act of Uniformity of 1662 might severely weaken it, they were to be badly disappointed. As is so often the case, the movement appears to have thrived on persecution, and the strong position that the Presbyterians were to establish in the town in the 18th century ensured that the Anglican church would never be able to regain the pre-eminence it had once enjoyed before the Civil War. Within months of the passing of the Toleration Act in 1689 the local Presbyterians had opened their first chapel on High Pavement, less than 200 yards from the premier Anglican Church of St Mary, from which the Presbyterian ministers, John Whitlock and William Reynolds, had been expelled in 1662. We have seen already that the registers of High Pavement Chapel reveal a remarkably high number of merchant hosiers, as well as framework knitters. The Chapel was consequently able to produce many of the town's wealthiest citizens, many of the aldermen and senior councillors, and two-thirds of the 18th-century mayors of Nottingham. Membership of the Chapel could clearly confer political benefits as well as economic and spiritual ones. Moreover, in the Revd George Walker, the minister of High Pavement Chapel from 1774 to 1798, the Presbyterians enjoyed the leadership of one of the most outstanding dissenting clergymen of his day, and the town's reputation as a centre of radicalism at the end of the century owed a great deal to his influence.

The other dissenting groups which – like the Presbyterians – had flourished in the mid-17th century, including the Quakers and Baptists, appear to have been in decline for much of the 18th century. The numbers of nonconformist centres of worship in the county declined sharply between 1717, when the minister of High Pavement Chapel, John Hardy, drew up a list, and 1743, when Archbishop Herring conducted a visitation, and a revival does not seem to have begun until late in the century, when the success of Methodism seems to have inspired a more general revival of nonconformity.

At the end of the 18th century the Anglican Church was also in a long-established decline, at least in terms of religious enthusiasm and activity. Even as late as the 1840s the Church of England could be described by one contemporary as 'lethargic in the spiritual oversight of her flock' and of having only a very limited view of its role: 'the Church of England's conception of duty was but meagre; the three parish churches being content with the two Sunday services year in year out'. In the years immediately following the Restoration, however, the Anglican Church had been far from quiescent. The church of St Nicholas, which had been destroyed by Colonel Hutchinson during the Civil War, was rebuilt between 1671 and 1683, and the Anglican-controlled Free School was also extensively repaired in 1689 and largely rebuilt in 1708.

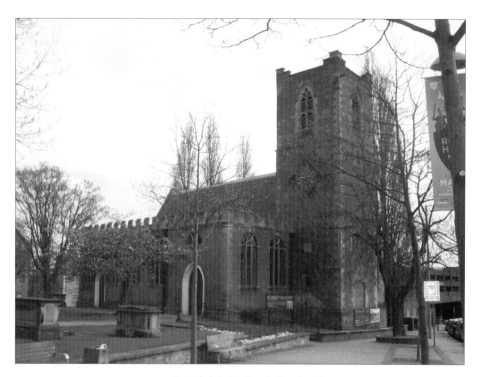

47   *St Nicholas' church, rebuilt 1671-83.*

But the Anglican Church failed to respond adequately to the rapid growth of the town during the 18th century, and came to be seen as increasingly remote from the lives of the majority of the town's poorer inhabitants. There was some expansion in the capacity of the three churches. The new church of St Nicholas, for instance, was first enlarged in 1756 by the addition of a south aisle and then again in 1783, when a north aisle was also added. However, no new churches were built during the whole of the century and any proposals to do so were certain to face strong opposition from the clergy of the existing churches in the town if they feared that their own churches might suffer a loss of income as a result.

However, from the 1740s onwards there was a new and steadily growing religious movement in the town, renowned for its spiritual enthusiasm, its sense of mission and its dedication to 'saving souls'. When John Wesley first came to the town, in June 1741, the first seeds of Methodism had already been sown the year before, when two of Wesley's followers – a Mr Howe and a Mr Rogers – had preached in the market place. And in Nottingham, among the framework knitters, framesmiths and other craftsmen and shopkeepers, he found a fertile ground. The little community of the town's first Methodists were meeting in Mr Howe's house when Wesley arrived, and it was here that he stayed and preached his first sermon in the town. A few days later, however, he preached in the market place 'to an immense multitude of people'. Wesley seems to have been well received, as was his brother, Charles, when he came to the town in 1743, but a year later, when Charles Wesley returned to the town, he found a much more hostile reception. He and the other Methodists who accompanied him were pelted with dirt, stones and pieces of wood. The Jacobin uprising of 1744-6, and Bonnie Prince Charlie's invasion of England in 1745, meant that, in the eyes of many, any challenge to the establishment at this time was akin to treason. For no other apparent reason, some people even seem to have believed that Methodists were in some way supporters of the Young Pretender. However, after the battle of Culloden of April 1746, and the removal of the Jacobin threat, attacks on itinerant Methodist preachers became much less common.

Throughout the 1740s and 1750s the Methodists continued to meet in the houses of members while money was collected and saved for the building of a small chapel. By 1764, however, sufficient funds had been collected to build a chapel, and the 'Octagon', as it was called, was opened that year just to the east of Milton Street, on a site now occupied by the Victoria Shopping Centre. It was licensed to hold services on 11 October. As the movement continued to grow, it quickly outgrew its first little chapel, and in 1784 the congregation moved into a larger chapel in Hockley. John Wesley was a frequent visitor, and preached many times in both chapels. When he made his last visit, in 1788, it was his 28th in 47 years. His *Journal* shows that he enjoyed coming to the town. He particularly appreciated the qualities of the poor working people who came to hear him. While on a visit to the town in 1777 he wrote in his *Journal*:

> There is something in the people of this town that I cannot but approve of. Although most of our society are of the lower class, chiefly employed in the stocking manufacture, yet there is generally an uncommon gentleness and sweetness in their temper, and something of elegance in their behaviour which, when added to solid, vital religion, make them an ornament to their profession.

48 *The Bluecoat Charity School, a print from Deering's* History.

Two years before Wesley's last visit the local Methodist leadership had agreed to co-operate with a number of wealthy local evangelicals, led by the Revd Walker of High Pavement Chapel, in opening what was at first called the General Town Sunday School. William Hallam of Kirton had opened a Sunday School at Moneyash in Derbyshire in 1778 and another at Mansfield Woodhouse in 1781, and it was probably his example that inspired this initiative in Nottingham. The education offered was free and the school was manned by volunteers. For most of the children who attended this was the only schooling they would receive, but they attended for the whole day and, if bright enough, quickly acquired a basic level of literacy, on which they might build in later years, together with an ability to 'sum' and a good knowledge of the Bible.

Before the opening of the first Sunday Schools almost the only other education provided for poor children was at the Nottingham Charity School, also known as the Bluecoat School, which had been established at Weekday Cross in 1706, 'supported by the contributions of the corporation and others'. This was established to instruct 50 poor children from the respectable, slightly better-off working classes, in the 'principles of religion, spelling and reading'. Its aims were clearly set out in its rules, published in 1793:

> The master shall teach the children the true spelling of words and syllables and stops, which are necessary to true reading. They shall also be taught to write a fair and legible hand and the rudiments of practical arithmetic ... And the mistress shall teach the girls to mend their own clothes, work plain work, and to knit. And both boys and girls shall be taught to sing psalms and a mannerly behaviour towards all persons; all of which being duly performed, will the better fit them for service or apprenticeships.

The Bluecoat School was seen as performing a valuable public service in preparing the children of the poor to be useful and well mannered, and the Sunday School movement quickly gained considerable support because it seemed to offer, at little expense, a similar service on the much larger scale that the rapidly increasing population required. For the vast majority of poor families the Sunday Schools represented the only hope their children had of receiving any education at all, but for many of those belonging to the 'superior classes' their support for both Charity Schools and Sunday Schools was mainly informed by their fear that unless the poor were given some education a fearsomely lawless and licentious generation would be created. One of those who were instrumental in ensuring Anglican support for the movement was the Archdeacon of Nottingham, Dr Kaye. The aim of these schools, he declared, was to:

> rescue children from ignorance, vice and idleness; to inculcate duties of industry and subordination ... to qualify them for the several relations of society; the preservation of health by habits of cleanliness and decency ... to change their mode of conduct, to curb the wildness of their tempers, and increase the respect due to superiors.

The success of the Sunday School movement in the town was remarkable, and very large numbers of children were soon enrolled, but the great majority of volunteer teachers were Methodists, and by 1792 it was being referred to as the Methodist School. The first school had been opened in the Exchange Rooms but as the demand for places increased the Methodist volunteers opened new schools in private houses and stockingers' shops, as well as at their chapel in Hockley, and one large class of 200 boys was taught by a Wesleyan in Green's cotton mill in Broad Marsh. By 1792 the 'Methodist School' had about 500 children enrolled, by 1796 there were about 700, and by 1802 nearly nine hundred.

What had begun as an example of evangelical cooperation now became entirely denominational. In 1798 the Independents of Castle Gate Chapel opened their own Sunday School, followed three years later by both the Particular Baptists of Friar Lane Chapel and the General Baptists of Stoney Street Chapel, and the parish churches of St Mary's and St Peter's opened their first schools in 1800 and 1801 respectively. By 1802 there were said to be 400 enrolled in the two Church of England Sunday Schools, 275 attending the Baptists' two schools and 150 attending the Sunday School run by the Independents. Altogether, including the children attending the Methodist schools, the Sunday Schools were offering a very basic education to about 1,800 children in the town, or about one in four of the 5-15 age group.

For the town's 'middling classes' who could afford to pay the school fees, there was the ancient and misnamed Free Grammar School (provided the parents were members of the Church of England) and, by the end of the century, a number of 'academies' or private schools, including the Nottingham Academy founded in 1777 and the Standard Hill Academy (as it would later be known) founded in 1797. In addition, the ministers of the Presbyterian Chapel on High Pavement had also established, probably soon after the founding of the chapel, their own Free School for the sons of members, paid for from the weekly collections and from the gifts of the wealthier members. In 1717 the running of this Free School was the particular responsibility of the assistant minister, John Hardy, and it seems to have enjoyed a high reputation in the town.

Leisure

For a great many of Nottingham's inhabitants, and particularly those who did not become Methodists, the town's very numerous inns and alehouses represented the chief means of escape from the long hours and drudgery of work. By the 1740s, tea drinking was also becoming extremely popular among all social classes, as Deering noted, not entirely with approval:

> People here are not without their Tea, Coffee and Chocolate, especially the first, the Use of which is spread to that Degree, that not only Gentry and wealthy Travellers drink it constantly, but almost every Seamer, Sizer and Winder will have her Tea in a Morning … and even a common Washerwoman thinks she has not had a proper Breakfast without tea and hot buttered white Bread …

Unlike many other manufacturing towns, in Nottingham many of the traditional popular recreations of rural England survived throughout the 18th century and well into the 19th. The failure to enclose the open fields and common lands that surrounded the increasingly overcrowded town meant that at least there were plenty of open spaces close to the town where families could enjoy a pleasant walk, where games of football and cricket could be enjoyed, and where races could be organised. Moreover, the slow arrival of the factory and the continuance of domestic and workshop production also meant that a high proportion of Nottingham's working people continued to enjoy rather more control over their lives and their hours of work than was the case in some other industrial towns.

The unenclosed Meadows were a particularly favourite resort for all those seeking a pleasant walk in the fields. Vast tracts of purple and white crocuses made this area a truly beautiful sight in March, enjoyed by all the town's inhabitants, and later in the year the wild lilacs flowered, covering more than 20 acres of the Meadows. Games of football and cricket were played in the Meadows and also on the Forest, to the north of the town. Games of 'long bowls' were played on the Duke of Newcastle's Park, to the west of the Castle, and foot races were also popular, drawing large crowds of spectators. In 1773 it was said that 15,000 people assembled on the Forest for a 10-mile contest between two of the most noted runners of the day. They ran entirely naked in an extremely good time: the winner completing the 10 miles in just over 56 minutes.

The Forest was also the home of the Nottingham Races. Horse racing is first mentioned in the corporation minutes in 1689, when the councillors agreed to buy a trophy to be run for 'as formerly there hath been'. When Defoe came to Nottingham he was impressed by the 'illustrious company' which gathered in the town in July for the races: 'eleven or twelve noblemen and an infinite throng of gentlemen from all the countries around'. He was also most appreciative of the charms of the ladies whom he met with: 'the train of coaches filled with the beauties of the north was not to be described'. The company may have become a little less illustrious by Deering's time, 20 years later, due to the competition of other race meetings, but the town's sportsman-MP, Sir Charles Sedley, succeeded in reviving its fortunes in the 1770s, making it once more a favourite meeting place for the region's aristocracy and gentry.

For most of the century the social classes mixed freely at the races. Large crowds gathered on the slopes of the Forest to watch the races, drink and gamble. By the 1770s, however, the Races' wealthier patrons were demanding that they should have a separate grandstand and an enclosure, where they could be confident of not having to rub shoulders with the 'lower orders'. A grandstand modelled on the one built at York was completed in 1777, at a total cost of £2,460, paid for mainly by the subscriptions of the nobility and gentry of the county and by the wealthiest inhabitants of the town, all of whom intended to avail themselves of its facilities.

Other popular entertainments in the town included the town's autumn fair, the Goose Fair, which at this time was still principally a livestock and produce market; bull-baiting at the *Leather Bottle Inn* in Burton Leys; and cock fighting, which was to be found in most of the town's larger inns. Cock-fighting competitions were sometimes organised between Nottingham and other towns, when as many as 70 or 80 birds might be entered. The events were advertised in the local newspapers and could attract large crowds from the surrounding countryside as well as from the town.

For Nottingham's more genteel society a game of bowls had long been thought an appropriate pastime. In 1609, when the first detailed map of the town was drawn, a bowling green was shown to the north of the Sand Field, on the north side of the town, and in 1709 the corporation agreed to pay £10 towards the cost of creating a new bowling green close to 'the bleaching works', beside the river Leen, where there was already a spa and a small park, laid out two years earlier. Unfortunately, vandalism was a problem three hundred years ago as well. In 1709 the town crier was told to warn 'unruly Burgesses' against damaging this amenity. It had 'with great expence been Levell'd and made Commodious for Walks, and an Arbour and a great many young Trees have been sett and planted there'. By Deering's time, 30 years later, this was known as the Town Green, and other bowling greens had been opened at St Ann's Well and at Basford. Deering himself may have been an enthusiast for the game for he speaks warmly of 'the good company' and good meals that could be enjoyed at the greens but tells his readers that the best bowling green of all was two miles to the east of the town at Holme Pierrepont.

As the town attracted increasing numbers of the well-to-do of gentle birth and a prosperous bourgeoisie, in the early 18th century, so also did it gradually acquire a reputation for its polished genteel society, enjoying all appropriate amenities. By 1720 purpose-built Assembly Rooms had been erected, complete with fluted Corinthian columns, in Low Pavement. This was for the exclusive use of the town and county elite, but the shopkeepers and attorney's clerks were not slow to emulate their 'social betters'. By 1721 they had their own assemblies in a large room in Thurland Hall. By the 1740s assemblies were being held monthly. They were, above all, opportunities to be seen in the latest fashions, to dance, play cards and perhaps – for the younger generation – to meet a marriage partner. The assemblies held during Race Week or during the assizes were regarded as the high-point of the county's social calendar. A theatre had also been opened by the 1740s, on the west side of St Mary's Gate, and in 1760 this was replaced by a more grand and spacious playhouse, capable of seating an audience of more than 750. It was built by James Whitley, who ran a company of players, and it proved extremely popular. In 1778 it was further improved. Concerts, as well as plays, were often performed in the theatre, and concerts were also held in St Mary's church and at the Assemblies. In

49 *Eighteenth-century houses on High Pavement today.*

1772 the organist at St Mary's organised a particularly ambitious musical event. Three of Handel's great oratorios, 'The Messiah', 'Judas Maccabaeus' and 'Samson', were all performed in the church as part of a grand musical festival. Concerts were sometimes arranged to raise money for the General Hospital, which had been opened in 1782 and attracted considerable financial support from many of the county's and the town's wealthiest inhabitants. In 1782 an annual Assembly was introduced for the support of the hospital.

The General Hospital was built on land given by the Duke of Newcastle, in the old north bailey of the castle. Together with the two Assembly Rooms, the theatre, the Exchange building in the market place, and the new grandstand at the races, it represented the polite and pleasant face of Nottingham at the end of the 18th century, and some visitors still saw little else but this. But the food riots, election riots and the violent protests of desperately poor framework knitters told a different story. Moreover, the poverty which bred so much violence and anger would be an increasing problem in the first half of the next century,

50   *Eighteenth-century house on St James' Street; the home of the poet Byron, 1798-9.*

when one of its most dire consequences would be to continue the process of transforming Nottingham into a hideously overcrowded and unhealthy slum.

SEVEN
The Turbulent First Half of the Nineteenth Century: 1801-51

An Overview

The first half of the 19th century was for Nottingham a most unhappy and turbulent period. The rapid population growth of the later 18th century continued, stimulated now by the expansion of the town's newest industry, machine-made lace making, but for the town's older staple industry, hosiery, these were years of depression and decline. Throughout the 1820s, 1830s and 1840s the framework knitters suffered appallingly low wages and disastrously low living standards, and this in spite of valiant efforts to protect their position through trade unionism. Their condition was made worse by the dreadfully overcrowded and insanitary housing which their poverty obliged them to endure. The situation only began to be alleviated after the arrival of the railway finally prompted the enclosure of the town's surrounding open fields in 1845, which in turn released much-needed new land for building. The poverty and hunger of the framework knitters and their families formed the background to an era of violent Luddite attacks, a desperate uprising, and enthusiastic support for radical causes, including opposition to the New Poor Law, support for the Reform Bill of 1831-2 and, later, support for Chartism. The defining image of the period was the burning of Nottingham Castle in 1831, the home of the Duke of Newcastle, hated in the town for his opposition to the Reform Bill. In circumstances such as this it is hardly surprising to find increasing middle-class fears of growing criminality and immorality among the masses, which in turn prompted urgent steps to improve policing in the town, and to view church and chapel building, and the introduction of a very basic education for the children of the poor, as essential means by which to civilise the working classes and their burgeoning offspring. Even the leisure activities of working people came under closer scrutiny, and many traditional, popular but violent pastimes gradually disappeared in these years.

Population Growth

Between the first national census of 1801 and that of 1851, Nottingham doubled in size from 28,861 to 57,407, growing particularly rapidly in the 1820s, when the population rose by about twenty-five per cent, from approximately 40,000 to a little more than 50,000. But this was by no means the whole story, for the real growth of the town was much greater. While Nottingham proper was growing rapidly, the villages surrounding the town, on the edge of the town's open fields, were growing faster still, as many of the new lace factories were established here. In 1801 the combined population of Radford, Lenton, Sneinton, Basford and Bulwell stood at 7,429, giving a total population for Nottingham and its surrounding villages of 36,290. Within 20 years, however, the population of these industrial villages – or suburbs – had risen to almost 13,000, and in the next 10 years they approximately doubled again, to 25,444. By 1851 the combined population of the five 'villages' was 40,543 and the true total population of Nottingham was only a little short of 100,000. The town itself could not grow any more than it did in the 1830s and 1840s because, until enclosure finally came, it was trapped within its medieval limits, by its unenclosed open fields, with its population 'bursting at the seams' in rows of tiny back-to-back houses squeezed into every available space and many houses in multiple tenancy. During the years of most rapid growth, in the 1820s, the real growth rate (counting Nottingham and its industrial villages together) was not 25 per cent but about 40 per cent, very similar to the rates of growth found at this time in fast-growing northern cities such as Manchester and Leeds.

The Decline of the Hosiery Industry

For nearly 150 years the growth of Nottingham had been intimately related to the prosperity of the hosiery trade. Very early in the new century, however, this ceased to be the case. From about 1810 the town's former staple industry was in decline. From now on, and for many years to come, any prosperity would be largely due to the expansion of the machine-made lace industry. This new trade had its origins in the hosiery industry, and the first lace fabrics were manufactured on stocking frames, but the invention of the bobbin-net machine in 1809, by John Heathcoat, ushered in the beginnings of a completely new and separate industry.

The hosiery industry was dealt a devastating blow by a simple change in men's fashions. Inspired by the uniform of Prussian officers during the Napoleonic wars, men began to abandon stockings and knee breeches for trousers. The full impact of this on the demand for the framework knitters' labour was at first hidden by the shortage of labour caused by the wars. One 'Old Hosier' of Leicester later recalled for the *Leicester Mercury* that: 'During the whole of the period ... from 1800 to 1810 there was an incessant draft of framework knitters, as well as labourers of all kinds, into the army ... so numbers of agricultural labourers and boys ... crowded into the trade.' When large numbers of knitters were demobilised at the close of the wars the labour market was seriously overstocked, and many knitters found themselves out of work and forced to beg or enter the workhouse. Moreover, their misery was compounded by high food prices. In 1811 the harvest failed for the third year running, and it was to do so again in 1812. Wheat leapt to the famine price of 160s. a quarter, which meant the price of a quartern loaf increased from 1s. 1d. to 1s. 8d.

Hosiers in Nottingham and Leicester responded to mounting stocks of unsold stockings by lay-offs, and by cutting wage rates and switching from the traditional narrow frame (which produced a shaped stocking, needing only seaming to complete it) to the more productive wide frames. These had first appeared in the 1770s and produced a straight piece of fabric which was then cut up to produce the required shape. Between 1811 and 1817 angry and desperate village knitters, whose wages were generally even lower than those of the Nottingham or Leicester knitters, sought to stop wage cuts with a wave of frame smashing, directed particularly at the wide frames, which were seen as undermining the skills of the trade. These 'Luddite' attacks, as they became known, may well have succeeded in inhibiting the widespread adoption of the wide frame, but any successes they had in frightening the hosiers into cancelling wage cuts were short-lived.

A number of factors combined to ensure that the industry remained in a depressed and stagnant state until the middle of the century. One reason was the failure of working-class living standards to rise appreciably, if at all, throughout the first half of the century. Even at the time of the *Report on the Condition of the Framework Knitters*, in 1845, merchant hosiers could see little prospect of a permanent increase in demand. Another factor was the flight of enterprise and innovation, among both framework knitters and hosiers, to the lace trade. It would probably be no exaggeration to say that following the invention of the bobbin-net machine in 1809, every highly skilled and inventive stocking knitter moved out of hosiery and into the new lace industry. The contrast between the energy, optimism and innovation of the lace industry in these years, reflected in the remarkable number of workmen who succeeded in setting themselves up in business on their own account, and the stagnation of the hosiery industry is stark indeed.

The lack of enterprise of the hosiers in the 1840s was very obvious to the government commissioner who conducted the inquiry into the condition of the framework knitters. 'If I except one enterprising house at Belper, another or two at Leicester, and one or two elsewhere,' the commissioner reported in 1845, 'there are literally none in the trade who have added any important novelty to it for the last century.' The lace manufacturer William Felkin agreed, writing in his *History* that 'Novelty in design and beauty of execution was not attempted by more than four or five houses during the first half of this century.' The hosiers' failure to take a lead, together with the framework knitters' antipathy towards any innovation which might reduce their status, helps explain the failure of the industry to adopt either circular knitting or warp knitting, two innovations of the early 19th century which were taken up enthusiastically in other countries and which could have led much earlier to the adoption of factory production in the British hosiery industry. As it was, the first steam-driven hosiery factory in the country did not open until the Nottingham partnership of Hine & Mundella opened their first factory on Station Street in 1851 and filled it with circular frames, or, as they were popularly known, 'Monsieur Claussen's Roundabouts'.

One of the many Nottingham stocking knitters who quickly moved into the new lace industry, and prospered sufficiently to at least briefly enjoy the status of a master, employing 11 journeymen, was the hosiery industry's first historian and an early labour leader, Gravener Henson. While some of the country knitters organised themselves into Luddite gangs and attacked wide frames, Henson led repeated attempts to use peaceful means of persuading hosiers to stick to agreed wage rates. He first became involved in trade union affairs in 1809, when he was twenty-four. A dispute in one particular branch of the industry – the point-net branch – prompted Henson's fellow workers to ask him to be their spokesman. Although, like most other knitters in the town, his only formal education appears to have been at one of the town's Wesleyan Sunday schools, he proved himself to be highly literate and a forthright opponent in debate. His first strike, called in 1810 to stop wage cuts in the point-net branch, was unsuccessful, and he and fellow leaders were imprisoned for a month under the Combination Laws, which forbade workers to form trade unions or call a strike. The following year, however, he organised a knitters' committee to discuss with the hosiers their demand for more pay cuts in other branches of the trade. When the hosiers refused to speak to him or his fellow committee members, he tried to use the Combination Laws to convict four hosiers who had demanded the cuts. The magistrates turned him down because he could not prove in which parish the combination of hosiers had occurred, but undefeated, he then resolved to change the law itself and drew up a Bill to be introduced in the House of Commons in 1812 to ban low-quality hosiery, outlaw truck payments and protect agreed wage rates. This, too, was eventually rejected, and Parliament's response to further frame-breaking that year was to make it a capital offence.

When it became clear that Henson's Bill was likely to be rejected, the Nottingham hosiers feared that there might be violence in the town and urged Henson to use his influence to calm the situation. In spite of suffering yet another major disappointment he remained willing to attempt this for he believed that trade unionism, and not violence, was the best hope for improving the living standards of working men. His private view of Luddism, expressed earlier in a letter written in 1812, was that their attacks were 'a glaring outrage on humanity and social order' and he hoped that his Bill, which at that time was still before Parliament, would 'restore the distracted peace of the three [hosiery-manufacturing] counties'.

Even before his Bill had been introduced into the Commons he was also trying to establish a trade union for all framework knitters. This was a most ambitious project. It was centred on Nottingham but contacts were made with other hosiery-producing areas throughout the country, including areas as far away as Scotland, Godalming and Ireland. The Framework Knitters' Union, or Society of Mechanics, as it was also known, was prepared to organise strikes to stop pay cuts but it was also planned that it should operate as a friendly society, and that small sums of money could be given as travel grants to the unemployed and to sick and elderly knitters no longer able to work. Henson became joint secretary of the union, along with Thomas Large, another framework knitter, and their headquarters became the *Sir Isaac Newton's Head* public house. Their activities were quite open and well known to the hosiers and magistrates, and hosiers willing to pay agreed rates supported the union. However, when more frames were smashed in the Nottingham district, in 1814, it coincided with a strike organised by the union in the silk branch. Some of the hosiers and magistrates in Nottingham believed – without any evidence to support the allegation – that Henson and his union were also directing the frame-smashing. The Combination Laws were used to convict three of the strikers, and they were condemned to a month's hard labour. The union was broken up and its papers seized, and for the time being all hopes for a peaceful alternative to violence disappeared, and the Luddite attacks still continued. Henson was also now under a cloud of suspicion from which he never fully escaped, and while in London in 1817 he was arrested, imprisoned and cross-examined by the Home Secretary, Lord Sidmouth, who by this time had received numerous allegations against him. His private correspondence was again seized and examined but no evidence could be found against him and Sidmouth had to order his release. Another outbreak of Luddism had also occurred the year before, when considerable damage was done to the machinery of John Heathcoat at his factory in Loughborough. But this was to be the last, for in 1817 six young men and youths were hanged for their part in the attacks and three more were transported, and this proved to be an adequate deterrent.

Attempts to enforce established piece-rates through strike action were not abandoned, in spite of the Combination Laws, and in 1819 a union was again established linking knitters in Leicestershire, Derbyshire and Nottinghamshire. Large-scale strikes were organised in 1819, 1821 and again in 1824, but any successes achieved in forcing hosiers to pay higher rates were invariably short-lived, and the starving framework knitters were in no position to maintain a strike for many weeks. It was later said that the terrible memories of their suffering during the strike of 1824 prevented Nottinghamshire knitters from engaging in any further 'great turnouts' for more than 30 years.

Given the depressed state of the market for hosiery and the over-stocked nature of the labour market, it is hardly surprising that the knitters' actions proved unsuccessful. As Henson himself came to realise, the living standards of the framework knitters could only improve if the hosiers could rediscover the enterprise which had been so apparent in the previous century, but this would not come until the 1850s. In the meantime the framework knitters' living standards continued to decline, and they became a depressed and demoralised occupational group, clearly distinguishable, contemporaries claimed, from all other sections of the working classes. A Nottingham doctor told the Factory Commission in 1833 that he could always tell a framework knitter by his appearance. 'There is', he said, 'a paleness and a certain degree of emaciation and thinness about them.' Many years later William Booth, the founder of the Salvation Army, who was born in Sneinton in 1829, recalled that his mission to the poor had been first inspired by 'the degradation and helpless misery of the poor stockingers of my native town wandering gaunt and hunger-stricken through the streets'. In 1844 the dire state of the industry and the economic, social and physical inferiority of the framework knitters were so generally acknowledged as to prompt a parliamentary investigation.

The Growth of the Lace Industry

In 1804, when young John Heathcoat arrived in Nottingham, having just completed his apprenticeship as a framesmith, framework knitters and framesmiths had long been striving to produce new meshes on the stocking frame, in the hope of new and lucrative markets. Heathcoat, managed to design a completely new machine which was able to produce bobbin lace more cheaply, faster and with less effort. His patent, taken out in 1809, was constantly infringed as other mechanics sought to copy his invention, but after two court cases in 1816 and 1817 he was able to establish a system of licensing which allowed a great many small-scale producers to set themselves up in business using his techniques. By 1819 there were said to be 200 such small-scale entrepreneurs in Nottingham alone, mainly enterprising former framework knitters and framesmiths who were able to scrape together the necessary capital. But his success bred jealousy and his unpopularity probably accounts for the Luddite attack on his factory at Loughborough in 1816. By this time, however, his constant legal battles to enforce his patent rights had already caused him to make plans to leave the area. In December 1815 he bought a large disused cotton mill in Tiverton, in Devon, and shortly after the Luddite attack a few months later he left the East Midlands forever.

Unlike the traditional stocking frame, Heathcoat's machines could be driven by water or steam power. The small-scale entrepreneurs who were now moving in to this new industry were able to rent both space and steam power in factories in and around Nottingham. This practice was known as 'stall-holding' and was probably first organised by local auctioneers of machines, who advertised space for machine-buyers. The earliest mill to be let for this purpose was Green's Mill in Broad Marsh, which had been built for steam-powered cotton spinning in 1791 but had closed down in about 1814. The first specialist lace factory built in Nottingham was Kendall and Allen's Leen Side mill built in 1825 with a small 14hp steam engine, but other, larger, mills were also being built in the '20s just outside Nottingham, at New Lenton and Radford, and a little later at Carrington and New Basford. The Lenton mill, built in 1822-4, was later turned over to stall-holding. The largest lace mill in the Nottingham area was James Fisher's mill, which opened in New Radford in the '20s. In the early 1840s he was probably employing more than 500 people. None of the Midlands producers could yet compete in scale of production, however, with Heathcoat's factory at Tiverton, which at this time had about 850 people on its payroll.

The outstanding – but very temporary – feature of these early years of factory production in this new industry was the high number of very small-scale producers. While the hosiery industry stagnated, the lace industry was bursting with energy and the town was filling with self-made men. When William Felkin organised a survey of the industry in 1829, he found nearly 1,200 independent lace-machine owners, of whom only seven were not originally working artisans. The 1820s was a boom period when scores of men came into the industry hoping to make their fortune, and among them were extremely talented mechanics who were able to make significant advances in lace-machinery technology. The boom years were brief, however, and in the 1830s the industry suffered a sharp check, caused partly by competition from France, and many of those who set themselves up in business in the 1820s were to suffer bankruptcy in the 1830s. Enough did survive and prosper, though, to feed the myth of Samuel Smiles' self-made man, enunciated in his best-selling *Self-Help*: 'what some men are, all without difficulty might be'. Many believed whole-heartedly in this, including Felkin himself. The son of a poor Baptist preacher and framework knitter, he was one of many whose hard work helped him cross the line from artisan to master, and to become a highly respected figure in Nottingham society, becoming mayor of the town in 1851 and 1852. As the following extract from his *History* indicates, he never tired of pontificating on the rewards of hard work and perseverance:

> And inasmuch as I know what it is to labour with the hands long hours and for small wages as well as any workman to whom I address myself, I am emboldened to declare from experience that the gain of independence or rather self-dependence for which I plead, is worth infinitely more than all the costs of its attainment.

Few of those who came into the industry in the 1820s had much commercial experience, and this was probably one reason why lace exports did not expand as rapidly as might have been expected. However, Felkin believed that three-quarters of output was being exported in 1832. Exports to France were limited by Heathcoat's decision in 1818 to open a factory in France himself and a number of his Nottingham rivals also set up lace factories in the region around Calais. Exports to the Continent were considerably advanced, however, by the efforts of a number of German merchants who migrated to Nottingham in the 1830s and 1840s to exploit the opportunities for selling Nottingham lace across the German states and elsewhere in Eastern and Central Europe. Great quantities of Nottingham lace were also soon being exported to the USA, Peru and Melbourne, while the largest manufacturers, such as James Fisher, had established permanent agents at New York by the 1840s. At first, most of Nottingham-made lace was sold through London merchants in the Wood Street and Cheapside area of the city, as much of her hosiery had always been, but a number of manufacturers began to keep sales offices in the area around St Mary's church, particularly after the arrival of the Midland Railway in 1839 and the introduction of a cheap and reliable postal service in the 1840s. During the 1840s and 1850s the largest firms began to build prestige warehouses and offices in the area, and it was at this time that Nottingham's Lace Market could be said to have come into being. So many firms were opening warehouses in the area in the 1840s that the *Nottingham Journal* could pronounce in June 1847 that, in the newspaper's opinion, 'Mary Gate is the seat of the Lace Market.'

The wages paid in the lace industry were generally considerably higher than most framework knitters could earn. While the latter could rarely hope to earn more than 12s. a week, most skilled men in the lace trade probably earned between 15s. and 20s. in the period 1812 to 1820, and quite a lot more during the boom of the early 1820s ('the twist net fever'). During the 1820s Heathcoat was said to pay his skilled men between 30s. and 60s. a week, depending on their strength and skill. In the 1830s, however, when demand slackened, wages sank back to pre-boom levels. Moreover, long hours had to be worked in the lace factories. It was common practice for the men to have to work two five- or six-hour shifts a day, amounting to 10- or 12-hour days, and some complained of having to work 14 hours a day. The dislocation caused by working broken shifts, the disruption to family life and the night work involved were all much resented and prompted a petition to the House of Commons in 1845 which bitterly complained about the practice. Conditions which had been acceptable when wages were high, and when there was a real prospect of workmen being able to set themselves up in business and become 'their own boss', were no longer bearable now that wages were lower and all realistic hopes of independence had gone.

Working-Class Housing

During the first half of the 19th century the quality of working-class housing in Nottingham was among the worst in the country. One of the principal reasons for this was the appalling poverty of the framework knitters but another, equally important, factor was the unnecessarily high price of land in the town. In 1800 the price of building plots in the town had been rising sharply for many years, but they had received an especial fillip in 1787 when the corporation rejected a proposal to enclose the open fields and meadows surrounding the town. Unfortunately no records survive of the meeting at which the corporation discussed this issue, but of the 18 councillors present 14 voted against and four abstained. The corporation saw itself as defending not only their own considerable and often lucrative rights, but those also of the burgesses in general, and they were right to believe that the majority of the burgesses shared their view. When one of the promoters of the enclosure stood for election to become a senior councillor, shortly afterwards, he was decisively rejected by the burgesses.

The consequences of this decision were dire but eminently predictable. The few closes and small orchards that still existed, mainly on the east side of the town, now disappeared as their owners succumbed to the temptation of unprecedentedly high prices, and to make a profit on their investment every builder and bricklayer who ran up a row of houses had to squeeze as many as possible into the smallest space, and keep his other costs as low as possible. Altogether, 1,886 houses had been built in the last 20 years of the 18th century and the great majority of them were extremely small and built back-to-back, in long courts, reachable only by passing through a dark and narrow tunnel. By 1812 300 such courts had been built in the town, and by the mid-19th century 8,000 back-to-back houses, built around many hundreds of courts, constituted the main housing stock of the town.

When the water engineer Thomas Hawksley was invited to give evidence to the *Royal Commission on the State of Large Towns and Populous Districts* in 1844, he produced an illustration and plan showing a typical Nottingham court that lay behind Rancliffe and Harrington Streets, in the Broad Marsh area of the town. Each house consisted of three rooms, one on top of the other, and each room only about eight feet six inches wide and 10 feet deep. Some of the houses were built immediately above the privies, with only the floorboards separating the ground-floor room from the stench and filth beneath. In many cases the courtyards on to which the houses faced were in perpetual shade, screened from the sunlight even on the brightest of days by the height of the houses, and most were unpaved. In the absence of any regular system of waste collection, house

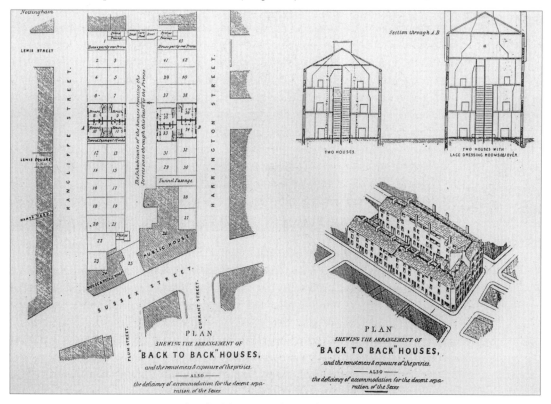

51   *Back-to-back housing in the Broad Marsh area, 1844.*

refuse was simply dumped outside the houses, in the courtyards and streets, in large heaps for the local children to play in. Here the refuse would be allowed to accumulate and grow until eventually the refuse heaps acquired value as manure, when they would be carted away by the 'muck majors', the local manure collectors, and a new heap would begin to form.

One of the Assistant Commissioners who had heard Hawksley's evidence, James Ranald Martin, shortly afterwards came to the town to see the town's working-class housing for himself. His report fully supported the evidence of Hawksley. The houses of the poor were, he reported, 'damp and uncleanly', and the courts:

> noisome, narrow, unprovided with adequate means for the removal of refuse, ill-ventilated, and wretched in the extreme, with a gutter, or surface-drain, running down the centre; they have no back yards, and the privies are common to the whole court; altogether they present scenes of a deplorable character, and of surpassing filth and discomfort.

Thomas Hawksley's example of a typical Nottingham court showed 43 houses sharing a dozen privies but a survey conducted by the corporation in 1847 found that in some cases courts had been built with fewer privies than this and some were without any privies at all, including a block of 38 back-to-back houses. In spite of the revelations of the 1844 Commission, the gentlemen who conducted the inquiry in 1847 were not always prepared for the appalling conditions they found. In some courts the privies were without doors, they reported, and absolutely filthy, and the stench emanating from them caused them to be 'scarcely approachable'. Some were broken and the contents of some drained into the nearby houses. Numerous cesspools were found and in some courts pigsties and slaughterhouses were also located among the houses, adding large accumulations of blood and offal to the rest of the noisome filth in which the inhabitants had to somehow live.

The appalling impact of such conditions on the health of the community had long been known, although not yet fully understood. In the summer of 1832 Nottingham suffered its first and most deadly attack of cholera. Between early July and October that year more than 900 cases were reported. Of these, 330 proved fatal, and the great majority of fatalities were in the grim and filthy courts of the southern and eastern parts of the town, and particularly in those courts where there had been a heavy influx of poor Irish families in recent years. As a result a new cemetery was opened and some efforts made to improve sewage disposal, but 12 years later the system of sewage disposal was still being described as 'very defective and unsystematic', and the corporation itself admitted that the River Leen was 'the Great Drain of the Town'. Thomas Hawksley had constructed an effective system of waterworks in 1830, close to Trent Bridge, but most of the courts still lacked water pumps and consequently clean water and cleanliness were regarded as luxuries that few of those living in Nottingham's back-to-backs could afford.

Hawksley calculated in 1844 that, as a result mainly of the very high infant death rates, the average life expectancy of a working man born in a Nottingham slum was barely more than 20 years, or only about half that of one born and brought up in the countryside. In one of the worst areas of the town, Byron Ward, on the north east side of the town, life expectancy at birth was calculated to be only 18.1 years. Cholera had a considerable shock-effect but, apart from the epidemic year of 1832, it was never one of the major killers in the town. One disease that was a constant scourge, however, was typhus, which was carried by lice and thrived particularly in filthy conditions. In July 1847 it was reported that in the previous 12 months approximately nine hundred cases of typhus fever had been treated in the town.

The poverty of the inhabitants meant that more than one family might occupy one tiny house, or a large family that had no space to spare at all nevertheless was obliged to take a lodger or two to help pay the rent. In 1832 one group of 833 houses was found to contain 947 families and 4,283 people. Many of these were poor Irish immigrants. In one court it was reported that 90 people were occupying just 11 rooms. Many similar examples can be found in the enumerators' returns for the 1851 census. In Lewis Square, for example, in the Broad Marsh area, a 33 year-old dyer, James Reyder, his wife Hannah, a 31-year-old lace mender, and their five children, shared their little house with Hannah's father, brother and two sisters. Families with six or seven children still at home were not at all uncommon, and lack of space meant that three or four children would often be obliged to share the same bed.

As the town grew dirtier and more crowded, so those who could afford to move away from the town centre did so. The first signs of a 'middle-class retreat' were apparent in the 1790s when Park Row was developed on the western edge of the town, and 10 years later the Duke of Newcastle had the Standard Hill area divided into 32 plots and sold off for

52-3 *Housing in the Park today.*

54   *Lenton Hurst, a large house, built for one of Nottingham's upper-middle-class families at Lenton, now in the grounds of Nottingham University.*

high-quality housing. The Ropewalk, overlooking the old castle deer park, but by now known simply as 'The Park', was developed as a middle-class suburb in the late 1820s and early 1830s, and from the turn of the century large houses for the town's middle-class elite were also being built further out of the town, at Lenton; some still stand today as part of the University of Nottingham campus.

By the 1830s the centre of Nottingham was almost entirely filled with rows of working-class houses, with alleys and courts squeezed into every possible space, while the middle classes were now to be found only on the western edges of the town and in the villages beyond. The town centre was by now so crowded that the rate of growth in the 1830s and 1840s was much less than it had been in any decade in the previous 60 years. Consequently there was also now no space in the town for the new factories required by the rapidly expanding lace industry, and almost all had to be built just outside the town. While Nottingham's population grew by less than 2,000 in the 1830s, the population of the surrounding villages increased by almost 9,000, and most of the new arrivals were employed in the new lace factories. Enclosure acts in the 1790s made possible the development of three new villages, right on the edge of Nottingham's still unenclosed open fields, at New Sneinton, New Radford and New Lenton, and a little further away to the north New Basford was also growing rapidly in the 1820s and 1830s, and entirely new settlements were being developed at Carrington and Hyson Green. The housing being erected for the lace workers in these villages was considerably better than that available to the poor framework-knitters in the town. Cheaper land and the higher wages of the lace operatives meant that these houses were not back-to-backs, but were laid out with at least a small front garden and a backyard.

The Coming of the Railway and the Enclosure of the Open Fields

The corporation lacked the powers – and probably also the inclination – to involve itself in proposals for housing or sanitary improvements in the town, but when it was removed in 1835 by the Municipal Corporations Act, the new elected council was also given no power to bring about real improvements in the state of the town. However, the elections for the new council did bring about a considerable change in personnel, for only nine members of the former corporation were elected to the new 42-member council, and this new body would prove rather less determined than its predecessor to resist proposals to enclose the town's open fields and meadows. It was recognised, however, that opposition to any such proposals was still very strong among the burgesses, and those councillors who were willing to support a change of policy knew that they would have to tread very warily.

Only two years before the winding up of the old corporation it had yet again repeated its opposition to enclosure. The issue had arisen on four occasions in the previous 32 years, in 1804, 1806, 1813 and again in 1833, but the opinion of the majority of the councillors had not changed. The case for enclosure seemed, to its advocates at least, to grow stronger with every passing year as the town descended steadily into an embarrassing and lethal squalor. Enclosure, it was claimed in 1833, would enable the town's lace industry to stay within the town and (bearing in mind the cholera epidemic only the year before) it would also 'be the means of averting the spread of any epidemic by enabling future Buildings … to be erected in more open, airy and healthy situations'. The corporation, however, was having none of it.

Ironically, when the first steps were finally taken for at least a partial enclosure of the town's fields it was for neither of the reasons given in 1833, but rather as a consequence of plans to bring a railway line into the town from Derby. Proposals for such a railway were presented to the new council only a month after it had taken office, early in 1836. It at first hesitated to support the plans, wary of the opposition from both the Nottingham Canal Company and the Trent Navigation Company, as well as from burgesses unwilling to see common lands disappear under railway sidings and goods yards, but after much criticism for its timidity in the *Nottingham Review* and a stormy council meeting, a number of councillors began to have a change of heart. Before the end of 1837 it had been decided to draw up two Enclosure Bills for presentation to Parliament: one to enclose the West Croft to the south of the town, to allow land for the proposed route of the railway and a station, and another for the enclosure of just 18 acres of land between Derby Road and Park Row, to allow the creation of a small estate of superior dwellings for the town's middle classes. By resisting calls for a general enclosure the new corporation managed to minimise opposition from the burgesses and the two Bills became law in 1839. A little later, on 30 May 1839, the first train pulled into the new stone-built Greek Doric-style station, just 40 minutes after leaving Derby, and in the same year a beginning was made in laying out the town's first middle-class suburb, centred on the new Wellington Circus.

A downturn in the textile industries prevented further developments in the next few years but the evidence presented by Hawksley to the Royal Commission in 1844, together with his evidence to a House of Commons Select Committee the same year, made a strong case for a general enclosure of the town's common fields. The town's Whig newspaper, the *Nottingham Review*, now also took up the cause and printed every word of Hawksley's evidence. By the end of 1844 the town was deeply and bitterly divided but the Whig majority on the corporation was moving towards supporting an Enclosure Bill drawn up by a small group of Hawksley's supporters, and at a noisy, ill-tempered meeting in March 1845 the corporation voted to back the Bill. It was presented to Parliament and, in spite of numerous counter-petitions from the burgesses, became law in June 1845.

For many of the Whig councillors who supported the measure, it was expected that this victory would now lead rapidly to a solution of the town's housing problems and, in particular, of chronic overcrowding, without the need for further improvement measures in the worst affected areas. This optimism, however, was misplaced for it assumed that the poor framework knitters would be able to move into the new and better housing which could now be built on the former open fields. Those who held this view overlooked the other major cause of the problem, the appalling poverty of the inhabitants of the slums, and they assumed, erroneously as it proved, that house prices would fall once the enclosure released plenty of new building plots for sale. On the other hand, the Enclosure Commissioners did set minimum standards for the building of new houses when the enclosed land was released for building on. Sewers now had to be laid, roads had to be of at least a certain minimum width, and the notorious back-to-backs were banned. But unfortunately the poor inhabitants of the slums would not be able to afford to move out and live in the new houses.

Partly to raise money for the enclosure, the Commissioners also sold more land to the Midland Railway Company, which was keen to extend its existing line from Derby on to Lincoln, and the Nottingham and Lincoln Railway opened in August 1846. The existing station was now rather inconveniently placed, however, as the new line ran to the south of the building, rather than through it, and trains to and from Lincoln had to back into and out of the station. The solution was to abandon the station built only nine years earlier and build a brand new one, at the eastern end of Station Street, and this opened in May 1848.

The full impact of the arrival of the railway would only be felt gradually, during the second half of the century, as many more lines were opened, but the immediate effects on the town's communications were dramatic and very obvious. The building of a line from Derby to Rugby in 1840 meant that from this time Nottingham was linked by rail to London – a journey of 5½ hours, or less than half the time of the fastest coach – and in 1848 another line was opened to Mansfield, and in 1850 another to Grantham. The 1820s and 1830s had been the golden age of coach travel but this was a world already fast disappearing by the mid-century. In the mid-1830s a stream of coaches ran daily in all directions from the town's coaching inns, from the *Lion Hotel* on Clumber Street, the *Milton's Head Inn* on Milton Street, and from the *Black Boy Inn* and *Maypole Inn*, both on Long Row. But the sights and sounds of this morning bustle and ritual – the clatter of the horses' hooves and the blasts of the coachman's horn – were becoming a mere memory by 1850. In 1853 only one coach service still survived, the Sheffield coach, via Mansfield and Chesterfield, but this also vanished shortly afterwards.

Radical Nottingham

Nottingham's reputation for radical activity and violent politics was already well established at the beginning of the century and the events of the next half-century would do little to contradict that impression. Strong anti-war and anti-government sentiment ensured that the election of 1802 was one of the most violent yet seen in the town. Daniel Parker Coke, who had represented the town in the House of Commons since 1780, had made himself unpopular in the town in some quarters, particularly among working people and some members of the corporation, by his support for a number of repressive measures introduced during the previous Parliament. Anti-government feeling was also sharpened by severe economic distress. Poor harvests had pushed the price of wheat to starvation levels the year before and the resulting famine had been followed by a typhus epidemic in the poorer parts of the town. The Whig majority on the corporation were keen to run a candidate against him and found a wealthy West India merchant, Joseph Birch, to stand at the last moment as a Whig-Radical candidate. Birch, however, was from Liverpool and was unknown in Nottingham, and it was very soon quite apparent that he could not hope to unseat Coke by fair means. His enthusiastic supporters therefore quickly devised strategies to obstruct all those who favoured Coke. Voters were threatened and insulted as they entered the polling booth and Coke himself was the painful target of a shower of stones as he arrived in the market place. Unable to compete, he withdrew from the contest, and Birch was duly declared elected, alongside the other candidate, Admiral Sir John Borlase Warren. His victory was then celebrated a few days later, on the anniversary of the fall of the Bastille, by a procession in which Birch was carried on a chair through the town, preceded by 24 young ladies dressed in white, with flowers in their hair and laurels in their hands, singing the *Marseillaise* and *Millions be Free*.

Birch had not long to enjoy his success, however, for Coke petitioned the House of Commons against the election on the grounds of intimidation and rioting and his case was upheld. In March 1803 the election was declared void and a new election set for May. Coke also persuaded the Commons that the election had shown that the town's magistrates, most of whom were Whigs, were either incapable of maintaining good order or unwilling to do so, and that the county magistrates, most of whom were Tories, should be given equal jurisdiction in the town. This seemed a major blow to the independence of the town and the Whig corporation suffered another defeat at the end of May when, in a remarkably peaceful contest, Coke defeated Birch and regained his seat.

The radicals in the town would not achieve an election victory for another nine years, but in the intervening years the movement remained active and well supported. The outbreak of war with France in 1803 and subsequent fears of invasion prompted a change of radical focus. With France now under the military dictatorship of Napoleon and threatening invasion, there was less emphasis on the ideals of the French Revolution, and the *Marseillaise* was never again sung in procession through the town. Instead, local radicals turned their attention back to an earlier cause, the need for a drastic reform of Parliament, and it was partly for this reason that Charles Sutton founded the radical *Nottingham Review* in 1808, with is office and printworks in Bridlesmithgate. When Parliament was dissolved in 1812 Coke decided to stand down and urged his supporters in the town to vote and campaign for his chosen successor, Richard Arkwright of Cromford, the son of the inventor of the water-frame cotton spinning mechanism. When the election was called the local radicals were determined to find a candidate who would stand on a pro-peace and pro-parliamentary reform platform to run against Arkwright, who was absolutely opposed to both. They had learnt from previous disappointments the need to have a credible local candidate with considerable social standing, and they found their man – at the last possible moment – in Lord Rancliffe of Bunny Hall. Rancliffe defeated Arkwright with almost 300 more votes and came second to the Whig incumbent, John Smith – another member of the banking family – who had been first elected in 1806, when Borlase Warren had stood down. Coke retired from politics in 1812 because he believed that his support for the war had made it impossible for him to hold the seat, and he was probably right. At the end of the year a petition calling for peace attracted between 5,000 and 6,000 signatures, while a counter-petition, supporting the continuation of the war, was signed by only 700.

At the time of Rancliffe's election the town was suffering the effects of a severe depression in the hosiery industry, and this had prompted a number of hosiers to try to reduce costs by cutting wages and producing cheap 'cut-up' stockings produced on wide frames. Some historians have seen the so-called Luddite attacks of some desperate framework knitters on the property of wage-cutting hosiers as being politically motivated. Although we can imagine the hatred that many poor and starving men must have felt for an unsympathetic government, whose only response to their plight was to make frame-breaking a capital offence, there is no evidence that the attacks were anything other than an attempt to intimidate the hosiers into restoring previous wage rates – which were already pitifully low –

Frame - Breaking.
£.200 Reward.

WHEREAS, on Thursday Night last, about Ten o'Clock, a great Number of Men, armed with Pistols, Hammers and Clubs, entered the Dwelling-house of *George Ball*, framework-knitter, of Lenton, near Nottingham, disguised with Masks and Handkerchiefs over their Faces, and in other ways,---and after striking and abusing the said *George Ball*, they *wantonly* and *feloniously* broke and destroyed five STOCKING FRAMES, standing in the Work-shop; four of which belonged to *George Ball*, and one Frame, 40 gage, belonging to Mr. *Francis Braithwaite*, hosier, Nottingham: *all of which were working at the FULL PRICE.*

NOTICE IS HEREBY GIVEN,

THAT if any Person will give Information of the Offender or Offenders, or any one of them who entered such Dwelling-house and were concerned in such Felony, he or she shall receive a Reward of

£. 200,

to be paid on Conviction, in the Proportions following, (viz.) £50 under the King's Proclamation, £25 from the Committee of the Corporation of Nottingham, and £125 from the said *Francis Braithwaite*.

WE, the under-signed Workmen of the above-named *George Ball*, do hereby certify that we were employed in working the under-mentioned Frames, on the Work and at the Prices hereinafter stated, when the Mob came to break them,—that we had never been abated in our Work, either by Mr. Braithwaite, the hosier, who employed the Frames, or by the said *George Ball*, our master ; of whom we never complained, or had any Reason so to do.

QUALITY OF WORK.	PRICE.	WORKMEN.	OWNERS.
40 Gauge, Single Shape, Narrowed Two-plain,	Maid's, 29 Shillings per Dozen,	Thomas Rew,	Mr. Braithwaite.
36 Gauge, Single Shape, Narrowed Two-plain,	Men's, 29 Shillings per Dozen,	John Jackson,	George Ball.
38 Guage, Single Shape, Narrowed Two-plain,	Maid's, 26 Shillings per Dozen,	Thomas Naylor,	George Ball.

NB. The other two Frames were worked to another Hosier, but at the Full Price.

THOMAS REW,
JOHN JACKSON,
THOMAS NAYLOR.

Nottingham, 25th January, 1812.

55   *A reward notice for information leading to the conviction of frame-breakers, issued in January 1812.*

and to end the use of the hated wide-frames, which were rightly seen as undermining the skills of the trade. The first outbreak of frame smashing began in Arnold, in March 1811, after a large number of angry framework knitters had gathered in the marketplace in Nottingham to protest against wage cuts. About two hundred frames were smashed in the next few weeks but peace seemed to have been restored following the arrival of extra troops in the town and the enrolment of special constables in April. Further wage cuts prompted more frame-smashing incidents, however, in November, and again the attacks began in Arnold but this time spread quickly to other villages near Nottingham, to Hucknall, Kimberley, Kirkby and Sutton-in-Ashfield. During the winter about two hundred frames were being broken every month, and when the attacks died down in the following February it was said that the Luddite gangs had smashed more than a thousand frames. More troops were drafted into the area and more special constables were sworn in, but no one could be caught. More attacks occurred the following winter, but on a smaller scale, and then again in the spring of 1814 and, for the last time, in the winter of 1816-17.

Although Luddism was almost certainly what contemporaries called a 'knife and fork' issue, the same desperate hunger and misery that prompted some to resort to frame-smashing also prompted some framework knitters to join the ill-fated 'Pentrich Rising' in the spring of 1817. Believing that they would be joined in Nottingham by many thousands of other like-minded revolutionaries, Jeremiah Brandreth, of Pentrich in Derbyshire, led about three hundred men from Pentrich and other villages towards Nottingham on the night of 9 June. They expected to be able to seize control of the town before marching on London to inspire a revolution that would overthrow the government. Shortly after passing through Eastwood, however, they were met by a detachment of hussars from Nottingham and about eighty were arrested, including Brandreth, who was later executed along with two others, while 14 other men were transported to Australia.

The Pentrich Rising was a symptom of the commonly held (but inaccurate) belief that Nottingham was a town full of determined revolutionaries. Support for parliamentary reform, however, was genuinely widespread and growing stronger. News of revolution in France, in July 1830, and the overthrow of the reactionary Charles X, brought calls for parliamentary reform back to the top of the political agenda. Following the adoption of the cause by Earl Grey's Whigs (if only as a useful stick with which to beat the Tory government) the Whig-dominated Nottingham corporation organised a public meeting in October to call for the town's support for reform as well, and more than 8,000 townspeople promptly signed a pro-reform petition.

The fall of the Tory government in November, and the assumption of power by the Whigs, gave the movement additional impetus, which then received another boost with the General Election in April 1831, when Grey won an overwhelming majority. In Nottingham the two Whig-Radical incumbent candidates (Rancliffe and Birch) were returned unopposed, although this was due in no small part to the Whig corporation's practice since 1817 of establishing its control over elections by enlarging the number of Whig voters. This was achieved by granting the right to be an honorary freeman of the town to Whigs living outside Nottingham, even if they had no connection with the town whatsoever. Such, however, was the enthusiasm for the Reform Bill that when news reached the town on 8 October that the House of Lords had rejected it rioting broke out in the town. The situation was made more dangerous because the market place was full of villagers who had come in that day for the Goose Fair. After a huge meeting in the market place the following Monday morning (10 October) a group of protestors marched first to Colwick Hall, the home of a Nottingham magistrate known for his opposition to the Bill, and tried – unsuccessfully – to set it on fire. They then returned to the town and made their way to the castle, an equally well-chosen target as its owner, the Duke of Newcastle, had been one of the Bill's most determined opponents in the House of Lords. The castle was empty, unguarded and very soon on fire, creating a spectacular sight which would never be forgotten by all those who witnessed it. The perpetrators could not be identified, but three men were hanged for the attack on Colwick Hall and for burning down a silk mill at Beeston. This had been attacked shortly after the burning of the castle and had also been targeted because it belonged to a local Tory known for his opposition to the Reform Bill.

A Nottingham Political Union had been formed to support the Bill, and to unite 'the middle and lower classes of the people', in March 1831, the same month Grey had first presented his Bill to the House of Commons, and within nine months it had more than

56   Nottingham Castle, set on fire during the Reform Bill riots of 1831.

2,500 members. But enthusiasm soon turned to dissatisfaction. When the Bill was finally passed, on 4 June 1832, it was soon seen by radicals among both the middle and working classes of the town as a bitter disappointment. Working men had not been given the vote and the number of voters in Nottingham was enlarged only a little. The issue was therefore far from closed. The *Nottingham Review* continued to call for further reform and the Nottingham Political Union remained in existence. Here, as in many other towns, the great enthusiasm once evinced for the Reform Bill movement would soon be recreated and channelled afresh into support for a much more radical movement, the campaign for votes for all men, which became known as Chartism.

For poor framework knitters and their families, as for the handloom weavers of Yorkshire and Lancashire, the Chartist movement represented the promise not only of the vote but, more importantly, of a better life, in which they could, to quote one Chartist speaker, 'furnish their houses, clothe their backs, and educate their children' and, he might have added, fill their stomachs. Nottingham was not one of the first major towns to hold a pro-Charter meeting, but the enthusiasm for the movement among the town's working men and women was never in much doubt. In spite of wet weather at least 3,000 people attended a Chartist rally on the Forest in November 1838. It was organised by a small committee of local Chartists, led by James Sweet, which met regularly in his shop in Goose Gate. Among those attending the November rally were members of the Nottingham Female Association for Obtaining the People's Charter, which was already reported to be holding regular weekly meetings. The *Nottingham Review* declared its support and published with approval the Six Points of the Charter. A further large-scale meeting was held in the market place in February 1839, followed by a great Chartist rally on the Forest in May, and when the first Chartist petition was presented it was claimed that 17,000 of the 1,250,000 signatures came from Nottingham. However, when the House of Commons rejected the petition out of hand, by a crushing margin of 235 votes to 46, enthusiasm and hope dwindled, although for a while well-attended meetings were held in the market place to discuss the 'National Holiday', or general strike, called for by some delegates at the National Chartist Convention in Birmingham.

Nationally, the movement died away in division and indecision during the summer and autumn, and in Nottingham – as elsewhere – only came back to life as a consequence of the acute trade depression of 1841-2, which forced many thousands out of work across the country, prompted wage cuts, and drove vast numbers of men, women and children to seek relief from the hated new workhouses, or 'Bastilles', as they were popularly known. When the new Chartist leader, Feargus O'Connor, came to the town in February 1842, he received a rapturous welcome. This time an even larger petition was presented, with 3,000,000 signatures, in May 1842, and although this was also decisively rejected by the Commons, by 287 votes to 49, the movement locally was given a considerable boost by the decision of one of the leading figures in the campaign, Joseph Sturge, to put himself forward as a candidate in a by-election in August. Sturge was an immensely able middle-class Birmingham Quaker who had earlier that year founded the Complete Suffrage Union, dedicated to uniting the working and middle classes behind the cause of universal suffrage. Hopes that Sturge could win were boosted by the arrival of both Feargus O'Connor and the Leicester Chartist Thomas Cooper to speak for him, and although he was defeated, the margin was narrow: a mere 84 votes out of 3,686 cast. Local support was then further encouraged by news of an outbreak of strikes in August across Lancashire, Yorkshire, Staffordshire, Warwickshire and Wales. Although the strikes were triggered by wage cuts, the rejection of the Charter had stirred up working-class anger and the strikes were often accompanied by pledges that the workers would stay on strike until the Charter was law. Inspired by these developments, local Chartists called a meeting on 18 August 'to promote a general strike … until the document known as the People's Charter become the law of the land', and on 23 August about five thousand Chartists assembled on Mapperley Plains. The meeting was peaceful but the magistrates were anxious to disperse the crowd, fearing that violence might follow. The Riot Act was read and when the crowd did not immediately disperse troops were ordered to make arrests. About four hundred were arrested and marched away to the House of Correction. Thoroughly incensed by this behaviour, a section of the crowd then began to stone the troops until they were forced to scatter by sabre-wielding cavalry.

The Battle of Mapperley Hills, as this violent episode became known, marked the end of the Chartist movement in Nottingham for almost five years, and when it revived, in the summer of 1847, it was again partly as a consequence of severe trade depression and resulting high levels of unemployment. Enthusiasm was also rekindled by an election, but this time it was O'Connor himself who stood as a Chartist candidate, and he was victorious. As economic conditions deteriorated in the winter of 1847-8, so support for

this third Chartist campaign grew, and news of yet another revolution in France, in February 1848, was also encouraging. An enormous national petition was again drawn up, and on 10 April, the day assigned for a huge Chartist rally on Kennington Common in London and the presentation of the petition to the House of Commons, it was agreed that in Nottingham there should also be a great Chartist rally. About four thousand Chartists attended to hear cheerful, optimistic speeches, and to the surprise of the magistrates the event remained peaceful and without incident, as was also the case in London. Fearing disorder, three troops of yeomanry were held in readiness nearby, in Gedling, Wollaton, and at Trent Bridge, to reinforce the troops stationed in the barracks, and a fourth troop of yeomanry waited in reserve further away, at Gamston, near Retford.

As was the case nationally, the rejection of this third petition by the Commons would effectively bring an end to the Chartist era in Nottingham; although its ideals lived on it would never again be a powerful mass movement. Moreover, Feargus O'Connor was able to make very little impact in Parliament and, as a sad postscript to Chartism, especially in Nottingham, in 1853 he had to be removed from the House of Commons and taken to a lunatic asylum, where he died two years later.

Although for the town's many radicals the failure of yet another attempt to obtain the vote was a bitter disappointment, the 1840s had seen one very important achievement, and a major blow to the privileges of the landed classes, namely the success of the Anti-Corn Law League in persuading Parliament in June 1846 to repeal the Corn Laws. Although a distinctly middle-class movement, it had considerable support from the working people of Nottingham, for whom there could hardly be a more important issue than the price of bread, which the Corn Laws were alleged to have kept artificially high to protect the rent rolls

57   *Statue of Feargus O'Connor, in the Arboretum.*

of landowners. In February 1842 it was reported that as many as 8,000 people had attended an Anti-Corn Law meeting in the town and later in the year, when the movement's leaders, Richard Cobden and John Bright, visited Nottingham on a speaking and money-raising tour, about £1,300 was raised from local businessmen. The corporation was slow to show its support, however, and did not send its own Anti-Corn Law petition to Parliament until February 1846.

Moreover, Chartism continued to have some influence in local politics for many years to come. The local leader, James Sweet, still considered himself a Chartist in 1872, and the support of local Chartists was vital in ensuring the election of the Radical Liberal Sir Robert Clifton in two extremely violent parliamentary elections in 1861 and 1865. Nottingham's reputation for radicalism would die away in the more prosperous years of the second half of the century, but it was still sufficiently alive even in 1885 to persuade the trade union leader, John Burns, to stand as a candidate for the Social Democratic Federation for the constituency of Nottingham West in the general election that year, and although he did not win the seat, he did win a respectable 598 votes.

Poverty and the New Poor Law

The enthusiasm which so many working people in Nottingham showed for Chartism in the 1830s and 1840s owed much to the fact that it was so closely associated with hatred of the New Poor Law, which had been passed in 1834. The cruel humiliation of the poor, which was a consequence of the application of the New Poor Law, made it an obvious target for Chartist leaders such as O'Connor and Cooper. The sight of extremely thin, starving unemployed men begging in the streets in the winter of 1839-40, because they dared not apply for relief to the workhouse, touched the heart of General Sir Charles Napier, who had been sent to Nottingham to take control of the troops stationed in the barracks. Writing in his journal on 2 December 1839, he was clearly shocked and angered by what he saw and by the lack of humanity shown by many of the well-to-do whom he met in the town:

> The streets of this town are horrible. The poor starving people go about by twenties and forties, begging, but without the least insolence; and yet some rich villains, and some foolish women, choose to say that they try to extort charity. It is a lie, an infernal lie, neither more nor less; nothing can exceed the good behaviour of these poor people, except it be their cruel sufferings.

The workhouse was full and outdoor relief was only available to the families of able-bodied men if they were prepared to undergo the 'labour test', that is undertake heavy manual labour. The Overseer of the Poor, Absolem Barnett, insisted that when the workhouse was full the poor must be found employment, however unpleasant, and that only by doing such work could the poor demonstrate that they were truly in need. A great many Nottingham people agreed with him for in the spring of 1837 £5,000 was raised in subscriptions to pay for 1,000 men to be set to work digging out soil to build a new road across Mapperley Common. Barnett's critics pointed out that the poor framework knitters, in particular, were rarely strong enough to do such work. Not only were they weak and starving, but, working in crowded, ill-ventilated and dirty houses, they were notoriously unhealthy and many were consumptive. For such men Barnett's 'labour test' was cruel and dangerous punishment for extreme poverty and destitution. Nevertheless, the policy continued, and in the spring of 1840, with unemployment remaining high and the workhouse still full, 500 of the unemployed were again set to work on the Mapperley Common road project.

Subscriptions were also raised, however, in times of crisis such as this to provide bread, soup and blankets for the destitute. Nearly 7,000 people, or 13 per cent of the population, were said to have benefitted from this in the winter of 1841-2. Trade tended to improve in the next few years but a sharp slump in the spring of 1848 caused unemployment in the textile trades to leap again. By this time the new Union Workhouse had been completed on York Street, designed to accommodate 1,150 paupers, or more than twice the capacity of the old St Mary's workhouse. It was reported in April 1848 that 1,600 were packed into it and many more destitute families were again relying on soup kitchens as their only means of survival.

Napier himself was instrumental in helping set up subscriptions in Nottingham for poor relief in December 1839. Like many other members of the higher classes he blamed the Chartist troubles on the New Poor Law, which he believed was driving hungry men to desperate measures. On 3 December he recorded his conversation with the mayor about organising a subscription and then added:

the excellent mayor, Mr Roworth … joins me in all my opinions as to the thrice accursed new poor law, its bastilles and its guardians. Lying title! They guard nothing, not even their own carcasses, for they so outrage misery that if a civil war comes they will be immediately sacrificed.

It was partly because of such views – as well as the enormous cost involved – that many of Nottingham's ratepayers objected so strongly to the building of the new York Street Union Workhouse, which was begun in 1840 and completed in 1843 at a cost of £17,500.

The very low wages earned by many, particularly framework knitters and casual labourers, meant that even in good years, when there was plenty of employment, the rent could only be paid and just enough food and clothing purchased if every member of the family who could possibly be found work did so. The 1851 census shows that in the poorer districts even children as young as seven were sent out to work and by the age of 10 or 11 all children of poor families would be expected to be able to contribute at least a little to the family income, girls principally as domestic servants, cap makers, lace dressers and lace menders, and boys as errand boys and labourers.

Crime and Punishment

The rapid increase in the town's population in the first decades of the 19th century, together with so much poverty, greatly exacerbated the problems of crime. What had been a relatively minor problem in the town in the 18th century rapidly became a major cause of concern. Nationally, the growth of crime in urban areas in these years was an important reason for the decision of the new Whig government to introduce the 1835 Municipal Corporations Act, which abolished the unelected corporations which had governed the towns since medieval times and introduced in their place elected bodies, accountable to the ratepayers.

The inadequacy of policing in the town under the old corporation was spelt out clearly by John Blackner in 1815. During the hours of daylight the police force consisted of just three full-time paid policemen plus a rather larger number of part-time, unpaid, volunteer constables, and at night they handed their responsibilities over to the ancient institution known as the Watch, and it was this that gave most concern. Blackner wrote:

> The reader will judge for himself, whether this town is properly watched during the night, when he considers that about 35,000 inhabitants are scattered through upwards of 400 streets, lanes etc. and that nine or ten men, four of whom watch the market-place, are employed to walk almost twenty streets.

It was also extremely dark in most of the town's streets at night. Gas lamps were erected to give some light in the market place in 1819 but few other streets were lit and anyone venturing out at night had to carry a lantern.

The traditional view was that criminality could be best kept to acceptable levels by a policy of severe deterrence. By the end of the 18th century a considerable range of offences might merit either the death penalty or transportation, and lesser crimes were usually punished either by a spell in the pillory or a public whipping. Until 1827 men and women convicted of committing capital offences in the town were usually executed on Gallows Hill, at the junction of Forest Road and Mansfield Road, but from 1831 executions took place beside the wall of the House of Correction, on the corner of Glasshouse Street and St John's Street. 'New Drop Corner', as it soon became known, was visible to large crowds in both these streets and along Parliament Street and Broad Street. Those condemned for crimes committed in the county were instead executed on the steps of the Shire Hall on High Pavement, and again large crowds could usually be expected to witness the event and, hopefully, be deterred from committing offences themselves. The gaol, beneath the Guildhall at Weekday Cross, was mainly used to house debtors and prisoners awaiting trial, transportation or execution. Other offenders were housed in the House of Correction. When John Howard, the prison reformer, visited it in 1776 he described it as consisting of 'two rooms, no fireplaces, a dark dungeon down nine steps'. In 1825 a 30-foot treadmill was installed so that the inmates could be set to work pumping water into the town.

Following the election of the new corporation in December 1835 it made sure that one of its first acts was to set up an improved policing system. A Watch Committee was constituted and new appointments of constables were soon made. Only three constables were again appointed for daytime duties but at dusk they were replaced by a dozen constables who patrolled the streets until 10.30 p.m., when they were replaced by a 50-strong night force. Unfortunately, many of the latter soon proved unsuitable and had to be replaced by constables willing to enforce the law more rigorously, and the numbers of both day and dusk police also had to be soon increased. At first the new constables enjoyed little respect and assaults on the police were common, but by the middle of the century this was beginning to become less of a problem as the police earned both greater acceptance and respect. Punishments were also becoming less brutal as attitudes to prisoners changed. The pillory ceased to be used in 1808 and public whippings came to an end in the 1830s. Public hangings continued until 1868 but were rare in Nottingham from the 1830s.

Church, Chapel and School

The fear of growing uncontrolled criminality among the poorer classes was one of the most important motivating forces behind both the church and chapel building of the evangelical revival, which began in the late 18th century, and the accompanying campaign to provide at least a basic civilising education for the poor by means of Sunday Schools. When Horace Mann published his Religious Census in 1851, however, it was found that, as in other cities and large towns, the working classes were largely absent from the pews of both Anglican churches and nonconformist chapels. By comparison with many other towns and cities, Nottingham's evangelists were actually doing rather well, with about forty two per cent of the town's population attending at least one service on Census Sunday (30 March) compared to a national average of about thirty-nine per cent, but it was mainly the middle classes who were filling both churches and chapels. The Sunday School movement could report a similar story. The Nottingham Sunday School Union was established in 1810 to encourage the opening of more schools, both in the town and in the rapidly growing surrounding villages, and by 1833 there were more than 20 Sunday Schools in the town with a total enrolment of 6,726. This was a great achievement but it still meant that large numbers of the town's children were receiving no education at all. Some children did not go to a Sunday School because their parents could afford to send them to a day school instead, but most of those who were missing from the Sunday School registers were the children of the poorest families. The children whose fathers were casual labourers or framework knitters had to be sent out to work as soon as they possibly could be. For them and their parents schooling of any sort belonged to a different world to which they did not feel they had access. Even if they were not too exhausted to go to a Sunday School, they were simply too poor; they were

58   *St Barnabas Roman Catholic Cathedral today; designed by Pugin 1841, consecrated 1844. Joseph Hendren, the first Roman Catholic bishop for the new diocese of Nottingham was enthroned in 1851.*

often without shoes, dressed only in ragged 'hand-me-downs' and very dirty. Cleanliness was a luxury which they could rarely enjoy.

The statistics for Sunday School attendance in the 1830s also reveal that the great majority of children who attended were going to a school run by a nonconformist chapel. A survey published in 1833 showed that only 1,678 children were attending one of the Church of England schools but about 4,500 children were enrolled in one of the many nonconformist schools, while another 200 attended the Catholic School and 336 adults were enrolled in two adult schools. These figures clearly suggest that by the 1830s the nonconformists had won the allegiance of the majority of the town's churchgoers, and this was confirmed by Mann's census 20 years later. Whereas about 7,800 people attended at least one Anglican service on Census Sunday in 1851, approximately twice that number were attending one or more of the services provided by one of the nonconformist chapels.

The rapid growth in the Methodist church in the town in the late 18th century continued throughout the first half of the 19th, and by 1851 there were almost as many Methodists attending church on Census Sunday as there were Anglicans. Moreover, most of the other, older, nonconformist churches had also expanded their numbers considerably and between them they could also boast more than 7,000 attendances in 1851. The local Roman Catholic community was also growing rapidly by the 1840s, partly because of an influx of Irish immigrants following the potato famine. The first Catholic chapel had been opened in 1790 but as numbers had grown a larger chapel had been opened on George Street in 1828, and in 1841 a plot was acquired on Derby Road for a still larger building, designed by A.W.N. Pugin. This proved enormously controversial and the incumbent of St Mary's, Archdeacon George Wilkins, made numerous speeches while the new church was being erected attacking Catholicism, many of which were well publicised in both the *Journal* and the *Review*. The church, St Barnabas, was completed in 1844, and in 1851 it became the cathedral for the newly created Roman Catholic diocese of Nottingham.

The Roman Catholic and nonconformist churches had both been far more responsive than the Church of England to the increase in the population of the town. By 1851 there were seven Anglican churches but 22 nonconformist places of worship. The first new Anglican church, St James's on Standard Hill, a growing middle-class area, was consecrated in 1809, but its promoters had had to contend with the most determined opposition from the clergy of the three existing parish churches of St Mary, St Peter and St Nicholas, all of whom feared a resulting loss of income. This delayed further church building until after the government made grants available in 1818. In 1822 the Catholic-hating vicar of St Mary's, George Wilkins, supported the building of a new church, St Paul's on George Street, but only on the condition that it was consecrated as a chapel of ease so that the income of his own church should not be affected. This was the first attempt by the Anglican church to provide for one of the new working-class areas and the parishioners were described by the Church Aid Society in 1840 as 'very poor, ignorant and immoral'. However, while the Methodists and Baptists pushed ahead opening ever larger chapels – the newly enlarged General Baptist chapel at Plumptre Place opened in 1834 accommodated 1,400 – the Anglicans made slow progress and no more Anglican churches were built until after the enclosure of Burton Leys in 1839, when Holy Trinity was opened, funded by middle-class subscriptions. Two years later, the Nottinghamshire Church Extension Society was founded to help finance church building, and in 1844 a second church was opened in a working-class area, the church of St John the Baptist on the south side of the town, close to the river Leen.

Rivalry between nonconformists and Anglicans also extended to the provision of day schools, which both denominations were quick to establish. The first Anglican elementary day school for boys opened on High Cross Street in 1811, the same year that the Anglican National Society was formed, dedicated to encouraging education 'according to the principles of the Church of England', and a National School for girls followed shortly afterwards on Rutland Street. The nonconformists, however, had already established a boys' school in 1810 although it only gained a permanent home in 1815, when a property was obtained in Derby Road, with encouragement and guidance from the nonconformist British and Foreign School Society established the year before. A nonconformist Girls' School was not opened until 1820, in Houndsgate, and two more nonconformist schools were opened in 1831 and 1835, in Barker Gate and Canal Street. From 1833 government grants were available to help meet building costs where subscriptions were already being raised, but the Anglican church, with greater financial resources, was in the better position to benefit from these. Consequently a second Girls' National school was opened on Barker Gate in 1835, an infants' school at St Paul's Church on George Street in 1840 and a boys' department was added to the Girls' School in 1845. The Trinity and St John's schools then followed in 1847 and St Mark's in 1850.

Concern that many of the children from the poorest families were still not receiving any education led the banker J. Smith Wright to open the first Ragged School in Nottingham in 1847, as a Sunday School in a first-floor room in a tenement in Sherwood Lane, off Charlotte Street. In 1852 this moved to a new building on Glasshouse Street and soon afterwards became a day school. This hoped to attract the poorest children by offering free meals at least twice a week as well as a free elementary education, but only about two hundred children could be accommodated.

A large number of private day schools were also to be found in the town but the quality of education provided varied enormously, and many were simply baby-sitting services with little or no education on offer. Anyone, however illiterate, had the right to open a school. The 1851 Education Census found about a hundred private day schools in the Nottingham Poor Law district, and most of them were small, occupying only one or two rooms, over a shop, in a converted chapel or a former warehouse.

Some private schools seem to have established a good reputation locally for the quality of post-elementary education provided for the sons of the town's middle classes, including the Nottingham Academy and the Standard Hill Academy. Responding to popular demand for a commercial education both they and the ancient grammar school offered principally an education in the three R's. The old grammar school was described in 1816 as a 'useful seminary for teaching boys English grammar, reading, writing and arithmetic … but its former celebrity in classical learning is at an end'.

Leisure

The success of the evangelical revival in the town could be measured not only in the number of new churches, chapels and schools that were opened in these years, but also in terms of its impact on the leisure activities of the townspeople. There was now a new seriousness among the middle classes and a concern as to how the Almighty might view any activity. Consequently many popular middle-class entertainments of the previous century were now less well patronised. The theatre was one example. By the 1820s the St Mary's Gate Theatre was only used for about three months of the year and was rarely full. The reason given by one performer who came regularly to Nottingham in the 1820s was that 'the greater part of the middle classes [are] now dissenters, and averse to theatrical performance'. The Assemblies were also becoming less popular and in 1835 the Assembly Rooms were sold to the News Society. Although a few of the most popular balls continued to be held, the rooms were from now on used mainly for concerts, exhibitions, public meetings and private societies, including the literary society, the chess club and a lodge of freemasons.

While dances and plays became less popular, improving and educational activities flourished. By 1815 there were half a dozen circulating libraries in the town and in the following year the Nottingham Subscription Library was founded. In 1821 it bought Bromley House on Beastmarket Hill and this quickly became a focus for the cultural and intellectual life of the town. The number of educational voluntary societies in

59   *William Clarke.*

the town also grew rapidly in the 1820s. Two of the most popular were the Literary and Science Society, founded in 1824, and the Literary and Debating Club, founded in 1837.

The pleasures of the working classes also came under close scrutiny. The large numbers of nonconformists on the corporation meant that those leisure activities which met with considerable evangelical disapproval were unlikely to survive to the mid-century. Those entertainments which did survive tended to be those which could be said to have an educational purpose, such as Wombwell's menagerie, which came to the town every year from 1805, and introduced Nottingham's inhabitants to lions and tigers, leopards and panthers, kangaroos and tropical birds. Some things were also simply too deeply entrenched in the traditions of the town to be removed, such as the Goose Fair, and one sport – horse-racing – although very much disapproved of by many, because it attracted gambling, pick-pockets and prostitutes, had far too much support among all classes to be removed.

Concern for public morality and Sunday observance had prompted the corporation to ban swimming in the rivers Trent and Leen on Sundays in 1780, and numerous constables had been appointed and paid to enforce the ban. Blood sports were disliked because of the cruel treatment of the animals involved and the gambling usually associated with them, and criticism was in many cases backed by legislation. By 1850 bull-running, cock fighting, bear-baiting and ratting had almost all disappeared, at least openly. Dog fighting continued on the Meadows but disappeared gradually after enclosure.

Cricket survived and flourished because it had support from all classes, could be controlled and did not tend to lead to riotous and senseless disorder. The first recorded match held in the town was against a team from Sheffield, played in 1771. Twenty years later, when a match was played in the Meadows against the gentlemen of the Marylebone Club, it was said that ten thousand people watched. Until the 1830s the games were played in open spaces, either on the Forest or in the Meadows, and large crowds of working people could watch without paying. In 1838, however, William Clarke, who had married the landlady of the *Trent Bridge Inn*, laid out a cricket ground behind the inn and charged spectators 6d. to watch the games. Working people objected and refused to pay and consequently only 10 major matches had been held on the new ground when Clarke left the town in 1846. The ground survived, and of course survives still, but the free matches once so much enjoyed by the poorest classes had gone forever.

Reports of the crowds' behaviour at the early free cricket matches usually stress their good humour and civilised behaviour. The same could not be said, however, for the traditional mass games of football, which could have limitless numbers of participants, had virtually no rules and invariably ended in numerous fights and injuries. By 1850 this ancient pastime had gone, but during the 1850s and 1860s football adopted a new, more civilised and controlled form, and the Nottinghamshire County Football Club would be one of the first of the new professional teams founded in the country.

60   *The* Bell Inn *today; William Clarke was the landlord in the 1830s, before he acquired the* Trent Bridge Inn*, and its appearance has changed little since Clarke's time. Some of its timbers, however, are medieval, and date from the 1430s.*

Another very popular sport that survived until 1850, albeit often illegally, was bare-knuckle boxing, and Nottingham was proud to produce at this time one of the nation's foremost practitioners of the art. William Thompson, better known as 'Bendigo', was probably the greatest prize fighter of his generation. He was born in New Yard, behind Parliament Street, on 11 October 1811, and became a prize fighter when he was 21. This traditional working-class sport had once enjoyed considerable patronage from the gentry and aristocracy but by the 1830s their role had been largely taken by the local publicans and innkeepers. One of Bendigo's most celebrated fights was his first contest against another local boxer, Ben Caunt, a miner from Hucknall, and throughout the 1830s and 1840s the two men fought on numerous occasions and became celebrated local heroes. In some respects Bendigo's life as a boxer encapsulated many of the worst features of working-class life which the evangelicals found most challenging and most hateful: violent, drunken and disorderly. Bendigo was frequently arrested for drunk and disorderly conduct and was sent to the House of Correction on no less than 28 occasions. But they could also be proud of the transformation he achieved after retiring from the ring, for he became a reformed character and an evangelical preacher.

The public house was at the heart of working-class life. It was the chief means by which to escape from the monotony of work and the stench and cramped conditions of the house and court, a centre for entertainment in a game of quoits or skittles, and the headquarters for trade unions and friendly societies, money clubs and Chartist meetings. And there were plenty of drinking places to choose from. In 1828 there were said to be 180 drinking establishments in the town and after the passing of the Beer Act in 1830, which encouraged the setting up of beerhouses, the number leapt to 225 by 1832, and went on growing in the next two decades. Attempts by evangelical reformers to set up libraries in public houses were only very partially successful and in 1850 only six public houses had working men's libraries, with 5,000 books between them. Moreover, the temperance movement remained a minority interest for the working classes. In 1832 there were eight temperance inns in the town and by 1853 there were thirteen. A Teetotal Society was only formed in 1851.

EIGHT

The Creation of Greater Nottingham

Population Growth and Boundary Extension

Rapid population growth from the mid-century, together with a major extension of the town's boundary, meant that by 1881, with a population of 186,575, Nottingham was the eighth largest town in the country, large enough to be thought of as a city in all but name. Then, in June 1897, as part of Queen Victoria's Diamond Jubilee celebrations, it was granted the status of a city in name as well. By this time the city's population was well in excess of 200,000 and still growing fast. At the time of the 1901 census it stood at 239,743, and in the next 10 years it would grow by another twenty thousand. By the time of the outbreak of the First World War, in 1914, Nottingham was truly 'Greater Nottingham', and a quite different community from the relatively little, but grossly over-crowded, town of the 1840s, with a population of less than 60,000 and still trapped within its medieval limits, surrounded by its unenclosed open fields.

The developments of the second half of the century were made possible by the Enclosure Act of 1845. The impact of the enclosure of the town's open fields and meadows during the 1850s and 1860s was little short of dramatic. The lack of space for new building had kept the town's growth rate down to less than four per cent in the 1830s, an increase in 10 years of less than 2,000 people, but as the Enclosure Commissioners began to make new land available for building new houses, so the town grew rapidly again. During the 1850s the population grew by 17,000 and almost 8,000 new houses were built on the newly enclosed land (a 43 per cent increase in the housing stock) covering much of the Clay and Sand Fields to the north of the old built-up area, and beginning to also cover the Meadows and the West Croft to the south. During the next decade the process continued, although a little less rapidly, and by 1871 the population had risen by a further 12,000, to nearly 87,000. Some of the worst slum housing in the old town area was demolished, but a great deal still remained and most of the new houses being built both on the Clay Field, between Mansfield Road and St Ann's Well Road, and on the Meadows, was of poor quality, designed for low-income working-class families. The latter was also an area subject to periodic flooding and this problem, a cause of the most enormous misery for the inhabitants, would not be solved until the next century.

PLAN OF THE TOWN OF NOTTINGHAM from the best Authorities Containing all the new Streets and EVERY RECENT ALTERATION PUBLISHED FOR DEARDEN'S History and Directory OF NOTTINGHAM 1844

61 Map of Nottingham, 1844.

BYRON WARD

ST ANN'S WARD

SHERWOOD WARD

PARK WARD

EXCHANGE WARD

ST MARY'S WARD

EAST CROFT

CASTLE WARD

CLAY FIELD

SAND FIELD

PARK

MEADOWS

The industrial villages that surrounded the town also continued to grow steadily and by 1871 Radford, with a population of more than 15,000, had overtaken both Newark and Mansfield to be the second largest township in the county. By this time the five satellite communities of Radford, Basford, Lenton, Sneinton and Bulwell had between them a population of more than 51,000 people. Moreover, now that Nottingham's former open fields were being built upon, the boundary between the town and its villages was fast disappearing and Nottingham was becoming a conurbation in all but name. An extension of the borough to bring the satellites within the town's boundaries, and thus to create

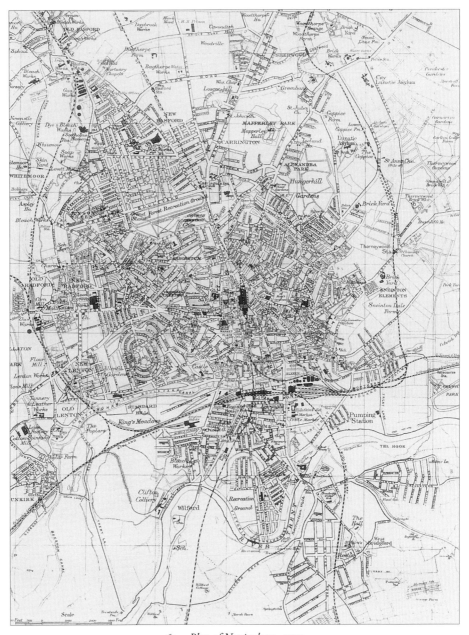

62 *Plan of Nottingham, 1902.*

Greater Nottingham, was the logical next step, and in 1876 the corporation had a Bill drawn up aimed at achieving this. The Bill passed quickly through its various parliamentary stages and the new borough came into being on 1 November 1877. As well as incorporating Radford, Basford, Lenton, Sneinton and Bulwell, the new boundary also took in that part of Wilford that lay to the north of the river Trent, creating a town of almost 11,000 acres, unimaginably bigger than the town had been only 30 years earlier. As the town – and then the city – continued to grow, so many of the green areas that still lay within the extended boundaries in 1877 disappeared under ever more acres of tarmac, bricks and mortar, and by 1911 Nottingham's population had reached 259,901 people.

The city's growth in the second half of the 19th century was due partly to the continuing expansion of the lace industry, which in 1900 was world-famous and at the peak of its prestige, and also to the growth of Nottingham's other staple industry, hosiery, which finally adopted steam-powered factory production in 1851. By the 1880s the nearby coal industry had also expanded considerably to become a major local employer, and three new industries – cigarettes, cycles and pharmaceuticals – were being established in the town by men of entrepreneurial genius, who by 1914 had already created large-scale businesses of national importance. After the First World War, when the city's textile industries declined, Player's cigarettes, Raleigh cycles and Boots the Chemists would become the new staple industries of the town and the new foundations of its 20th-century prosperity.

The Hosiery and Lace Industries

The opening of the first hosiery factory in the town, on Station Street, close to the Midland Railway Station, by Messrs Hine & Mundella in 1851, did not rapidly lead to a transformation

of the industry. The profits to be made from factory-made hosiery were not encouraging and the larger Nottingham hosiers proved to be too conservative, too cautious and to have too large an investment in the traditional hand-operated stocking frame industry to follow Hine & Mundella's lead. In 1844 it had been calculated that three Nottingham firms, Hine & Mundella themselves plus I. & R. Morley and Heard & Hurst, owned between them 7,700 stocking frames, or a very large proportion of all the frames to be found in the town and the surrounding villages. Moreover, a general improvement in living standards among all classes in the country in the 1850s and 1860s brought about a remarkable late recovery in the demand for traditionally made hosiery, and something of an 'Indian Summer' for the long-oppressed poor framework knitters. The rapid decline of the traditional industry came only in the 1880s, when increasing

63   *Interior of a framework knitters' workshop,* c.1930.

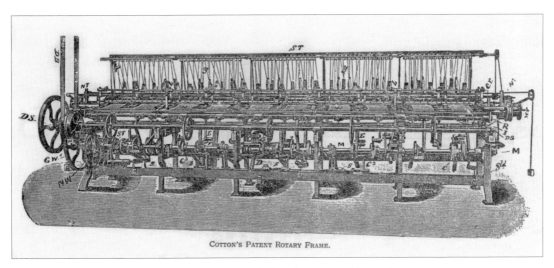

COTTON'S PATENT ROTARY FRAME.

64 *A Cotton's patent machine, c.1890.*

competition both at home and in export markets squeezed out many of the framework knitters, but even in 1892 there were still said to be 5,000 traditional stockingers in the midland counties, most of them employed by I. & R. Morley, who in 1899 still employed almost four thousand.

Most of the firms that followed Hine & Mundella's lead in the 1850s were relatively small-scale businesses, renting factory space and steam power in an existing lace factory, and most lacked the capital or commercial connections and expertise to last long. The company that came to dominate the Nottingham hosiery industry at the end of the century, I. & R. Morley, did not open its first factory until 1866, on Manvers Street. Thereafter, growth was rapid. In 1875 the firm built its second factory, at Heanor, in Derbyshire, and in 1879 another factory in Nottingham, on Handel Street. Other factories were then built in the next few years at Loughborough, Sutton in Ashfield and Leicester, and a number of factories and warehouses of other firms were also bought up. At the turn of the century the firm employed more than 3,000 men and women in seven factories and another 1,200 in their two warehouses in Wood Street in London and Fletcher Gate in Nottingham, as well as the 4,000 framework knitters mentioned above.

Most of the Nottingham hosiery factories were relatively small scale, employing only a few hundred workers at most. The largest factory in the town was probably that built by Rogers, Black & Co. in Dame Agnes Street. This firm specialised in the cheaper cut-up section of the trade and employed more than 1,000 women operating rotary machines that produced large rolls of fabric which were then cut up and sewn to make a wide range of garments, including vests, pants and combinations, as well as stockings. I. & R. Morley refused to manufacture what they regarded as an inferior article and preferred to specialise in the fully fashioned trade, using the Cotton's patent machine, which employed mainly male operatives. The invention of the overlocking machine in 1887, greatly improved the quality of cut-up work and by the end of the century the number of female employees was increasing rapidly, but at the expense of men.

Most lace factories were also small. In 1876 a parliamentary commission found that the average factory employed less than 40 people. Much of the work of lace finishing, mainly lace clipping and scalloping, was done by women in their own homes, but increasing numbers were also being employed in many of the new prestigious warehouses being built near St Mary's church in the 1850s and 1860s, creating the Lace Market, for which Nottingham was becoming famous. High tariff barriers checked the export market for a number of branches in the 1870s, but one part of the trade continued to flourish: the manufacture of lace curtains. The first machines for making lace curtains were developed in the 1840s by a group of enterprising mechanics, and the success of this new venture was quickly established when the firm of Heymann & Alexander won a gold medal for their product at the Great Exhibition at the Crystal Palace in 1851, together with a large order from the Queen for lace curtains for Buckingham Palace. Within a few years no home, however large or small, would be deemed

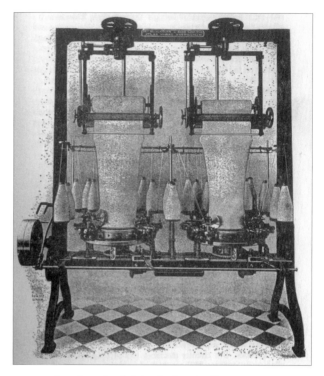

65   *A two-headed circular knitting frame, c. 1890.*

66   *The former 19th-century lace warehouses that line Broadway today, the site of the 17th-century mansion, Plumptre House.*

properly furnished without at least one pair of Nottingham lace curtains. Wright's *Directory* of 1910 listed 41 lace curtain manufacturers.

The success and importance of the lace industry from the middle of the century was most clearly trumpeted by the grandiose warehouses built for the town's larger lace manufacturers. The Adams & Page warehouse designed by local architect T.C. Hine has been described as 'the flagship of the Lace Market'. Opened in 1855 on Stoney Street, it stood six storeys high and was built in Hine's 'Anglo-Italian' style, with a grand central entrance up a flight of steps and an imposing E-shaped frontage laced with Ancaster and Derbyshire stone. Almost as impressive was the warehouse built at about the same time by Hine for Messrs Birkin & Co., immediately to the north of St Mary's church and on the site of a fine 17th-century mansion known as Plumptre House, which had been demolished shortly before, when a new road, Broadway, was also cut through the grounds of the former mansion. By the time Edward Salmon's map of Nottingham appeared in 1861 the extensive grounds of Plumptre House – one of the last open spaces in the centre of the old town – had been completely built over by warehouses, many of them designed by Hine. Richard Birkin was one of the pioneers of mass-produced lace, having built his first lace factory in 1827, at New Basford, but the firm only moved into lace curtain manufacturing in 1869, the year before Richard's death. Under his successor, Sir Thomas Isaac Birkin, the firm invested heavily in this profitable new line and became the largest producer of both lace curtains and fancy lace in the country.

Other Industries

One of the more positive features of Nottingham's economy at the end of the 19th century was the considerable diversity of occupations and industries now to be found in the city and the immediate surrounding area. Professor Chapman lists 40 major Nottingham companies valued at more than £100,000 at the turn of the century. The largest firm, by some distance, was the hosiery manufacturer I. & R. Morley, valued at about £2,000,000, but only nine of the other firms listed were either hosiers or lace merchants and manufacturers. Second in the list (according to their valuation) was Boots, by this time a firm owning a chain of chemists' stores as well as a manufacturer of pharmaceuticals, and the third largest was the Stanton Ironworks of Ilkeston. Other firms listed included five breweries, four of which were valued at more than £400,000 each, and five coal mining companies, all of which had benefitted from the growing demand for coal prompted by the expansion of factory production in the city since the 1850s. Two cycle manufacturers also make the list, Humber of Beeston and the Raleigh Cycle Co., whose main factory was now at Lenton, together with John Player & Sons, tobacco manufacturers, valued at £200,000. Two engineering works are also included but, perhaps rather surprisingly, only one textile machine maker, John Jardine & Co. The conservative and cautious tendencies of many of the city's larger lace and hosiery manufacturers was probably partly to blame, and particularly I. & R. Morley's antipathy towards rotary hosiery machinery.

One textile firm listed that was neither a lace nor a hosiery manufacturer was that of William Hollins & Co., 'spinners, weavers and clothing manufacturers'. This had been, until 1890, a Mansfield firm specialising in spinning cotton and merino for the hosiery companies. In that year, however, it branched out into producing a wool and cotton mixture of its own which it called 'Viyella', which it then had woven into fabrics and made up into

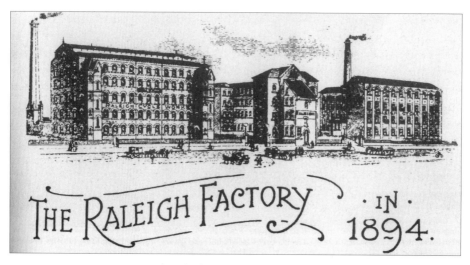

67   *The Raleigh Factory in Russell Street, 1894.*

shirts and nightshirts which it sold direct to the trade, backed by very successful advertising. This success meant that by 1900 it was already one of the largest textile companies in the region, valued at about £350,000, and after the First World War it would continue to enjoy remarkable success.

One leather manufacturer is also listed, John and Edward Turney's leather works. This firm was established in 1861 on 'Sneinton Island', between the river Trent and the canal, and by the 1890s employed about 450 workers. Sir John Turney, who was in sole control by this time, was said to have designed much of the firm's machinery himself. Partly because of his attention to detail and inventive skill, his factory was renowned for the remarkable absence of the unpleasant smells usually associated with leather works. Sir John was also a major figure in the public life of the town, becoming a councillor in 1873, and later mayor, and receiving the freedom of the city for his services in 1916.

Three other entrepreneurs not only established new businesses in the town in the last quarter of the century, but enjoyed such an unusual degree of success that their firms had already become household names throughout the country by 1900. John Player started selling tobacco as a sideline in his shop on Beastmarket Hill, which specialised in agricultural manures and seeds. So great was the demand that after a few years tobacco sales became his sole business, and in 1877 he bought William Wright's tobacco manufactory in Broad Marsh, a firm established in 1823 which by this time was employing 150 workers. By selling his tobacco in branded packets, rather than loose from jars, and by heavy investment in advertising, he was able to quickly establish himself as one of the largest tobacco manufacturers in the country, second only to Wills of Bristol. Within four years his business had outgrown the Broad Marsh factory and he began to build a new factory and warehouse at Radford. By 1901 the firm was employing 1,200 people, making it the largest employer in the city, and by 1914 the number of employees had more than doubled again. John Player did not live to see this success, however. In 1884, three years after building his first factory at Radford, he died of liver cancer, at the age of forty-five.

The founder of the Raleigh Cycle Company, Frank Bowden, was also a man of great energy and enormous entrepreneurial talent. He had already made a fortune for himself as a lawyer in Hong Kong when he returned to England and took up cycling to improve his health.

The cycling boom of the 1880s had prompted numerous craftsmen in the town to set up cycle-manufacturing workshops, but Bowden was particularly struck by the reliability of the safety bicycles being made by three young men, Woodhead, Angois and Ellis, in a workshop in Raleigh Street, and he saw a business opportunity which he could exploit. Bowden bought the business in December 1888, which was then producing only two or three cycles a week, invested £20,000, and created the Raleigh Cycle Company. The new firm was very soon producing 12 cycles a week. It was clear to Bowden, however, that the potential demand was enormous and in 1891 he increased the capital to £100,000 and acquired a five-storey former lace factory in Russell Street. The labour force was increased to 200 and output rose to 60 cycles a week, but this too was quite inadequate and in 1896 he opened his first purpose-built factory at Lenton. By the turn of the century his firm was making 10,000 bicycles a year. Demand for cycles in Britain began to diminish in the next few years, and many cycle manufacturers went bankrupt during the Edwardian era. Bowden managed to increase output and maintain profitability, however, by raising productivity and by a determined drive to secure new markets abroad. By 1907 the Raleigh Company was making 30,000 bicycles a year, and selling them not only in almost every European country but also across the world, and particularly in India and China. Consequently demand continued to rise and by 1912 Bowden's firm was making 50,000 machines a year.

Jesse Boot, the founder of Boots the Chemists, was the most successful of all Nottingham's late Victorian entrepreneurs. Born in Hockley in 1850, his father died almost penniless when he was only 10 years old and three years later he had to leave school to help his mother run the family herbalist business. Mary Boot sold potions and pills in a little rented shop in Goose Gate, made up from the herbs she and her son collected in the surrounding country lanes. While still in his teens he took over the management of the shop and to boost profits began selling a wide range of household items. Goose Gate was one of the poorest shopping districts in the

68   *A Raleigh cycle advertisement, 1897.*

town but young Boot was confident that he
could make the business prosper if he could
sell goods more cheaply than other shops. An
advertisement from the early 1870s read:

> M. & J. Boot, the Household Stores, 16
> Goose Gate, Nottingham. Who sells all
> things cheaply, not one or two as other
> traders do. Over 2,000 different articles
> in stock.

He also recognised that working people
were beginning to buy patent medicines
rather than traditional herbal remedies, and
in 1874 he decided, in his own words, 'to
enter the proprietary medicine business',
but he would buy in bulk so that he could
undercut other chemists' shops. He later
recalled these early days:

> there was nothing at all remarkable about
> my methods. They were simply the
> application of common sense. I found
> that everywhere articles, especially drugs,
> were being sold at ridiculously high prices,
> and were sold without any regard to
> neatness and attractiveness. My idea was
> simply to buy tons where others bought
> hundredweights or less, thus buying much
> more cheaply, and making all the articles I
> sold look as attractive as possible.

Lack of capital delayed the launch of
his bulk-buying, cut-price, sales initiative,
but in February 1877 a series of large,
bold advertisements began to appear in
the *Nottingham Daily Express,* the first of
which announced 'PATENT MEDICINES
RETAIL AT WHOLESALE PRICES'
and offered 128 separate items at greatly
reduced prices. The impact was immediate.
Within a month he was taking £40 a week,
twice his previous turnover, and by May he
was taking £100 a week. His name was by
now well known throughout the town and
every Saturday there were queues outside his

69 *Jesse Boot's first shop, Goose Gate.*

70   *Jesse Boot, c. 1880.*

Goose Gate shop as country people came into town looking for the latest bargains he had on offer. Boot was untiring in publicising his business. To continue the sales drive he used eye-catching window displays, countless bill posters, newspaper advertisements and even a brass band. His first purpose-built shop was opened in 1884, with huge windows, but still in Goose Gate, but soon new branches were being opened in other parts of the town, factory space had to be rented to manufacture many of the preparations being sold, and from 1884 all of his shops began to include a dispensary. By 1893 there were 33 shops, most of them in the Midlands, including seven in Nottingham.

His marriage to Florence Rowe, the daughter of a St Helier stationer, in 1885, brought not only personal happiness but also further commercial success, for Florence was also a born entrepreneur and just as determined and enterprising as her husband. Overcoming her husband's reluctance, she soon ensured that at least a part of every Boots shop contained stationery, fancy goods, pictures and books, and by 1900 her stationery department accounted for about a quarter of the turnover. By this time the capital value of the Boots Pure Drug Co. was put at £1,155,000, second in the city only to I. & R. Morley, and at the beginning of the year the firm had 181 shops

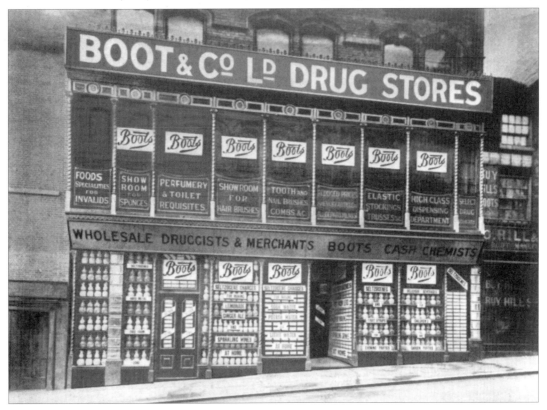

71   *Boot's first purpose-built shop, opened in Goose Gate, 1884.*

across the country. During the next few years growth continued rapidly. During 1900 Boot acquired a chain of 60 drug stores in London and the south of England, and by 1901 the empire numbered 251 branches; by 1914 there were 560, many of them newly built and very substantial department stores standing in prime sites. A knighthood in 1909 was followed soon afterwards by the opening of the most prestigious shops yet, on Princes Street in Edinburgh in 1911 and on Regent Street in London in 1912. By 1914 retail sales had risen five-fold since the turn of the century, to almost £3,000,000, and in Nottingham alone 2,700 men and women were employed in the company's offices, warehouses and factories.

Boot's first 'factory' opened in 1885, consisting of a number of ground-floor rooms of a back-to-back terrace in Angel Alley, close to the Goose Gate shop, but two years later he began renting three rooms in a lace factory in Island Street, and in the next few years, as the business grew, so the number of rooms occupied in the Island Street factory increased, until in 1892 he had acquired the entire mill. In 1895 a second factory was acquired in Parkinson Street but this addition was also soon inadequate and a few years later Boot began buying or leasing the warehouses, factories and back-to-back cottages squeezed into the land between the Midland Railway line and the Nottingham Canal, and gradually converted almost all of them to his own use before 1914. The former hosiery factory of Hine & Mundella, on Station Street, became his head office and in 1914 he opened his first purpose-built laboratory and drug warehouse on Island Street.

'Improvements' and the Changing Appearance of the City

The city into which Jesse Boot had been born in 1850 had changed considerably by the time of the outbreak of war in 1914. Not only was it much larger, both in terms of its boundaries and its population – which now stood at more than 250,000 – but the appearance of large areas of the city had also been transformed. The creation of the Lace Market near St Mary's church was one of the most notable developments but, in addition, road widening schemes had by 1914 greatly improved communications within the city, as had the arrival of the electric tram; and the last of the town's 30 windmills, which had long stood on Tollhouse Hill, had been demolished as early as 1858, replaced by the new steam-powered mills. The expansion of the town in the second half of the century also necessitated an enormous increase in the number of new churches and chapels built by Anglicans, Roman Catholics and nonconformists, and also of new schools, although from 1870 elementary schools were becoming increasingly the responsibility of the new Nottingham School Board, rather than of the churches. The growth of the town also prompted the building of a new Guildhall on Burton Street in 1887-8, and the old Guildhall at Weekday Cross (the site of a guildhall since at least the 14th century) was demolished shortly afterwards to make way for the Great Central Railway line. Ambitious proposals for a new Exchange and market centre, however, put forward in 1857 by the architect T.C. Hine, were rejected by the corporation. Nevertheless, the town centre was much altered by the building of new-style shops, banks and offices designed by exceptionally gifted local architects such as Hine, Watson Fothergill and Alfred Waterhouse. Moreover, some of the appalling back-to-back courts of the old town had by 1914 disappeared as a result of slum-clearance schemes from the 1870s, including the notorious Rookeries to the north of Long Row, while others had succumbed to the arrival of the Great Central Railway line and the building of the Victoria Station in the 1890s.

In 1914, however, enormous housing problems still remained. The demolition of slum property often led to even more overcrowding in the courts that survived, if the inhabitants were unable to afford the rents of the better-quality housing being built. In 1914 most of the city's back-to-backs still survived and many still lacked piped water, adequate ventilation or sanitation facilities, and consequently outbreaks of typhoid fever were still common well into the 20th century. But much improvement was achieved and much of the credit for this must go to two men in particular, the city's first borough surveyor, Marriot Ogle Tarbotton, who was appointed in 1859, and the city's first Medical Officer of Health, Dr Edward Seaton, appointed in 1873. Tarbotton's greatest achievement was perhaps the building of a new Trent Bridge in 1871, but he also played a major role in the corporation's decision to buy the gasworks in 1874, which he then managed, and it was his initiative that prompted the corporation to also purchase the waterworks in 1880, building new works on Mapperley Plains and a pumping station at Papplewick shortly afterwards. His work to improve the town's system of sewage disposal began as soon as he was appointed, when he ordered the culverting of the river Leen, which had long been a stinking open sewer for the town, but it reached fruition with the opening of a 900-acre sewage farm at Stoke Bardolph in 1880.

Tarbotton was also responsible for many road improvements in the town. Nottingham was notorious in the 1850s for the narrowness of its streets and for the great difficulty that carts and carriages found in reaching the centre of the town, especially from the south. Within a year of taking up his post, Tarbotton had made a beginning to the Victoria Street project, replacing the steep and narrow Chandler's Lane to cut through the new road and thus greatly reduce the strain on Bottle Lane. In 1865 he undertook the widening of Lister Gate and the following year he had numerous properties on Sheep Street purchased and demolished so that this little alley – only 10 feet wide – could be replaced by market street. Wheeler Gate was also considerably widened at about the same time. During the 1880s Tarbotton also gained the corporation's support for a series of wide new roads designed to link up the disparate parts of the newly extended city. The first to be completed was Gregory Boulevard, followed soon afterwards by Castle Boulevard and Lenton Boulevard, Vernon Road and Radford Boulevard.

Among those who could be most grateful for Tarbotton's efforts were the horse bus drivers and the tramway companies. The rapid growth of the town meant also a rapid growth in the numbers of commuters. The first horse buses were running regular services in the early 1840s and by the 1870s there were services to Basford, Lenton, Sneinton and West Bridgford. The first horse-drawn tram route was opened in 1878, from St Peter's church to the Midland Station and the Great Northern Station, and a service to Carrington and Basford followed soon afterwards. Complaints about the cost and quality of the tram routes prompted the corporation to take control of the Tramways Company in 1897 and to almost immediately begin laying out new tram routes and to draw up plans for electric trams. As if to mark the dawning of a new age, as well as a new century, the first electric tram began service on 1 January 1901, running from the market place to Sherwood. By this time the first motor cars had also arrived in the town and the Humber car-building works had opened in Beeston in 1898. The first motor bus service began in 1906, running from the market place to the *Crown Hotel* on Carlton Road, and two years later the Barton company was established, running its first motor-bus service from Long Eaton to the Goose Fair in the market place. The all-conquering future of this new mode of transport, however, could not yet be foreseen.

Dr Edward Seaton was, like Tarbotton, a man of considerable energy and determination, and both men assisted and encouraged one another in their efforts to bring 'improvements' to the town. On his appointment in 1873 the two men immediately began work on a report on the health of the town, and bluntly told the corporation that 8,000 houses were simply not fit to be lived in. Many houses in the old town were not connected to the town's sewers and at least 200 in the Meadows had been built below the flood level of the river Trent. A Bill to clarify and extend the powers of the corporation to improve lighting, sanitation, water supply and housing was then drawn up and, fully supported by the corporation, passed swiftly through Parliament to become law in August 1874. With this backing, plus the Artisans' Dwellings Act of 1875, which allowed local authorities to undertake large-scale demolition of slum property, Seaton persuaded the corporation to purchase and demolish housing in a number of particularly unhealthy areas of the town. His greatest success was to have 100 houses and six common lodging houses demolished in the 'Rookeries', between Long Row, Market Street and Upper Parliament Street, and then to redevelop the site, with King Street and Queen Street cutting through the cleared area. He left the town, however, in 1884, long before this project was completed. It was said that he was angered by the corporation's refusal to raise his salary, but it was known that he was also disillusioned by the depressing tendency of many of those whose condemned housing was demolished to simply move into other slum properties in the town, rather than into what he regarded as cheap but sanitary housing.

Church, Chapel and School

Although Nottingham's Anglicans could be pleased that the proportion of the town's population attending a place of worship on Census Sunday in March 1851 was higher than the national average, they could only be dismayed that only about a third of those who did attend were to be found in one of the town's Anglican churches, and that the rest were attending Methodist, Baptist, Congregational, Roman Catholic or Unitarian services. At least equally worrying, however, was the failure of any of the denominations, and particularly the Anglicans, to claim the allegiance of more than a very small minority of the working classes.

Horace Mann's Religious Census of 1851 came as a wake-up call to Anglicans and nonconformists alike, but whereas it had been the nonconformists, and especially the Methodists, who had shown the greater initiative and energy in the first half of the century, now it was the turn of the Anglicans to take the lead. The New Parishes Act of 1856 made it possible for large urban parishes like St Mary's to be subdivided into much smaller parishes, and, if sufficient money could be raised, for a new church and elementary school to be built for each new parish. By 1871 St Mary's parish had been subdivided seven times, seven new churches and numerous new schools had been built, and six of the seven parishes were in distinctly working-class areas. By 1870 the Anglicans had 22 elementary day schools in the town and well over 5,000 pupils; with far less resources the nonconformists could not compete and boasted only eight schools and about 1,200 pupils. This still left many children in the poorest parts of the town receiving at best only a Sunday School education, or even no education at all. But the nonconformists were not slow in building new chapels, and again it was the Methodists who were most active. Between 1851 and 1881 they built 20 more chapels and missions and by 1881 there were 45 Methodist chapels in the extended borough. But in spite of all this effort the churches were only running to stand still, and as far as winning back the allegiance of the working classes was concerned they were not succeeding. A survey published by the *Nottingham Journal* in December 1881 showed that approximately 47,000 people were probably regularly attending a church or chapel every

Sunday, almost twice the total calculated by Mann 30 years earlier, but whereas in 1851 the total population of the town was 57,407, by 1881 (with the size of the borough now considerably extended) it was 186,575. In short, Nottingham was becoming, like most other cities, an increasingly secular community. Whereas in 1851 about 42 per cent of the population had attended church or chapel, now only about 25 per cent did.

Throughout the next 30 years or so, both Anglican clergy and nonconformist ministers recognised that one of the most difficult challenges they faced was to reach out to working people and demonstrate to them the relevance of Christianity to their lives. One initiative with this aim in mind was the Spiritual Aid and Church Extension Society, set up by the Bishop of Lincoln for the town in 1882. Mainly as a result of this, not only were more churches built but also temporary iron churches, which could be set up quickly and cheaply where necessary and staffed by young, energetic and determined clergymen, who saw themselves, quite accurately, as missionaries into the slums of England's cities. By the end of the century there were numerous iron mission churches in the city, some Anglican, others Methodist or Baptist. There were, however, no more church and chapel censuses before the outbreak of war by which to measure their effectiveness.

By the 1880s the churches were also gradually ceasing to be the principal providers of elementary education. The great efforts of the churches before 1870 meant that in Nottingham the shortfall of school places was far less than in many other towns of similar size. The Nottingham School Board, established in 1870 under Forster's Education Act to 'fill the gaps' in school provision, found that the 'gap' in Nottingham was relatively modest. It was reckoned that about another 1,200 places had to be provided to meet the needs of children up to 13, and Nottingham's first two Board schools were subsequently built on Bath Street and Huntingdon Street. When the town's boundaries were extended in 1877, many more 'gaps' appeared and much new school building quickly followed. Some voluntary schools were also transferred to the School Board and by the end of the century it was providing nearly 29,000 school places in 36 schools, or about twice the number being provided by the churches.

The Nottingham School Board proved itself to be a model for other school boards. It was run by remarkably enterprising and energetic men with a broad and ambitious vision of the importance and possibilities of education far beyond the remit granted in 1870. New 'higher grade' schools were opened for 15- and 16-year-old pupils and existing schools for older, more able, pupils were taken over and given excellent facilities, including well-equipped science laboratories, swimming pools and gymnasia. One of these schools, People's College, also became a centre for training teachers and a generous salary structure ensured able young people were attracted to train for the profession. An ambitious programme of adult education was also offered in the evenings and a free school meals service was introduced in the Board's elementary schools.

Two of the leading figures on the School Board, Canon Francis Morse of St Mary's church and the Revd J.B. Paton of the Congregational Church, were also among a group of local commercial and professional men who successfully lobbied for the opening of a University College for the town in 1881, and managed to persuade the corporation to give substantial financial support for the venture. Civic pride also played its part in prompting the corporation to find the £50,000 required to pay for a handsome High Gothic building on Horse Fair Close, which incorporated a public library and museum as well as a university college. Such

72   *The High Gothic entrance to the former University College on Shakespeare Street, erected in 1897; now part of Nottingham Trent University.*

73   *The east wing of the former University College.*

generous support from a municipal corporation was at this time quite unusual, and possibly unique. When Treasury inspectors reported on the College in 1897 they noted that such patronage, reflecting as it did the support of the community for the needs of higher education, 'is a very remarkable thing … being thus supported by the rates [it] may be said to be the most democratic institution of the kind that we have seen'. There were at first four professorships, covering language and literature, physics, maths and mechanics, chemistry, metallurgy and natural science, but other subjects were also soon added. Students were entered for degree examinations set by the University of London. Today the building is part of Nottingham Trent University.

Students of the higher grade schools whose parents could afford to send them away to university usually transferred to the old Boys' High School, or Free School (as it was also known), for their last two years of schooling. As a fee-paying, private, school, the Boys' High School was now thriving. Its premises were also much improved when, in 1868, it moved from the bustle of the Lace Market in Stoney Street to its present site near the Arboretum. Working-class children were allowed to apply for scholarship places. In 1875 the Girls' Public Day School Trust helped establish the fee-paying Girls' High School, but this remained a strictly middle-class institution, with no scholarships offered to allow bright working-class girls an opportunity to attend. Like the Boys' High School, the Bluecoat

74 *The former School of Art, opened in 1865 at a cost of £6,000. It is now, appropriately, the School of Architecture, Design and the Built Environment of Nottingham Trent University.*

75 *A mid-19th-century print of Nottingham's Arboretum.*

School also moved out of the town centre in the wake of the Enclosure Act, leaving the old building at Weekday Cross for a new, more spacious school building on Mansfield Road, designed by T.C. Hine, in July 1853.

Land made available by the enclosure was also used by the corporation in 1865 to provide a new site for the School of Art, on the corner of Waverley Street and Peel Street. This had been first established on Heathcote Street in 1843 in an attempt to foster the talent and design skills so much needed in the local lace industry. By the 1850s, it was becoming increasingly a drawing school for the middle classes, and attracting fewer artisans. With a move to new premises and the appointment of a new principal, it was hoped to re-establish the school's close links with the town's textile firms, and to some extent this did happen, but the school remained in financial difficulties until it was taken over by the corporation in 1888.

Recreation

We have seen that evangelical concern to control and civilise working-class entertainment and leisure pursuits was already an important driving force behind the development of some new leisure activities in the town, and the disappearance of others, before the middle of the century. Ideally, many believed, leisure for all classes should be undertaken peacefully, it should not disrupt business, and it should not promote the consumption of strong liquors, gambling, fighting or any other sinful activities; instead, it should be educational and improving. Thus, as cock fighting, bear and bull baiting disappeared, so attempts were made to establish artisans' libraries in local pubs, and in 1837 the Nottingham Mechanics Institute was founded, dedicated to the cause of education for the working classes. The Institute flourished, but not quite as its founders had hoped. Its membership was made up mainly of members of the lower middle classes, and for most its chief attractions were not the educational lectures but the entertainment it provided. Among those who performed at the Mechanics in its early years were Charles Dickens, who read *Christmas Carol* in 1858 and returned on a number of occasions, and the most famous soprano of the time, Jenny Lind, popularly known as the 'Swedish nightingale'.

When the Arboretum was opened in 1852 it was hoped that it would serve an educational function as well as a recreational one, and the plants and flowers were therefore labelled with information about their origins and size. The Arboretum was a relatively new idea; the first one in the country had been opened in Derby in 1840. It partly reflected a growing appreciation of the benefits of healthy exercise for both the middle and the working classes, and the desire of many to find a happy and healthier alternative to the public house. Shortly before this, in December 1850, the town's first public baths had been opened on New Bath Street, and many of those who welcomed this facility saw it also as a means of popularising healthy exercise and communal leisure, although the failure to change the water in the pool more than once a week did cause some to doubt just how healthy such exercise might prove.

A concern to promote worthy, educational, leisure activities also helped drive forward the initiatives to open the first free museum in 1867, the first public library a year later, in Thurland Street, and the Museum of Fine Art, housed in the recently restored Nottingham Castle, in 1878. Two of the most significant developments in middle-class culture in the town, however, were marked by the opening of the Theatre Royal in September 1865 and of the Albert Hall in 1876, with the latter claiming to be 'the finest concert hall in the Midland

76   *View from the Arboretum today; the tower and spire of All Saints' church can be seen through the trees. The Arboretum today is a sadly neglected and litter-strewn area.*

77   *The Arboretum lake and fountain today. The artificial lake and nearby aviary are original features of the Arboretum.*

counties'. The opening of the Theatre Royal was not without controversy, for it incurred the strong displeasure of a number of the town's dissenting clergy, some of whom roundly condemned the unwelcome development from their pulpits. It survived, however, to become an important cultural centre for the town, famed for the wide variety of its productions, from Shakespeare to post-Christmas pantomimes. The Albert Hall, with seating for 2,550, was originally intended to be a Temperance Hall but its function was changed before the work was completed. A revival in interest in music, and particularly in large-scale choral music, had led to the formation of a local choral society, the Nottingham Sacred Harmonic Society, in 1856, and it was entirely appropriate that the Albert Hall opened with a performance of Handel's *Messiah*, with the chorus largely supplied by the Sacred Harmonic Society. After a fire had destroyed much of the building in 1906 it was rebuilt with a larger hall, paid for largely by Jesse Boot, and Boot insisted – among other things – that cheap seats had to be made available to attract the working classes.

The modern game of football came into being as the older, unregulated and often very violent village game was tamed and transformed by the formation of the Football Association, and by the agreement, reached in 1863, to draw up and publish *The Laws of Football*. Nottingham was among the first towns in the country to establish two affiliated teams. A group of businessmen and cricketers had already set up the Notts. County Football Club in 1862 and three years later a group of young people attached to St Andrew's church on Mansfield Road set up a rival team, playing their matches on the Forest and hence naming themselves Nottingham Forest FC. At this stage football was still a middle-class activity, but in the next few decades its popularity amongst the working classes grew steadily. Both of the city's professional teams at first played their matches at a number of grounds, but Forest eventually settled at the City ground in 1898. Notts. County played at the Trent Bridge Cricket Ground from the 1880s but moved to the present Meadow Lane site in 1910.

When cricket moved from the Forest in 1838, where working people had been able to watch the games without charge, to William Clarke's ground at Trent Bridge, where he charged a 6d. entrance fee, many working people strongly objected and the numbers watching the games at first fell dramatically. Cricket, however, became respectable, the crowds were almost invariably orderly and well mannered, and the success of the county team in the 1880s made the likes of Alfred Shaw and William Gunn national as well as local heroes, to middle and working classes alike. At this time Nottinghamshire was the most successful team in the country and repeatedly won the county championship.

The popularity of both football and cricket as spectator sports by the 1880s owed much to the rise in working-class incomes and reductions in the working week. Both factors also played a part in ensuring the enormous popularity of railway excursions by this time.

Not included in the Subscription.

MECHANICS' HALL, BOXING NIGHT,
WEDNESDAY, DECEMBER 26th, 1906.

Grand Christmas Performance of Handel's

"The MESSIAH"

∴ Artistes. ∴

Miss HELEN JAXON
Miss EDITH CLEGG
Mr. ERNEST PIKE
Mr. WATKIN MILLS

Band and Chorus of 300 Performers.

Leader of the Orchestra -	Mr. H. LYELL-TAYLER
Organist -	Mr. F. WYATT, F.R.C.O.
Solo Trumpet -	Mr. MARK HEMINGWAY
Conductor -	Mr. ALLEN GILL.

78 *Programme for Handel's Messiah at the Mechanic's Hall, 1906.*

A few local firms had begun treating their employees to an annual outing in the 1850s, but excursions on a very large scale, when it seemed as if the whole town was emptying, came only after the passing of the Bank Holiday Act in 1870. This piece of legislation, together with cheap excursion trains, made it possible for working people to leave the town for a day and enjoy a complete break from work. The seaside was an especially popular destination but not even the railway company could have predicted the success it would enjoy with Bank Holiday excursions from Nottingham and other Midlands towns to the little village of Skegness, when it extended a single-track line to this obscure 'watering place' in 1873. Skegness quickly became 'Nottingham by the Sea'. On August Bank Holiday 1874 10,000 people arrived in the village and the agent of the Earl of Scarbrough, who owned the village, immediately saw the potential to develop a successful seaside resort, and one of the first to purchase building plots in the new town was the Nottingham architect T.C. Hine. By August Bank Holiday 1882, when 20,000 people took excursion trains to Skegness, the rapidly growing seaside resort had rather more to offer the visitor: three new hotels, a fine walk beside the sea wall, a newly built pier extending well out to sea (at high tide), Pleasure Gardens complete with artificial lake and pavilion, and brand-new swimming baths. There was still, however, only a single-track line into the town and, as a result, the *Skegness Herald* reported that the last train back to Nottingham did not leave until 2.30 on Tuesday morning, with 'many hundreds spending the night in waiting rooms or in the streets'.

Among the most popular of all forms of working-class entertainment throughout these years, much to the disgust of many of the town's more serious and sober citizens, was the music hall. The earliest appeared before the middle of the century, wherever innkeepers created a temporary stage and invited travelling entertainers to perform for their customers. Members of the audience would also be invited to 'do a turn', rather like a karaoke night today. The success of such ventures encouraged the building of purpose-built music halls, such as St George's Hall, which opened in 1854, and later the Malt Cross on St James's Street

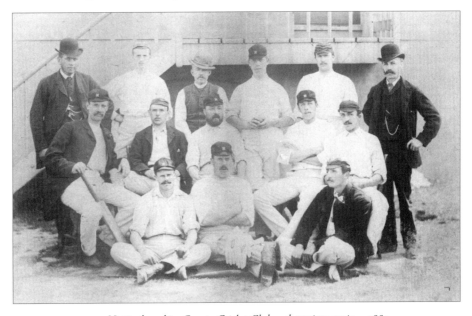

79 *Nottinghamshire County Cricket Club – champions again – 1884.*

80   *Star Court Yard, Mount Street, c.1910.*

and the Crown and Cushion on Fletcher Gate. The introduction of fire regulations in 1878 led to the closing of some of the least salubrious halls and tavern concert rooms, but most of the music halls survived and flourished, always rather rowdy and not altogether respectable.

The popularity of the music hall, and its survival up to and beyond the First World War, was seen as a defeat by many who wished to control and civilise working-class culture, and the same could also be said of the popularity of the public house. In 1864 there were 389 drinking establishments in the town, including 169 beerhouses. After the extension of the borough boundary in 1877 there were six hundred. Although a temperance movement had been established in the town in the 1830s it would seem to have been in decline by the 1860s. However, the plethora of clubs and societies to be found in the town in the Edwardian era did include many that still promoted the cause of temperance. One club for which this was particularly important was the Morley Club, to be found on the corner of Shakespeare Street and Mansfield Road.

The Edwardian era also saw the emergence of a completely new form of entertainment, and one which would – after the First World War – replace the music hall as the most popular form of entertainment of all. The first 'moving pictures' seen in Nottingham were the two- or three-minute bioscope films being shown in music halls, travelling circuses and in a tent at the Goose Fair from the turn of the century. The first purpose-built cinemas, or 'electric palaces', only appeared in about 1910. Among the first were the Victoria Electric Palace, which first opened on Milton Street in 1910, Hibbert's Pictures on Shakespeare Street, and Pringle's Picture Palace on Goldsmith Street, which also opened in 1910 and was the largest of the early cinemas, boasting a grand balcony and seating for 850 people. By the time war broke out Nottingham had seven picture houses, and as soon as the war was over the number would begin to rise rapidly again.

Nine

The Twentieth Century and Beyond

The First World War

The outbreak of war with Germany on 4 August 1914 was greeted with much enthusiasm in the city. Young men rushed to join up and 'join the fun' before it was all over. The 7th Sherwood Foresters, the 'Robin Hoods', were soon marching through the city centre, past thousands of cheering onlookers on their way to Belgium, and the corporation resolved on 5 October to raise £500 for the Belgian Refugees' Fund. Altogether, during the next four years, about 40,000 men and women from Nottingham would join the colours and serve in the armed forces.

Although the government was at first keen to encourage a 'business as usual' attitude to the war, and hoped to avoid either conscription or rationing, the impact of the war was soon being sorely felt, for it was not long before the local press began to print long lists of casualties, and the full horror of trench warfare – or at least something approaching it – began to be appreciated. Moreover, there were plenty of visual reminders too, for in April 1915 the workhouse infirmary was converted into a military hospital and it was not long before blind, maimed and wounded soldiers became a common sight at the city's railway stations, on their journey to the hospital from the Western Front.

The impact of the war on the city's industries was almost immediate, especially on the hosiery industry. Local firms were soon tendering for, and receiving, enormous orders from the War Office for socks, underwear, pullovers, balaclavas and gloves. During the early summer of 1914 many hosiery factories were reported to be working on short-time but by the following January almost all had full order books. By May 1915 the *Nottingham Daily Express* was reporting that at least a quarter of the city's knitting machines were employed on government contracts, and that 'in spite of the increased productive capacity of this district for the supply of hosiery, the demand continues to be greater than the possible output, and most firms are only booking fresh business for delivery at a long period ahead ... orders are already being placed for the spring trade of 1916'. Such was the increase in demand that a number of firms enlarged their factories or built new ones. In July 1915 it was reported that the city's largest firm, I. & R. Morley, had doubled their capacity at their factory at Heanor, where they already employed 1,500, at a cost of £11,000.

81   *Nottingham's first woman taxi driver, March 1916.*

Although the public's enthusiasm for recruitment campaigns began to wane in 1915, as the real nature of the conflict became more apparent, the corporation remained determinedly patriotic. In April 1915 it authorised the Mayor's Recruiting Committee to spend up to £1,000 on activities to raise the Nottingham Brigade Royal Field Artillery and the Nottingham Bantam Battalion, a special battalion for men who were not tall enough to be accepted by other regiments. The Nottinghamshire Volunteer Regiment was also strongly supported and, as the numbers coming forward were beginning to fall off, a Local Recruiting Appeal Committee was set up by the corporation in November 1915.

As more men went to war so their wives and sweethearts found themselves called upon to 'do their bit' and volunteer for munitions work and other occupations women had never done before. Women had always been heavily employed in the city's textile trades but there were some branches, such as warehouse work and the operation of the heavy Cotton's patent knitting machines, which the local trade unions had always managed to keep exclusively for men. In 1915 many workers were prepared to strike rather than let women take over these jobs, whatever the shortage of male labour. The union leaders were generally less militant, however, and in December 1915 an agreement was reached that women could be employed provided they were 'physically fit', paid the same rates as the men, and employed only for the duration of the war. Even before the end of the month the local press was reporting that the shortage of male labour in the hosiery trade was 'largely surmounted'. This was something of an exaggeration. During the rest of the war many firms were only able to meet their demands by requiring very long hours of work from their employees, both male and female. Overtime, double shifts and Sunday work all became routine experience for thousands of workers, and holidays were largely foregone.

Two of the largest munitions factories established in the area were the shell-filling works at Chilwell, a few miles to the west of the city, which began production in March 1916, and the National Projectile Factory opened by the Cammell Laird Company a few months later in the Meadows, at the end of King's Meadow Road, on a site leased by the corporation. The Chilwell factory complex was enormous, covering 200 acres of green fields, but it was built in less than six months between September 1915 and February 1916. The new Minister of Munitions, David Lloyd George, was desperate to increase the production of shells following the heavy criticism of the government in 1915 for failing to supply sufficient ammunition to the army on the Western Front, the so-called 'shell scandal'. By October 1916, when it was in full production, the factory employed about 4,000 men and 2,000 women and was producing 130,000 shells per week. The employment of women was absolutely vital to achieve this output, but when the factory was being planned the employment of women had not been anticipated. Most of the 2,000 women employed came by special trains from Nottingham, Ilkeston and Derby. Few had worked in a factory before. Some had never worked before, many had been in domestic service, and even more had been out-workers in the lace industry.

When the first women started work, in April 1916, they were employed as crane drivers in the Filled Shell Store. One of the first to be employed was Lottie Wiggins of Lenton. She later recalled her first day at work:

82   *Chilwell Munitions workers, 1916.*

We were told to report for duty next morning at 6.00 am at the office. Along with eight other girls we were taken over to … the Filled Shell Store and to our consternation we were told we were to be trained to drive the overhead cranes which were suspended on rails in the roof of the building. We could hardly believe our eyes, we had to ascend a ladder to man the crane and descend by way of a rope. I was never very brave but … if I failed to mount the ladder I would be out of work and this I could not face, I had my board to pay, so up I went, but it was some time before I mastered the rope.

With the beginning of the Battle of the Somme, two months later, the weekly demand for shells increased rapidly and so, too, did the hours that had to be worked, as Lottie recalled:

We were on eight hour shifts at first but this was changed to twelve hours, this meant two shifts instead of three. Twelve hours Monday to Saturday then we changed to eighteen hours going on duty at 6 o'clock Saturday evening and working to 2 o'clock Sunday afternoon when the opposite shift would take over and work through until Monday at 6.00 am, when we would resume normal twelve hour shifts.

The Cammell Laird factory was also enormous, covering a site of more than 13 acres and employing by the end of 1916 about four thousand women. As at Chilwell, most of the women had never worked in a factory before. At first, just two types of shell were produced, 6 inches and 9.2 inches, but from 1917 the factory also started to manufacture guns. Long before the war ended, it was reported, many of the women had become highly skilled operatives, with some achieving the high status of toolsetter.

The work was dangerous and unhealthy. Those employed in the TNT Mill at Chilwell suffered from TNT poisoning and an undisclosed number of employees died as a result

83   *The Filled Shell Store at Chilwell; the store covered 8½ acres and held 700,000 filled shells.*

84 *Nottingham's first motorised ambulance.*

of this in the first months of the factory's operation, prompting rapid improvements in ventilation and dust removal procedures. In the Chilwell Melting Room, where the shells were filled with Ammonia Nitrate and TNT, it was reported in 1916 that not all the men and women wore protective face masks, even though the fumes given off damaged their skin and many complained of constant nausea. Those who worked as shell-fillers, and were therefore in direct contact with TNT, became known as Chilwell Canaries because their hands, faces and hair quickly developed a strange yellow hue.

If anyone had any doubts about the dangers the munitions workers faced they were dispelled on 1 July 1918, when an explosion in the mixing house at the Chilwell factory killed 134 people and injured 250, 50 of them extremely seriously. Most of the dead were too badly burnt to be identified. The precise cause was never established. The government's principal concern was that production should begin again as soon as possible, which it did. Just three days after the explosion, filled shells began to leave the factory again, on the same day that the first of many funerals were held. The great counter-offensive which would drive the German army almost back to Germany, and force its surrender, was about to begin and the British army needed every shell that Chilwell, Cammell Laird and every other munitions factory in the country could produce. In September the workers at Chilwell managed to break the factory's production record, filling 275,327 shells in a single week.

Other factories in the city also found themselves heavily involved in producing goods for the War Office. The Raleigh works at Lenton produced shell fuses and Boots had to expand their production facilities at Island Street very quickly, taking on hundreds more employees – mainly young women – to meet the demands of the forces. More than 900 women were employed in making box respirators to combat gas attacks and the firm also produced water sterilisers, anti-vermin powder, anti-fly cream and enormous quantities of aspirin and disinfectant.

For the first few months of the war the government was happy to maintain the myth of 'business as usual'. The Goose Fair was therefore able to go ahead in 1914 and in June and July 1915 the Royal Show was held at Wollaton Park. But this would be the last such major gathering and the Goose Fair was not held again until after the war. However, the first

Zeppelin raids did not appear until January 1916, when a Zeppelin was spotted following the line of the Trent, possibly looking for the Chilwell shell filling factory, which was then almost completed but not yet in operation. The city was fortunate to suffer only one serious bombing raid, in September 1916, when a Zeppelin managed to bomb buildings in Lister Gate, Greyfriar Gate, the Broad Marsh area and the Meadows. Considerable damage was done but there were mercifully few casualties.

By the autumn of 1916 the success of German submarines in sinking British merchant shipping in the Atlantic was causing growing alarm, and consequently the winter of 1916-17 saw food shortages becoming an increasingly serious problem. Measures were taken by the government to boost food production, to encourage more women to help on local farms and take over the work of men who had been conscripted, and to control food supplies to try to prevent serious hunger. From August 1917 the corporation was required to set up a local Food Control Committee responsible for ensuring that all districts of the city received an adequate supply of food. As a result of this the first communal kitchen in the city was opened in January 1918, providing a plate of Irish stew for 4d. To publicise the event the mayor and mayoress were both invited to attend and both pronounced the stew 'excellent'. Other communal kitchens were soon being opened in other parts of the city, organised by a special Mayor's Food Committee, but later in the year the Ministry of Food began issuing ration books. Fuel was also in very short supply by 1917, and therefore extremely expensive. To guard against profiteering and to try to ensure at least a limited supply at a reasonable price, a Coal Prices Committee was also set up by the corporation in October 1917.

By this time many local families had suffered the loss of loved ones and there were many private stories of sacrifice and heroism, but one local young man's daring, bravery, patriotism and, eventually, sacrifice captured the public imagination like no other. On 19 February 1917, 20-year-old Flight Commander Albert Ball was honoured with the freedom of the city, in a ceremony at the Exchange Hall, for his 'splendid services' in the Royal Flying Corps. He had already received the DSO with two bars, the Military Cross and the Russian Order of St George for his bravery and remarkable success in shooting down enemy aircraft. He had been born into a well-to-do family at 301 Lenton Boulevard (now Castle Boulevard) but the family moved shortly afterwards to a large house in the Park. His father was a successful local businessman, Albert Snr, who was also a member of the corporation. In many ways he was the perfect hero: polite, modest, popular, young, very good-looking and extremely brave; a true *Boys' Own* hero. Tragically, like so many other young pilots, he was not to see the end of the war, dying in a dogfight over the Western Front on 7 May 1917. He was buried in German-occupied France but accorded full military honours by the German army, and German officers attended his funeral in full parade dress and allowed Allied prisoners to also attend. Shortly after his death he was awarded the VC, and after the war a statue of him was erected in the grounds of the castle, unveiled by the Chief of the Air Staff, Sir Hugh Trenchard, and his portrait was hung in the Council House.

Tales of heroism were important in maintaining morale and a sense of common purpose at a time when long casualty lists published in the local papers, long hours of work, food and fuel shortages, high prices, blackout restrictions and fears of Zeppelin raids all conspired together to induce war-weariness and depression. And for the government, the maintenance of public support and belief in the war were vital, not least to ensure financial backing for the fighting. In February 1918 a special Tank Week was organised to encourage investment

Part 131. THE FIGHT FOR THE DOMINION OF THE AIR. 7d. Net.

The

GREAT·WAR

THE STANDARD HISTORY OF THE ALL-EUROPE CONFLICT
Edited by H·W·Wilson, author of
"With the Flag to Pretoria", "Japan's Fight for Freedom", etc.

Captain Albert Ball, D.S.O., M.C.,
Notts and Derby Regt. and R.F.C.   Won the D.S.O for successfully attacking six enemy machines in one flight.

85   *Portrait of Albert Ball, VC.*

in War Bonds. A tank was brought into the city and placed in the market place as a focus
for the appeal and a week later the mayor was able to announce that the enormous sum of
£2,700,000 had been raised.

At the beginning of 1918 there seemed little prospect of a swift end to the war. No
one could have foreseen the rapid collapse of the German army in the late summer and

autumn of that year. Even as the war reached its last stages, a new and equally deadly enemy was sweeping across the continent, 'Spanish Flu'. This would prove to be the world's greatest pandemic since the Black Death, and Nottingham, like every other major city in the country, suffered a considerable loss of life. The outbreak of war had prevented the corporation from continuing its policy of large-scale slum clearance and house building, and only piecemeal demolition had been possible in the last four years. Many thousands of people therefore still lived in overcrowded and insanitary conditions, ideal for the spread of disease. Young children and babies were especially susceptible and the infant death rate, which had been falling before the war, now briefly rose again. Altogether, during 1918 and 1919 the 'Spanish Flu' killed 1,350 people in the city.

Not even 'Spanish Flu', however, could prevent the city from celebrating the end of the war. Soon after the news of the Armistice reached the city, on 11 November 1918, gaily coloured bunting appeared everywhere, factory hooters were sounded and crowds came out on to the streets to celebrate, with children and adults waving flags. The official celebrations were delayed until after Germany had signed the humiliating Treaty of Versailles six months later, and a memorial to the many thousands from the area who had given their lives in the First World War was not unveiled until July 1928. This was (and still is) a grand memorial triple arch designed by the city engineer, T. Wallis Gordon, on the Trent Embankment. The arch forms the entrance

86   *Statue of Albert Ball, VC, in the grounds of Nottingham Castle.*

to the Victoria Embankment Gardens. Much of the cost was met by a gift from Jesse Boot. The original proposal, to erect a memorial column in the centre of the market place, with a bronze figure symbolising peace on the top of the column, had proved to be extremely unpopular and had to be abandoned.

The 1920s and 1930s

The rapid rates of population increase which had so characterised 19th-century Nottingham were not continued into the new century. A falling birth rate meant that the population of the city grew only modestly between the wars, from 259,901 in 1911 to 276,189 by 1931. The Second World War prevented a census being taken in 1941 but in 1951 the city's population had only risen to 306,008, an increase in 40 years of less than 18 per cent (and this increase was largely owing to the extension of the city boundary in 1932). The number of households in the city, however, grew much more rapidly, from 60,070 in 1911 to 70,740 by 1931 and to 93,491 by 1951. Rising living standards and changing social values were causing a steady decline in average household size, from 4.33 in 1911 to 3.9 by 1931 and 3.27 by 1951, and the consequence was an ever-increasing demand for more housing. Moreover, during the inter-war years this demand was made all the greater by the recognition that a very high number of the city's existing houses were no longer fit for human habitation. A Housing Committee report in 1919 identified seven areas of the city, containing nearly 9,000 houses and more than 12,000 people, as unhealthy, and a further 3,000 individual houses, containing nearly 11,000 people, were described as not fit to be lived in. So serious was the situation, indeed, that the Ministry of Health gave this as the principal reason for turning down the corporation's application to extend the city boundary in 1920.

This humiliating rejection stung the corporation into action, with the lead taken by Alderman William Crane, the very energetic chairman of the Housing Committee. The powers granted by the Housing and Town Planning Act of 1919, to build houses in large numbers which could be let by the corporation at a subsidised rent, were eagerly taken up, and ambitious plans were drawn up to meet the Ministry's criticisms, to improve the city's sewage system and undertake a large-scale programme of slum clearance. The result was a huge increase in the city's residential area; it approximately doubled in 20 years. By 1939 17,461 new houses had been built by the corporation on 20 new estates, mostly on 'green-field' sites, representing about two-thirds of all new houses built in these years.

The first of the new housing estates were built on the northern edges of the city. In 1919 the corporation bought two sites at Sherwood and Stockhill Lane, and Crane and his Housing Committee ensured that the plans for these and later estates should meet high standards. The new houses were an enormous improvement on the Victorian slums which were by now being demolished in Narrow Marsh and Carter Gate. They were semi-detached and each had a separate kitchen and living room, an indoor toilet and bathroom, and also a generous garden. Also, the estate plans had to include schools, playgrounds and shops, and in some cases allotments and bowling greens, and the housing density was strictly limited. The maximum allowed was 12 houses per acre. In the city's worst slum areas there

87   *New housing on Stockhill Lane; the architect's drawing.*

88   *Sherwood Estate houses.*

were often as many as 500 houses squeezed into a single acre. Many regretted the loss of neighbourliness but the new houses did much to improve the health of the community. At the same time rapid progress was being made in the older parts of the city to improve the sewage system so that every house had a water closet, and in August 1923 the city engineer was able to announce that the last pail closet in the city had been removed and replaced.

The next estate development followed in 1925. In September 1924 the corporation purchased the 16th-century Wollaton Hall and its surrounding park of almost 800 acres from Lord Middleton for £200,000. The Hall itself was converted into a natural history museum, which was opened in 1926, and most of the surrounding park was developed as a public recreation ground, playing fields and an 18-hole golf course. Some land was reserved for housing, and land sold off to private housing developers in the north-west corner of the estate enabled the corporation to finance the building of 1,000 working-class houses.

To continue the process of estate development and meet the demand for new housing, the corporation had to seek a limited extension of the city boundary in 1932. This was agreed, adding to the city the parishes of Wollaton and Bilborough to the west, part of Colwick to the east, and part of Bestwood Park and a small part of Arnold Urban District to the north. It was therefore mainly in these areas that most of the 1930s development took place. Part of the demand for new housing came from those families displaced by the continuing programme of slum clearance in the older parts of the city. Another Housing Act of 1930 gave a fresh impetus to the drive to rid the city of its appalling housing problems and in the next few years more than 2,000 houses were demolished, mainly in Barker Gate, Sussex Street, St James's Street, Colwick Street and Sneinton Market. Altogether, more than 7,000 people had to be rehoused.

As the city's population became more dispersed so the need to improve transport facilities also became more sorely felt. One of the first new roads to be built after the war was at Daybrook, where Valley Road was opened in August 1922, along the north side of the new Sherwood housing estate. Other new roads quickly followed, culminating in the completion of an outer ringroad in 1932. The gradual process of widening Nottingham's numerous narrow medieval streets had begun long before but there was still much to be done. A start was made in 1923 when the corporation agreed to widen the lower part of Friar Lane, from Beastmarket Hill to Friar Yard, but congestion dictated that a one-way system had to be introduced in 1924 for Clumber Street, Bridlesmith Gate and St James's Street. Trent Bridge was doubled in width in 1926 and more roads were widened during the remaining inter-war years, including Parliament Street and Huntingdon Street in 1932.

The electric tram was still synonymous with fast and reliable public transport when the First World War ended but its position was soon being challenged by the motor bus, which had made its first appearance in the city as early as 1906. In 1925 the corporation also approved the introduction of a trolley bus service, but this did not begin until April 1927, running along the Nottingham Road route to Basford. At this time there were still 200 electric trams at work in the city but the competition of the motor bus and trolley bus caused their number to fall sharply in the next few years and in 1936 the last tram was

89   *A second-hand goods market in Sneinton, c.1930.*

withdrawn from service. Like the very first electric tram, introduced in January 1901, it ran from the market place to Sherwood.

Throughout the inter-war years the public works undertaken by the corporation, including slum clearance, house building and road building, were seen as having a double value, as means not only to bring about much needed improvements for the city but also to alleviate the scourge of unemployment. The diversity of Nottingham's economy ensured that it did not suffer the punishing levels of unemployment found in the North East or in South Wales. Unemployment, however, was widespread, and in the depth of the Depression in 1933 20,455 people were out of work in the city. Nottingham's major industries enjoyed varied fortunes. The lace industry suffered decline and contraction, and those employed in the industry lived in constant fear of lay-offs and longer periods of unemployment. Changes in women's fashion meant less demand for lace and although the home market began to recover in the 1930s the overseas markets could not be regained. The hosiery industry, by contrast, enjoyed modest prosperity, helped partly by the rise in women's hemlines and the growing demand for stockings, but also by the introduction of new artificial fibres, such as rayon. Nottingham's most successful textile business between the wars was probably William Hollins & Co., which specialised in producing its own branded fabric for ready-made clothing. Such was the firm's confidence in the continuing success of its 'Viyella' fabrics after the First World War that it built a completely new glass and steel factory on Castle Boulevard in 1919, Viyella House, and then added a substantial extension in 1933. This quickly became a Nottingham landmark and although all of

90   *Viyella House today; now New Castle House and the offices of the Gala Coral Group.*

Hollins' concerns have now been closed down in Nottingham, Viyella House survives as a monument to the enterprise of the firm.

The city's three great 'success stories' of the late 19th century, Boots, Raleigh Cycles and Players, all survived the years of Depression remarkably well. Players had already become the city's largest employer at the turn of the century, and in 1914 employed about 2,500 people. Cigarette smoking became increasingly popular between the wars and the firm was able to continue to grow rapidly, with 5,000 employees by 1928 and 7,500 by 1939. The production of cigarettes on this scale necessitated the building of three new factories and a bonded warehouse alongside 'No 1 Factory' on Radford Boulevard.

Heavy investment in increased productivity ensured that Raleigh also expanded production. Frank Bowden died in 1921 but his son, Harold, who now took over the firm, quickly demonstrated that he had inherited his father's entrepreneurial flair. A visit to America by Harold Bowden to study Henry Ford's production methods led to the firm building an overhead factory conveyor at its Lenton works which was more than a mile long. Productivity was dramatically improved and Raleigh were able to cut the price of a standard bicycle from £14 in 1921 to £4 19s. 6d. in 1932. In 1920 the Lenton factory was already the largest cycle manufacturing works in the world, producing almost 100,000 bikes a year, but as the cost per unit of production fell, and with it the retail price of a bicycle, so demand and output continued to grow. By the 1930s it seemed as if every working man in the country had a bicycle. By 1936 Raleigh were making 400,000 cycles a year, and by 1938 almost 500,000. Other manufacturers could not easily compete and in 1932 Raleigh were able to purchase one of its larger rivals, Humber Cycles of Coventry, a firm founded 50 years earlier in Beeston, just to the west of Nottingham, which in 1900 had been a substantially larger business than Raleigh. Harold Bowden also experimented with the production of motor cycles, motor vans, light motor cars and motor accessories, but shortly before the outbreak of the Second World War he decided to abandon these and concentrate instead on the firm's core product.

American-style business practices also played an important role in ensuring the survival and continuing prosperity of Boots. Chronic arthritis forced Jesse Boot to retire in 1920 but instead of handing the business on to his son, John Campbell Boot, as was widely expected, he sold his controlling interest for £2 million to an American pharmaceutical company, the United Drug Company. Father and son had long had a tempestuous relationship and Jesse believed his son to be a spendthrift who could not be trusted with the business. The family were horrified but it proved to be a good business move. Young executives were now sent to America to learn American retail innovations, less profitable products were identified and cut out, and expenses were brought under firmer control by a new system of territorial general managers. Rising sales led to further factory and warehouse building in the streets around the Midland Railway but by 1927 it was clear that more space and better-designed factories were needed. Louis K. Liggett, the head of the United Drug Company, appointed John Boot vice-chairman of the company and it was John Boot who now supervised the search for a new site. A large area of open fields was chosen beside the Trent at Beeston and the first building, a large soapworks, opened in 1930. Boot, however, had very ambitious plans and this was only the first part of a major complex of factories and administrative offices. The 'Wets' factory, designed for the production of liquid goods, creams, toiletries and sterile products, opened in 1933 and the 'Dries' factory, specialising in medicated confectionery

91   *An advertising brochure for the Raleigh three-wheeled car, the 'Safety Seven'.*

and powders, was completed five years later. The 'Wets' factory was (and still is) especially impressive, built in steel and glass to a pioneering design of Sir Owen Williams, one of the most highly respected architects of the inter-war years. While this work was going on the American Depression was causing Liggett's business fortunes to suffer a dramatic decline, forcing him to sell Boots, and in 1933 John Boot, now the 2nd Lord Trent following his father's death in 1931, had the enormous satisfaction of buying the company back. In the same year he also opened the firm's 1,000th shop. The company was both prosperous and prestigious, although for Trent, surprisingly, it was always prestige that mattered more.

Although the success of Players, Raleigh and Boots ensured that Nottingham did not suffer the same levels of unemployment and short-time working as many other areas, there was still much poverty and hardship. In 1937 one quarter of the city's families had an income of less than £1 10s. a week. This was well below the average found in comparable cities such as Leicester or Coventry. Married women were not employed at all by many firms, including Players, Raleigh and Boots, and could only find work as out-workers for the textile trades, where the wages paid were even lower. In poor families children were still expected to leave school as soon as they possibly could so that they could earn a little money to help maintain the family finances, or to assist mum in looking after the younger children. Families had to be fed using the cheapest of scraps and leftovers from the fishmonger or butcher, and stale bread, stale cakes and bruised fruit were all highly prized by poor families. Many mothers went hungry to ensure their husbands and children were fed. The number of pawnshops in the city – 51 – gave some indication of the extent of poverty between the wars. Many families could only manage to feed themselves and pay the rent by regularly pawning their Sunday suits and wedding rings, redeeming them again on pay-day. And poverty and poor housing also ensured that the infant death rate in the city – although steadily falling – remained stubbornly above the national average throughout these years. Improvements in housing in the 1930s probably largely explain the tendency for the rate to fall in this decade, and also for falls in the number of deaths from tuberculosis and typical childhood diseases such as diphtheria, enteritis, measles and whooping cough, all of which had been a product of overcrowded and insanitary Victorian housing.

Low wages and unemployment, or the fear of unemployment, fuelled political divisions and political debate in the city, both in the council chamber and on the streets. A bitter dispute over pay and conditions in the mining industry led to a national miners' strike in April 1921. Public feeling was deeply divided. Local miners and their supporters held rallies to explain and defend their cause but many members of the public condemned

92 *The new Boots 'Wets' factory, shortly after its completion in 1933.*

their disruption of fuel supplies, especially when, after six weeks of strike action, the corporation announced that it would have to cut off gas and electricity supplies every day, between 4 p.m. and midnight, and coal was rationed by the corporation's Coal Emergency Committee. Feelings also ran very high in the city during the General Strike in May 1926, when corporation transport employees came out on strike in support of the miners, thus crippling the bus and tram service. Workers in numerous other firms also came out, and when some firms attempted to organise private bus services their buses were attacked and in some cases overturned. Large groups of angry workmen gathered at street corners to discuss events, and for a few days, until the General Strike was called off, there was a feeling – or fear – that almost anything might happen. Nottingham had been politically quiet for many decades, but for a few days in May it seemed to some as if something of the spirit of the days of Radical Nottingham, and of Reform Bill riots and Chartism, might have returned.

At least a temporary escape from the concerns and struggles of everyday life was offered by the picture house, or, as it came to be known, the cinema. In 1913 there had only been seven picture houses in the city but by the early 1930s there were more than 30 and by the end of the decade more than 40. In some parts of the city three or four cinemas could be found within 50 yards of each other. For adults and children alike the trip to the cinema was often the highlight of the week. By the 1930s it had replaced the music hall as the most popular form of entertainment and Hollywood stars had become idols for millions. It appealed to both middle and working classes for most cinemas offered a wide range of seat prices, with the cheapest only 4d. for adults and 2d. for children, prices which even poor families could usually afford. Every Saturday afternoon queues of children would gather excitedly, clutching their two pennies and waiting for the doors of their local cinema to open. Their favourite films were almost invariably the 'cowboys' and their heroes Ken Maynard, Hoot Gibson and, above all, Tom Mix. Many of the cinemas were not large and served a highly 'local' audience, and some could best be described as flea pits, perpetually smelling of tobacco, or worse. A few, however, were designed to be lavish 'dream palaces' and the first of these was the Elite Picture Theatre on Parliament Street, which could seat 1,600 people and opened in August 1921. Its promoters described it as 'the last word in amusement houses'. As well as a cinema, the Elite also offered its clientele a choice of three cafés, a ballroom and a pair of shops. Other large cinemas were soon to follow but the most prestigious in the 1930s was undoubtedly the Ritz, which seated 2,500 and opened on Angel Row in December 1933. By this time the 'talkies' had arrived and film-going was more popular than ever.

Another escape into a world of glamour and (hopefully) romance was offered by the Palais De Danse, which opened in April 1925, in Lower Parliament Street, on the site of the old House of Correction. Up to 400 couples could take to the floor at once, and dance to the music of Reuben's 'Savannahs'. The only drawback for the ladies was that men were in relatively short supply, outnumbered by four to one by the mid-1930s. To draw in the men a slogan proclaimed, 'If She's Beautiful – She Dances', and the man who wished to appear at his best beside his dancing partner could find every assistance in the men's cloakroom; here he could shave, have his shoes polished and have his trousers pressed.

Nottingham's two football teams were modest achievers between the wars, to be found mainly in the Second and Third Divisions, but they had both established a significant and loyal following well before the First World War, and once the war was over great numbers filled the terraces again. Unlike the cinema, football was an overwhelmingly male leisure activity, carrying male sociability out of the workplace and into 'spare time'. The writer J.B. Priestley, who attended a match between Forest and Notts. County in 1933, deplored what he saw as the 'commercialisation of leisure'; entertainment being provided for the people – at a price – rather than being created by themselves. This overlooked the enormous number of men and boys who played the game themselves at weekends and holidays in the town's parks and competed in local youth leagues. Football, it could be said, had succeeded among the working classes – at least the male section – where the churches had failed. The Nottinghamshire County Cricket Club also attracted large crowds to Trent Bridge, and, unlike the two professional football teams, it enjoyed considerable success, winning the County Championship in 1929 with players of outstanding calibre such as George Gunn, Harold Larwood, and W. (Bill) Voce.

Churches, schools and factories all organised football and cricket matches, as well as many other social and cultural activities. The Methodist churches were particularly active in this respect and many chapel-goers would later look back on this period as a golden age for chapel-led recreation. The Derby Road Methodist Church, for instance, organised a Sunday School, a guild, a women's meeting, a choir, a benevolent society and a Thursday evening fellowship. The Sherwood Methodists had their own troop of boy scouts, a drama group, a girls' club, a campfire gathering and cricket, tennis and badminton teams. The churches

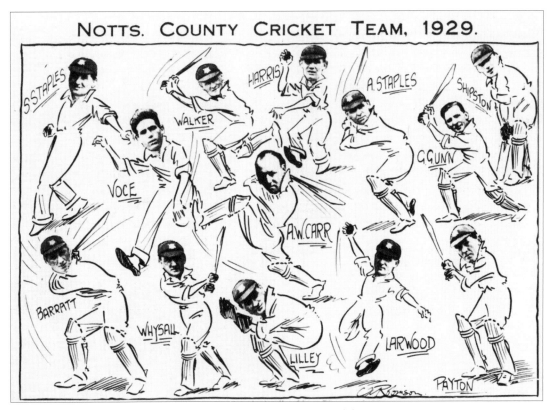

93   *Nottinghamshire County Cricket Club, 1929.*

were invariably most successful, however, in the better-off, middle-class areas, of the city, and in predominantly working-class areas, such as Hyson Green and Radford, voluntary organisations struggled to establish themselves or to hold on to their members.

A number of local firms organised leisure activities for their employees in the hope of fostering better shop floor relations and high levels of productivity. Jesse Boot had begun taking employees for social excursions in the nearby countryside in the 1890s, but between the wars the company regularly organised more ambitious outings on a very large scale. In 1924, for instance, eight special trains were chartered to take 5,500 employees to the British Empire Exhibition at Wembley. Employees were also able to use the sports grounds at Plaisaunce, Boot's house by the Trent. Players also organised a wide range of leisure activities for their employees, including a drama club, a flying club, a rifle club, flower shows and numerous sports events. Raleigh had its own sports ground at Coach Lane, in Wollaton, where employees enjoyed football, hockey, cricket and tennis.

Family holidays at the seaside were also still extremely popular, and Skegness maintained its position as Nottingham's favourite resort. Provided dad was in work, a considerable effort would be made throughout the year to save up enough for a week in a bed-and-breakfast at 'Skeggy'. The children would build their sandcastles, buy an icecream for a penny and have a ride on the donkeys while mum and dad enjoyed a well-earned snooze in a deck chair. One-day Sunday excursions also remained very popular. Queues would begin to form as early as 2.00 a.m. outside the Victoria Station on Milton Street, to buy a return ticket for 2s. 6d. and catch the first trains to the seaside. This would be a very long day. The last train back would pull into the station at midnight.

Another very popular entertainment, and a much older one, was the Goose Fair. It was held in the market place in October and was re-established by popular demand in 1919, having been suspended during the First World War. It had been for many years an eight-day event but had been reduced to three days in 1880 as a result of numerous criticisms that it disrupted the city's normal business, attracted criminals and prostitutes and encouraged heavy drinking and riotous behaviour. But it had been, and still remained, too popular to be banned completely. As the manager of a local factory had commented in 1879, the fair was 'a necessary relief from the cares and toils of business and the foul atmosphere of factory life'. Half a century later there were many local people, and not least the employees of local factories, who would have agreed fully with these sentiments. When J.B. Priestley came to the city in 1933 it was autumn and he managed to visit the fair. He enjoyed it no more than the football match, describing it as 'an assembly of devices, chiefly mechanical, contrived to attract the largest number of pennies in the shortest possible time', but he did acknowledge its importance to local people. It was, he said, 'one of the highlights of the year. They even speak of Goose Fair weather, that definite autumnal nip in the air ... it is as much a centre of interest in school as Christmas ... if there was not a school holiday the kids would take it anyway.'

By this time the fair was no longer held in the market place. It had been moved to the Forest in 1928 as part of a major redevelopment programme, involving also the transfer of the open-air market to Parliament Street, the creation of a processional way flanked by gardens and fountains on the site of the market place and, most ambitious of all, the demolition of the old 18th-century Exchange and the building of a new Council House. This was a brave and controversial decision for the corporation. The cost was especially controversial: approximately £500,000. The corporation had long been promoting Nottingham as 'the Queen of the Midlands', a term that seems to have been first used to describe the city in about 1870. Civic pride had been hurt by the government's refusal to allow the extension of the city boundary in 1920 and there were many on the corporation who felt the need for a grand gesture to assert the city's sense of self-worth. The architect who was already responsible for much of the new council-house building, Cecil Howitt, drew up the plans for the new building on the site of the old Exchange and for the new layout of the market area to the west. He succeeded where T.C. Hine had failed 70 years earlier because the political climate in the city was now favourable for such an ambitious and expensive plan. The old Exchange was demolished in 1926 and the new Council House was opened on 29 May 1929 by the Prince of Wales. Some have criticised the design, including Nikolaus Pevsner, who in 1951 dismissed it as an example of 'neo-Baroque display', adding 'the Ionic columnation is no more inspiring or truthful than the interiors'. Its Classical style, however, including a Wren-inspired dome, made for a prestigious building, with an impressive council chamber and offices, and it also incorporated an imposing arcade of shops. It provided, and still provides, a real focus for the city centre.

The developments in state education in the city between the wars were also seen by many as a major achievement, which re-established the reputation of the city as a centre of progressive education. The city's first ever Director of Education, A.H. Whipple, who was appointed in 1924, had very clear ideas about how the potential of all children could be best advanced through educational reform. His plan envisaged a considerable expansion in the provision of secondary schools dedicated to ensuring that all young people received

94 *The Council House in 2010; now somewhat overshadowed by the 'Nottingham Eye'.*

a good all-round education. Existing selective schools were phased out and new non-selective schools built. Where new estates had been built new schools were required and Whipple was able to use this as an opportunity to introduce his scheme, building 'families' of schools for each estate. Ideally, he argued, each estate should be served by an infant, junior and two senior schools, one for boys and one for girls, and in the evenings the senior schools could serve as community, as social and cultural centres, knitting together the population of the new estates to create a sense of community. The majority on the corporation liked Whipple's ideas and the first new schools began to be built soon after his appointment. By 1933, when the William Crane Schools opened to serve the new estate at Aspley, the reorganisation of the city's school system was complete.

95   *Bust of Lord Trent (Sir Jesse Boot) on University Boulevard.*

96   *The Trent Building, University of Nottingham, today.*

While Whipple's vision was being realised, Jesse Boot's last great ambition for his native city was also coming to fruition. In July 1928 King George V and Queen Mary formally opened the new University College of Nottingham on a new site at Highfields, to the west of the city, overlooking the Trent. Boot had bought the site intending to build an industrial village for his employees, but with the sale of his business to the United Drug Company the scheme had to be abandoned. The existing site of the University College in the city, on South Sherwood Street, was too restricted to allow the expansion needed if it was to achieve full university status. Boot read about the problems facing the University College's future expansion in a newspaper, in the summer of 1920, while trying to adjust to retirement from business in his newly purchased mansion on Jersey. He immediately saw an opportunity to both help his native city and achieve a spectacular building project. He summoned his old friend, Edmund Huntsman, a member of both the corporation and the College Council, to Jersey and offered him the Highfields site for the University and a cheque for £50,000. Further large gifts followed, totalling £150,000 and the grand scheme was launched. Although his sight was now failing badly and his body was racked with rheumatoid arthritis, Boot took an extremely active interest in the project. The architect for most of his more recent shops, Morley Horder, was commissioned to design the new buildings and the foundation stone for the Trent Building was laid by Viscount Haldane in June 1922. In the fields below the new university Boot had a public park laid out, complete with a 15-acre boating lake and a public swimming pool. The latter was an addition to the original plans, but as the work went on Boot made further additions, including college playing fields with a pavilion, engineering laboratories and a great hall. In 1926 he relinquished the chairmanship of the Boots Companies so that he could devote himself entirely to the completion of the project but by the time of the royal opening, two years later, his disabilities made it impossible for him to attend. The King and Queen visited him shortly afterwards, however, and took tea with him, and a few months later his generosity was rewarded with a peerage.

The Second World War

When Chamberlain broadcast to the nation on Sunday morning, 3 September 1939, announcing the outbreak of war with Germany, the news was not unexpected. Indeed, the country had long been preparing for what had come to seem inevitable, and this time there would be no pretence of 'business as usual'. This would be 'total war', involving everyone. From the outset the government took sweeping and unprecedented powers to mobilise the nation for its defence and survival, and no one could be in any doubt that the country faced one of the greatest crises of its long history.

The great fear, and a major reason why Chamberlain had tried so hard to appease Hitler and avoid war for so long, was aerial bombing. Expert advisors had for a long time been telling the Prime Minister to expect many hundreds of thousands of casualties in the first few weeks of war as a result of German bombing of Britain's cities. In the light of this, Air-Raid Precaution Committees had been set up in cities across the country, including Nottingham, many months before the outbreak of war, and on 1 May 1939, on instructions from the Home Office, these committees were converted into Emergency Committees, with wide-ranging powers. John Campbell Boot, 2nd Lord Trent, was appointed the Regional Commissioner for Civil Defence for the North Midlands, a post he held for the duration of the war, and the Principal of University College, H.A.S. Wortley, was appointed his Deputy.

These two, together with the ARP Controller for the city, effectively ran Nottingham for the next six years, much to the annoyance and frustration of many of the councillors, who found the corporation's loss of power difficult to accept. The first ARP Controller was the town clerk but in July 1940 the position passed to the Chief Constable and then about a year later to Lt-Com. G.J. Mackness.

All corporation building projects not already in hand were cancelled at the end of July 1939, and in August the art collection held in the Castle Museum was evacuated for safe-keeping and the castle handed over for military purposes. Plans for the evacuation of the city's children had been drawn up more than a year before and on the declaration of war these were now put into place. Two days after Chamberlain's broadcast, tearful children wearing identity labels and clutching their gas masks were queuing up outside their schools, ready to say goodbye to mum and board the evacuation bus, which in most cases was taking them just a few miles to live with strangers in nearby villages and small towns. Pregnant mothers were also urged to take advantage of this opportunity and altogether about five thousand mothers and children were evacuated. This was only about a quarter of all the children and young people of school age in the Nottingham evacuation zone and most of the city's children were never evacuated. Moreover, the great majority of those who left in September were back with their parents within six months. The terrible bombing campaign that had been so feared had not come and the

✗ EMERGENCY STORE CUPBOARD ✗

Compiled at the request of many of our clientele, the enclosed booklet—
"Suggestions for Emergency Store Cupboard," together with A.R.P. information on Home Storage of Foods, etc., is issued solely with the desire to render every assistance to those housewives who desire to create an Emergency Food Supply.

Issued in a handy wallet, we suggest this be retained for further reference.

BURTON'S
of SMITHY ROW and EXCHANGE ARCADE
NOTTINGHAM

Grocery & Provision Dept.   **AND OVER**
DIAL **2265** (3 lines)   **200 BRANCHES**

97   *An advertisement for an Emergency Store Cupboard booklet issued shortly after the outbreak of war.*

evacuation quickly came to be seen as perhaps an over-cautious measure that could be relaxed. Many of the city's schools had been either closed down or commandeered for war purposes during these first few months, but some now reopened, and by 1940 all schools that remained open had had bomb shelters erected to protect the children in the event of an air raid. However, the strains on the education system were enormous. A shortage of both accommodation and staff, as more teachers were called up for military service, meant that about 10,000 pupils in various parts of the city had to be taught in shifts, either in the morning or the afternoon.

All cinemas were also closed down when war was declared, but again the lack of action – the 'phoney war' – meant that they were soon reopened again, and in February 1940 it was also agreed that they could even open on Sundays, something the corporation had up to now always resisted. The need to maintain civilian morale was now recognised as being extremely important, but a request to allow cinemas to open on Sundays had also come from the military as large numbers of soldiers and RAF personnel were now stationed near Nottingham. The Goose Fair was also cancelled on the outbreak of war but it would not return for another six years.

A determined recruiting campaign during the last months of peace ensured that when war did come the ARP controller had a full team of volunteers in place. Partly to silence criticism from the corporation, the Emergency Committee sent the councillors a very detailed report in March 1942 outlining the work of both paid full-time staff and the local volunteers up to that time. The Air-Raid Warden Service was described as the 'eyes and ears' of the whole ARP network. Across the city 177 wardens' posts had been set up, staffed mainly by volunteers, and always open. A skeleton staff of full-time officers was supplemented by volunteers working on a day and night rota, and many more volunteers could be summoned at any time on the sounding of an alert. Also, as part of the service, 600 volunteers had been trained as unexploded bomb investigators, and many hundreds of people were part of the Fire Guard Organisation, again working on a rota, and charged with fire watching and fire prevention work, covering, in theory at least, every street and every business across the city. An Auxiliary Fire Service had also been set up at the beginning of the war, staffed increasingly by women, who were given training in maintaining the equipment and in dealing with incendiary bombs. The police were also trained in fire fighting, salvage work and rescue work, and it was their responsibility to operate the air-raid warning sirens.

One of the first priorities in 1939 was the provision of air-raid shelters. Under the Civil Defence Act of that year, all large businesses employing 50 or more people had to provide shelters for their staff, but it was the responsibility of the ARP service to cater for the rest of the population. Altogether nearly 38,000 shelters were provided: about 24,000 outdoor Anderson shelters and nearly 14,000 indoor Morrison shelters. Neither offered comfort. The Anderson shelters consisted of two curved sheets of galvanised steel bolted together and fixed over an excavated base, with a little extra protection afforded by piling the excavated earth over the roof. The Morrison was only three feet high and looked very much like a steel table, with its sides protected by a steel mesh. Domestic street shelters were also built, capable of sheltering many families, and large shelters were built for schools, hospitals, railway stations and other public buildings. Many people also built their own shelters and at the Bluecoat School the pupils dug their own cave shelter under the school, large enough to accommodate a hundred people.

When an air raid occurred a number of Civil Defence Services were called into action. As well as the fire service and police, volunteers who were trained in first aid, under the control of the Director of Medical Services, worked alongside a specialist volunteer Rescue Service, who were trained in extricating bomb-victims from damaged houses and consisted almost entirely of local builders and miners. The City Engineer's Department was responsible for emergency repairs to buildings, roads, bridges and sewers, but the military could also be called on to give assistance if necessary. As part of the Department's contingency

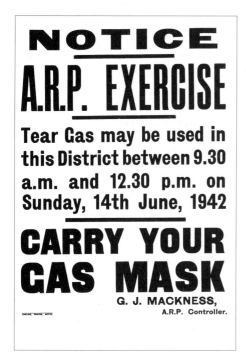

NOTICE

A.R.P. EXERCISE

Tear Gas may be used in this District between 9.30 a.m. and 12.30 p.m. on Sunday, 14th June, 1942

CARRY YOUR GAS MASK

G. J. MACKNESS,
A.R.P. Controller.

98 *ARP exercise warning notice, 1942.*

99   *Raleigh employees who had formed a company rescue squad, c. 1940.*

100   *Polish air force men parade in Market Square, 1943.*

planning three enormous steel spans had been purchased by 1942 to be used for repairs to Trent Bridge, should it be hit by German bombs.

Providing meals for those whose homes had been destroyed or badly damaged, and for the volunteers themselves, was a major concern. An emergency meals service was established, designed to function after a raid, when gas, water and electricity supplies had been destroyed. Emergency feeding centres were set up and staffed by the Women's Voluntary Services. In March 1942 there were 31 in the city, often located in schools that had been closed down at the outbreak of war, and school teachers worked with the WVS in manning them. There was also by this time five special restaurants recently opened, known as British restaurants, which provided hot meals for persons working away from home and anyone else obliged to eat out. So popular were these that in 1942 there were plans to open another four.

Food rationing was introduced early in 1940, at first only for sugar, butter and bacon, but soon also for many other items of food, and from June 1940 ration books were also needed for buying clothes and footwear. Fuel rationing meant that petrol was also in very short supply and both motor bus and trolley bus services had to be much reduced. Moving about the city at night was also made more difficult by the blackout, for people found themselves often in almost total darkness. Even traffic lights were hooded; no light was supposed to escape from the windows of nearby houses, and there were, of course, no street lights. Not surprisingly, the number of car accidents increased considerably.

101   *Houses destroyed on Hutton Street in a raid in January 1941.*

The first bombing raid came on the night of 30-1 August 1940, when high-explosive bombs and incendiaries were dropped on Mapperley and Sherwood, killing a baby and injuring 17 people. More raids then followed and the numbers of casualties steadily grew. The worst raid by far came on the night of 8-9 May 1941. The city was attacked by about a hundred German planes dropping nearly 500 high-explosive bombs and thousands of incendiaries. Very soon there were fires raging all over the city. Fire watchers and fire fighters struggled to put out the fires but at 4.10 a.m. a report to ARP Control stated that 12 major fires were burning in the city. A public air-raid shelter on Dakeyne Street took a direct hit, causing many fatalities, but the greatest loss of life occurred at the Co-op bakery on Meadow Lane where 49 people were killed and another 20 injured. The Notts. County football ground, which stood very close to the bakery, was also badly damaged. Altogether in that one awful night 151 people were killed and more than

102   *University College on Shakespeare Street after the raid of 8-9 May 1941.*

270 seriously injured. Many houses, factories and public buildings were destroyed or badly damaged and but for a great many acts of heroism the losses would have been even greater. Two churches were completely destroyed, St John's on Leenside and St Christopher's on Colwick Road, and St Mary's only escaped serious damage because of the prompt action of two firewatchers. The church was hit by an incendiary bomb but the firewatchers were able to keep the flames under control until the fire brigade arrived. Casualties would also have been much greater had decoy fires not been lit in open countryside in an effort to confuse the German pilots and lead them away from Nottingham. As a result of the fires many of the bombs fell on the fields of the Vale of Belvoir where the only reported casualties were two unfortunate cows and some chickens.

In his novel *Saturday Night and Sunday Morning*, the Nottingham-born writer Alan Sillitoe drew vividly on his own memories of working-class life in Nottingham during the war when he had his central character, Arthur Seaton, recall a bombing raid over the city:

He remembered his father digging up the back garden to plant an Anderson Shelter, Arthur stumbling into the hole and getting a clout for doing so. And later the family sat on the planks inside, coughing from the damp moist soil, scratching their scabied bodies, and listening to the weird-sounding hollowness behind Beechdale woods, his white-faced father rushing in at midnight, a teapot in one hand and half a dozen cups strung along the fingers of the other, having braved falling shrapnel to mash, back just in time to escape the Jerry plane that sprayed the factory with its machine-guns. In the long high-pitched whistle of a bomb the whole world was caught and suspended so that you just wondered, wondered, wondered, keeping quite still during the whistle, not breathing, not moving a finger, your eyes open wide, until the explosion on the railway yards or on a pack of houses in the next street made you glad to be still alive.

DIG FOR VICTORY

ON A

NOTTINGHAM
CORPORATION
ALLOTMENT

THE ESTATES COMMITTEE
HAVE PLOTS TO LET IN ALL DISTRICTS

Apply to—
ESTATES SURVEYOR
GUILDHALL - NOTTINGHAM

103 *Poster advertising new allotments for rent to 'dig for victory'.*

In spite of the bombing, morale generally remained high, and, under the leadership of Lt. Com. Mackness and his team, it is probably fair to say that the city remained united in its determination to meet whatever challenges and horrors the enemy threw at it. More raids followed and by the time the war ended more than 200 people had died in the raids and many more had been injured. There was, however, a widespread and grim determination to see it through, and a belief that almost everyone had a part to play in the struggle. School children collected scrap metal and waste paper, acted as 'knockers-up' to alert fire watchers, collected and delivered ARP helmets and other equipment, and dug up their playing fields to produce more food and 'dig for victory'. Women in the WVS put together food parcels and knitted socks, gloves and pullovers for the troops; men who were too old or too young to fight enlisted in the Home Guard, and as the war went on the numbers volunteering for ARP responsibilities continued to increase.

As in the First World War, the role of women was enormous. As well as maintaining their families, women joined the Land Army, the Auxiliary Territorial Service (ATS), and again took over the jobs once done only by men. Women became bus conductresses, railway station porters

104 *Women ATS volunteers at Chilwell, c.1940-1.*

and guards, and worked in munitions factories. At Chilwell the First World War shell-filling factory was considerably enlarged during 1940 and 1941 to become the country's principal ordnance depot, employing more than 16,000 people by 1943. Women were recruited not only to work in the offices but also to service tanks and drive lorries. By the end of 1943 4,000 ATS women worked at the depot, alongside 5,000 soldiers and 7,000 male and female civilians. The depot played a central role in the preparations for D-Day, packing and despatching more than 35 million items of kit and equipment for the Normandy landings. To celebrate the good work women were doing, the corporation organised a Women's Day in November 1941, culminating in a parade of women war workers through the centre of the city.

Many of the city's textile factories were soon working entirely on orders from the armed forces and Raleigh's factories were adapted entirely to munitions production, producing fuses, igniters, timers, cartridge cases, trench mortars and shells for anti-aircraft guns. Raleigh was now employing 9,000 men and women, and to meet War Office orders the factories worked night and day, and shifts could be very long.

When the news of Germany's surrender came, on 7 May 1945, huge crowds celebrated by singing and dancing in the Old Market Square in front of the Council House, which, for the first time in nearly six years, was lit up with flood lights. Churchill's victory speech was broadcast on loudspeakers the following afternoon, the official VE Day, before a short celebratory service of thanksgiving conducted by the Bishop of Southwell, community singing, and the King's speech at 9.00 p.m. There was great joy and great relief, but not everyone could celebrate. Many lives had been devastated by the loss of loved ones; the war was not yet over for Japan was yet to surrender, and VE Day was also, of course, the fourth anniversary of the awful night when so many had died in one bombing raid.

From Post-War Recovery to the Twenty-First Century

In some respects the challenges of 1945 were not unlike those which had faced the city after the First World War. In spite of the great achievements of the inter-war years there was still a shortfall in the number of houses in the city when the Second World War began and almost all house building had halted. Although the population of the city was growing only slowly in the 1940s and 1950s, reaching 306,008 in 1951 and then peaking at 311,899 in 1961, the number of households continued to grow more quickly, and the great task of clearing away and replacing unhygienic 19th-century slums was still far from completed. A thorough survey commissioned in 1947 reported five years later that more than 11,000 houses were in a poor or unfit state, mainly in the St Ann's area and the Meadows, and the situation of the latter was made worse than ever by the floods that followed the terribly cold winter of 1946-7. The floods, caused by a rapid thaw in the spring of 1947, led to polluted, sewage-laden water flooding 7,000 houses in the Meadows.

Government approval for tackling the city's remaining slums did not come until 1955. New house building, however, restarted soon after the war ended, with the erection of the first 'pre-fabs' on the Beechdale Estate in 1946. Prefabricated houses were soon also being built on a number of other pre-war estates and in 1950 a beginning was made on an enormous new council house estate at Clifton. The land had been purchased by the corporation in 1945 and in 1951 permission was gained to extend the city boundary yet again to incorporate Clifton and South Wilford. Slum clearance on a major scale only

105   *Women working on an ammunition assembly line at Raleigh.*

106   *Prefabricated houses on the Bilborough estate.*

107   *The cover of the 50th Anniversary Edition of Alan Sillitoe's novel about working-class life in 1950s Nottingham,* Saturday Night and Sunday Morning.

began in the 1960s when the corporation turned its attention to the areas of bad housing identified in the 1947 survey. During the 1960s and 1970s vast areas of late 19th-century housing were swept away by the bull-dozer. Tenants had complained for years about the lack of inside toilets, rotting window frames and damp walls, and a survey of the St Ann's district, undertaken by a Nottingham University adult education class in 1965-6, drew national attention to the poverty and deprivation of this area.

Most people were, however, much better off now than they had been before the war, and were well aware of it. A sense of this new working-class affluence was captured by Alan Sillitoe in another passage from *Saturday Night and Sunday Morning*, which was first published in 1958. Arthur Seaton is thinking about his work as a lathe operator in the Raleigh factory, where he usually earns about £14 per week on piece rates:

> The thousands that worked there took home good wages. No more short-time like before the war, or getting the sack if you stood ten minutes in the lavatory reading your *Football Post* – if the gaffer got on to you now you could always tell him where to put the job and go somewhere else. And no more running out at dinnertime for a penny bag of chips to eat with your bread. Now, and about time too, you got fair wages if you worked your backbone to a string of conkers on piece-work, and there was a big canteen where you could get a hot dinner for two-bob. With the wages you got you could save up for a motor-bike or even an old car, or you could go on a ten-day binge and get rid of all you'd saved.

The new affluence, which brought a considerable increase in car ownership from the late 1950s, together with continuing demands for new and better housing, and the need to compete with the retail and office facilities of other cities, all meant that both the appearance and the character of the city were beginning to change rapidly in the 1960s. High-rise blocks of flats began to replace the traditional terraced houses such as the one Alan Sillitoe had been born and brought up in; great blocks of multi-storied offices began to appear on the skyline; the first large shopping centre was built, familiar landmarks began to disappear; and new, much wider, roads were approved and built, in some cases cutting through and destroying forever the city's ancient street pattern.

One of the first major new developments was the demolition of the Victoria Station in 1967 to make way for the building of the Victoria shopping centre and a multi-storey block of flats. Also in 1967, and more controversially, part of a new inner ring-road system was completed with the opening of Maid Marian Way on the west side of the city centre. The aim of the planners was to reduce the pressure of traffic and ensure more rapid movement, but the new road was (and is) an ugly dual carriageway cutting through the middle of some of the city's oldest streets and leaving the castle remote and almost cut off from the centre of the city. Among the historic buildings demolished to build the road was Collin's almshouses on Friar Lane, a fine example of the town's heritage, dating from the early 18th century and – unlike the Council House – much appreciated by Pevsner, who had called them 'a lovely group, one of the best almshouses of its date in England'.

The Victoria Centre was welcomed by most shoppers as a positive development for the city, but to provide a second major shopping centre on the south side of the city, to be known as the Broad Marsh Centre, one of the city's oldest and narrowest streets, Drury Hill, had to be demolished. Moreover, for a while it seemed possible that one of the city's very few surviving medieval houses, a fine half-timbered 15th-century house on Middle Pavement known as 'Severns', might also go. The city's heritage was clearly under threat and public

108   *Drury Hill, 1969.*

criticism of the Broad Marsh development began to swell. A public inquiry was demanded but by the time this met, in September 1971, a 13-acre site for the project had already been largely cleared, including Drury Hill, and another part of the city's medieval heritage had already disappeared forever. The corporation did agree, however, to move 'Severns' to a new site, opposite the castle, where it would be safe from developers and planners.

The Broad Marsh Centre project went ahead and was opened to the public in 1974. The debate which it had inaugurated would have lasting and very positive consequences. Public concern for conservation issues could no longer be ignored by the corporation's planners and during the 1970s and 1980s there would be numerous examples of close co-operation between various local amenity groups and planners. Moreover, in 1971 members of the public and the corporation who were concerned about conserving the city's heritage received a powerful boost when new legislation made it possible for the corporation to 'list' buildings of historical or architectural interest to protect them from demolition or major external alteration. The character and appearance of whole areas of the city could also be protected by designating them as conservation areas. An early success for both co-operation and conservation came with the project to develop the Lace Market. This was clearly an area of considerable historical interest but also one that had long been suffering decline and neglect. A well-planned and sensitive restoration programme succeeded in transforming the Lace Market into an attractive mix of residential and commercial properties, able to draw people back into the city centre and thus begin to reverse a long-established trend. More restoration and conservation projects followed. The rather run-down Brewhouse Yard buildings, the Victorian Theatre Royal and the George Green Windmill were all successfully restored in the 1970s and early 1980s, and in 1972 a major pedestrianisation programme for the city centre was begun, including the ancient Bridlesmithgate.

109   *Bridlesmithgate today.*

110   *Slum housing in St Ann's in 1952.*

Consultation with residents was an integral part of the planning for the new houses built in the 1970s to replace the 19th-century slums being pulled down in the Meadows, but the inspiration for this had been the determination of St Ann's residents to have their say a few years earlier, when the corporation had announced their intention to clear their area. The result for both areas was low-rise housing, traffic separated from pedestrians, and the modernisation – rather than demolition – of some of the better existing housing. The inhabitants of both St Ann's and the Meadows were very clear about what they did not want: high-rise tower blocks. Those which had been built in the 1960s were in many cases very unpopular with their residents. The social and structural problems that plagued the Basford Flats, erected between 1967 and 1971, led to their early demolition in 1985.

Unfortunately, the new estates which arose from the rubble and ashes of the old slums had their own problems. It was not long before the designs of both the St Ann's and Meadows developments, with their rows of terraced houses, small gardens and narrow lanes, were being described as a paradise for burglars and muggers. Moreover, the design of the new estates and the destruction of the old slums (both before and after the war) also came to be at least partly blamed for what many long-term residents saw as the greatest change to affect family life in the city in the 20th century: the decline in neighbourliness. In her study of Nottingham social history, *Family life in the Twentieth Century*, Julie O'Neill concludes, after conducting many interviews with local people:

> Some link [the decline of neighbourliness] to the slum clearances of the 1920s and 1930s when inhabitants, formerly pressed together in inner city slums, were dispatched to distant council estates where each family was separated from its neighbour by a fence and garden. Others see increasing materialism or the isolating influence of television since the 1950s as responsible. Yet others blame the increasing diversity of the population whether in the form of the mixture of social classes in the All Saints area, or the mixture of cultures and races in St Ann's or Sneinton where the common bond of living in the same neighbourhood is outweighed by cultural and language differences. Whatever the perceived cause, there is a common belief that neighbourliness no longer exists.

A typical interview was with an elderly resident who fondly recalled the St Ann's estate in the 1950s and 1960s:

> It might have been a deprived area but the people were marvellous. They were always ready to help one another and nothing was too much trouble for them. There wasn't much money about but we were happy. And it was safe to walk the streets without being set upon by thugs and hooligans.

Some other planning developments have proved to be more successful. From the 1970s onwards, the preservation of the city's heritage would be a major priority and by the late 1980s there was also a growing awareness of the possibilities of exploiting the city's history and heritage for tourist purposes. The success of the Jorvik Centre at York encouraged a private company to open the 'Tales of Robin Hood' on Maid Marian

III   *The former Shire Hall, built 1770; now the Galleries of Justice.*

Way in 1989. This also proved to be remarkably popular, especially with families with young children, and, encouraged by this, the Castle Museum then set up, in 1990, a permanent exhibition on the 'Story of Nottingham'. In 1994 the system of caves that had, fortunately, been preserved under the Broad Marsh Centre, were opened to the public, and the following year the Galleries of Justice were opened in the Lace Market. This was the culmination of an imaginative project to restore the old Shire Hall and County Gaol, which had lain empty and deteriorating for many years. They were now turned into a museum of the law combined with a courthouse for schools to use for 'mock trials', to help pupils understand the workings of the law and practise their debating and adversarial skills before a real judge.

The opening of the Galleries of Justice was also part of the continuing work to revitalise the Lace Market. During the 1990s, and on into the new millennium, one of the major themes of the city's development has been the renewal of areas of the city centre which had become run down or derelict. Considerable central government support, coupled with private investment, has made possible the redevelopment of a number of previously neglected areas, including the former Boots Island Street site and the former railway and industrial land between Carrington Street and Castle Meadow. The latter area in particular has been utterly transformed. Of the new buildings erected here, the Inland Revenue Offices on Castle Meadow are particularly outstanding. The Amenity Building, which is at the centre of the project and includes a sports hall and restaurant, has been described by Professor John Beckett as 'the most exciting building in the city'.

112   *Nottingham Canal at Wilford Bridge Lock; now used for leisure craft and part of the renewal and restoration of the Castle Meadow area.*

113 *Weekday Cross today; part of the restoration and renewal of the Lace Market area. Restaurant seating now fills the area once occupied by the ancient market place.*

Attractive modern building designs have helped establish the city's image as vibrant and forward-looking, and even the city's chronic problems of traffic congestion have been eased at least a little by a park-and-ride scheme, by the introduction of the 'supertram', running from the north of the city to the centre, and by a one-way traffic system (although this does have the capacity to baffle any visitor to the city travelling by car without a satellite navigation system).

The changing and improving appearance of the city is also indicative of a more profound change. Like so many other cities in Britain in the last 30 years, the economic base of Nottingham has shifted significantly. Manufacturing has declined and the tertiary and service sectors have expanded enormously. Far more people are now employed in restaurants, bars and night clubs than in making cigarettes, and the once great Raleigh Cycle Company has almost disappeared completely from the city.

Today, no bicycles are made in Nottingham and the numbers employed by Players is a mere fraction of the workforce of earlier decades, down to about 700 in 2010. Of the former 'Big Three' only Boots – renamed Alliance Boots plc following a merger with Alliance UniChem in 2005 – remains a major employer of local people. The decline in the once mighty Raleigh Cycle Company has been swift and dramatic, and all the more so because for more than 30 years after the war it enjoyed considerable success. The company recovered quickly after 1945 and during the 1950s enjoyed an export-led expansion. After purchasing most of its rival firms it completely dominated the British bicycle industry in the 1960s, producing 80 per cent of all the cycles made in the country. Production, however, peaked in the late 1970s, when it was producing 4 million bikes per year. In spite of the popularity of completely new 'fun' models such as the 'Chopper', the firm's market share was slipping, down to 40 per cent by 1981. During the 1980s it continued to lose money, unable to hold its market share against low-cost foreign competition. By the mid-1990s it was maintaining about a one-third share of the £300 million UK market, but a further blow came at the end of the decade with the winding down of the mountain bike craze. Hopes that a management buy-out in September 2001 might save production in Nottingham were disappointed. Just a few weeks after the buy-out the new company sold its Triumph Road site to Nottingham University, and when environmental protection issues complicated a proposed move to a new site nearby, the management decided to end cycle production in Britain altogether and move instead to the Far East, where wage-costs were much lower. The last Nottingham-made Raleigh bicycle came off the production line in November 2002. When the factory closed it was employing 600 people and making 500,000 bikes a year.

Today the city's largest employer is the Queen's Medical Centre, popularly known as QMC, which was opened by the Queen in July 1977, to the west of the city centre, close to the University of Nottingham. This was an important national as well as local and regional development, for this was the first ever purpose-built teaching hospital opened in this country. Today it is the largest hospital in the UK and the largest teaching hospital in Europe. It has more than 1,300 beds, employs more than 6,000 staff and serves a very wide regional area.

The opening and subsequent expansion of QMC, together with the considerable expansion of Nottingham Trent University in the heart of the city, and the construction of a £50 million Jubilee Campus for Nottingham University (fittingly on the site of the former Raleigh factory) have greatly boosted the student population of the city since the 1990s, and this in turn has helped stimulate the city's night life and leisure and sporting facilities.

Two developments especially stand out: the opening of the National Ice Centre in 2000 and the construction of a new leisure complex, The Cornerhouse, opposite the Royal Concert Hall. The National Ice Centre was an especially ambitious project. Built on the site of the 1930s Ice Stadium, it cost £40 million, just over half of this being provided by a grant from the Lottery Sports Fund, and can seat 7,500 people for ice events and 9,000 for concerts. Nottingham is an especially appropriate city to boast such a facility for it is the hometown of Olympic ice-dancing champions Jayne Torvill and Christopher Dean. Long before their greatest triumph, at the Sarajevo Olympics in 1984, they had spent countless hours in practice at the old Ice Stadium, and in April 2000 Jayne Torvill cut the ribbon to open its successor.

Sporting achievement – however ephemeral – has long been part of the city's sense of its own importance and value, dating back at least to the 19th century and pride in the exploits of Bendigo and its great cricketers of the 1880s and 1920s. Torvill and Dean's success in the 1980s raised the national profile of the city, but other sporting achievements also helped, and none more so than those of Brian Clough's Nottingham Forest, who twice won the European Cup, in 1979 and 1980. Moreover, the opening of the Holme Pierrepoint Centre in 1973 made Nottingham the national centre for watersports and during the 1980s the county cricket club, led by Richard Hadlee and Clive Rice, twice won

114   *Nottingham Trent University.*

115   *The Royal Concert Hall.*

116   *The Cornerhouse.*

117   *The Nottingham Playhouse.*

THE TWENTIETH CENTURY AND BEYOND 185

the county championship and every other cricket trophy. Today, alas, the city's sporting achievements are less evident. The county cricket club remains in the county championship but there are grave concerns regarding the financial health of Notts. County, and the great days of 'Cloughie', when Nottingham Forest could compete with the finest football teams in the land and beat them, seem something of a dream as the team struggles (and in May 2010 nearly managed) to gain promotion to the Premier League.

The city also prides itself in being a cultural centre for the East Midlands, and for many years successive city councils have been keen to promote this aspect of the city's image. Plans drawn up in the late 1950s for the building of a new theatre, the first new provincial theatre since the war, were part of a conscious effort by the corporation to improve the city's cultural facilities and its importance to the surrounding region. A change in party control on the council almost wrecked the plans, but in 1963 the Nottingham Playhouse opened and, led first by John Neville and then by Stuart Burge, it managed to quickly establish and maintain a fine reputation for innovative and imaginative productions. The restoration of the Theatre Royal in the 1970s was followed in the 1980s by the addition of a completely new Royal Concert Hall, forming the Royal Centre. Both venues can stage very large-scale productions, including, for instance, in 2010, the Moscow City Ballet at the Theatre Royal and great orchestras, including the Hallé Orchestra, the City of Birmingham Orchestra and the London Philharmonic at the Royal Concert Hall. The Playhouse has tended to offer an eclectic mix of drama, contemporary dance, children's theatre and folk and jazz music.

There is, however, another, dark, side to the city's image. Like many other cities, Nottingham also has to cope with problems of crime, drug abuse, prostitution, poverty,

118 *The Theatre Royal.*

homelessness and unemployment, all of which are closely related. In 1993 a Salford University study described the city as 'a blackspot' and in 1996 it was claimed that Nottinghamshire had the second highest rate of crime in the country. The city's social problems were much increased in the 1980s, in spite of improvements in the quality of the city's housing, by high levels of unemployment and the enforced sale of council houses. A survey of 1995 revealed a close relationship between poor health and social deprivation and a huge difference between the health of those living in socially disadvantaged areas of the city and those in more affluent areas. Studies of criminality show a similar picture, with a high concentration of both offences and offenders' homes in low-status neighbourhoods, both in the city centre and on suburban council estates, and it is also in these areas that the majority of the city's illegal drug users are to be found. Newspaper reports of gangs and drug-related gun crime in the city, with shootings in St Ann's and the Meadows, have badly tarnished the city's image in recent years. Race relations have also been a major problem for many years, but relations between the police and the Black Caribbean community and the various Asian communities have improved since the 1980s. In 1981 there was serious rioting in the Hyson Green area and in 1986 there were more disturbances following a series of street searches and forced entries into people's homes.

Concern about high levels of certain types of crime led in 2003 to the launch of the 'Respect for Nottingham' initiative, involving the close co-operation of the Nottinghamshire Police and Nottingham City Council with the Nottingham Crime & Drugs Partnership, Nottingham City Homes, the voluntary sector and various other local agencies. By adopting a series of simple practical measures the group planned to reduce significantly the incidence of begging, street prostitution, drug dealing and drug misuse, anti-social behaviour and litter. Surveys of local opinion had identified these as issues of

119   *The Nottingham 'Supertram'.*

particular concern, and in 2006, when the plan was given fresh impetus, alcohol-related disorder, youth disorder and vehicle-related crime were added to the list. Reports of alarmingly high crime levels, however, continued to damage the city's image. A 2006 Think Tank Report claimed that the city had the highest rate of serious crime in the country, including the highest rate for murder and vehicle crime. The report was hotly contested, with many pointing out that it had been based on too low a figure for Nottingham's population (omitting Clifton) and that if the entire conurbation of Nottingham was considered Nottingham was only 15th in the national crime ratings.

Fortunately, the latest crime figures for the city are much more encouraging. At the end of 2009 it was reported that the total number of crimes committed in the city had fallen dramatically in the previous two and a half years, from 59,663 to 44,098, a drop of 26 per cent. Numbers for almost all offences were well down on previous years, most notably vehicle crime offences, which had fallen 41 per cent since 2007, and burglary offences, which were down 34 per cent. The Respect report for 2009 gives some reasons for this success. Much has been achieved by introducing new preventative measures, improving facilities for young people living in deprived environments, and by helping prostitutes and drug and alcohol abusers change their lifestyles. At least equally important has been the increase in the number of patrols by police, Community Protection Officers and Police Community Support Officers, the expansion in the use of CCTV cameras, encouraging the creation of more neighbourhood watch schemes and the full use, wherever appropriate, of Anti-Social Behaviour Orders. The campaign against litter and graffiti has also reported much success in many parts of the city, although the Arboretum remains sadly neglected and litter-strewn. Straightforward measures such as installing an extra 1,000 new litter bins have helped considerably in reducing litter in the city and Respect's target for 2011 is that Nottingham should be the cleanest in the country in 2011.

A brief but fair assessment of the current state of the city today was made by Jon Collins, the Leader of Nottingham City Council, writing the Foreword to the *Respect for Nottingham* report in 2009. He said:

> Nottingham has seen many changes and improvements over the years … Visitors flock to Nottingham for its historic attractions, shopping facilities and nightlife. We continue to be one of the leading cities and whilst we can list our achievements, we are aware that we need to continue our focus on tackling crime and anti-social behaviour.

120   *Street sculpture on Chapel Bar today, by Richard Perry.*

The latest development in the city's continuing process of renewal and regeneration came in November 2009, with the opening of a new art gallery, Nottingham Contemporary, at Weekday Cross, at the heart of the old city. The gallery opened with a very successful exhibition of more than 60 works by David Hockney, followed early in 2010 by a futuristic fashion show. The City Council has invested heavily in this £20 million venture and would dearly love the city to become known principally for such positive developments. If the current decline in crime levels can be maintained there must be every chance that it will.

BIBLIOGRAPHY

The following is a list of the printed primary and secondary sources used in the writing of this book, not including general histories. A much more complete bibliography for the history of Nottingham can be found in *A Centenary History of Nottingham*, edited by Professor John Beckett.

Printed Primary Sources

Anon., 'Copy (by Dr Charles Deering) of a Ms Account of Nottingham (1641)', *Transactions of the Thoroton Society (TTS)*, 2 (1898)

Bailey, T., *Annals of Nottinghamshire: History of the County of Nottingham including the Borough* (4 vols), Nottingham (1853)

Blackner, J., *The History of Nottingham*, Nottingham (1815)

Deering, C., *Nottinghamia Vetus et Nova or an Historical Account of the Ancient and Present State of the town of Nottingham*, Nottingham (1751)

Felkin, W., *History of the Machine-Wrought Hosiery and Lace Manufactures*, London (1867)

Field, H. (ed.), *The Date Book of Remarkable and Memorable Events connected with Nottingham, 850-1884*, Nottingham (1884)

Garmonsway, G.N., *The Anglo-Saxon Chronicle*, London (1972)

Henson, G., *History of the Framework Knitters*, London (1831)

Henstock, A. (ed.), *The Diary of Abigail Gawthern of Nottingham 1751-1810*, *Thoroton Society Record Series*, 33 (1980)

Hutchinson, L., *Memoirs of the Life of Colonel Hutchinson* (2 vols), London (1806)

Morris, J. (ed.), *Domesday Book, Nottinghamshire*, Chichester (1977)

Napier, W., *The Life and Opinions of General Sir Charles James Napier* (4 vols), London (1857)

Orange, J., *History and Antiquities of Nottingham* (2 vols), London (1840)

Stevenson, W. *et al* (eds), *Records of the Borough of Nottingham, I-IX*, Nottingham (1882-1956)

Thoroton, R., *The Antiquities of Nottinghamshire*, London (1677)

White, W., *History and Directory of the County of Nottinghamshire* (1832, 1844, 1853)

Wylie, W.H., *Old and New Nottingham*, Nottingham (1853)

Secondary Sources

Amos, D., 'Nottingham's Health Pioneer, Philip Boobbyer, Medical Officer of Health for the City of Nottingham, 1889-1929', *Nottinghamshire Historian (NH)*, 69 (2002)

Barley, M.W. 'Nottingham Town Wall,' *TTS*, 69 (1965)

Barley, M.W. and Straw, F.I., 'Nottingham', in M.D. Lobel (ed.), *Historic Towns*, I, London (1969)

Beckett, J. (ed.), *A Centenary History of Nottingham*, Chichester (2006)

Beckett, J., *Nottingham; An Illustrated History*, Manchester (1997)

Beckett, J. (ed.), *The Thoroton Society; A Commemoration of its first 100 Years*, Nottingham (1997)

Bosworth, A., 'Nineteenth-century churches in Nottingham', *NH*, 46 (1991)

Bowyer, C., *Albert Ball, VC*, London (1977)

Brocklesby, R., 'How they lived: William Robinson, sr., Nottingham Hosier', *NH*, 11 (1973)

Bryson, Emrys, *Portrait of Nottingham* (1974)

Chambers, J.D., 'Nottingham in the early nineteenth century', *TTS*, 45 (1941)

Chambers, J.D., *Modern Nottingham in the Making*, Nottingham (1945)

Chambers, J.D., *Nottinghamshire in the Eighteenth Century*, London (1966)

Chapman, S.D., 'The evangelical revival and education in Nottingham', *TTS*, 66 (1962)

Chapman, S.D., 'Working class housing in Nottingham during the industrial revolution', *TTS*, 67 (1963)

Chapman, S.D., *Jesse Boot of Boots the Chemists*, London (1974)

Chapman, S.D., 'The Genesis of the British Hosiery Industry, 1600-1750', *Textile History (TH)*, III (1972)

Chapman, S.D., 'Enterprise and Innovation in the British Hosiery Industry, 1750-1850', *TH*, V (1974)

Chapman, S.D., 'The innovating entrepreneurs in the British ready-made clothing industry', *TH*, XXIV (1993)

Chapman, S.D., 'Birkins; the last of the Old Nottingham Lace Manufacturers', *NH*, 74 (2005)

Chapman, S.D., 'Sweated labour in the Nottingham lace industry', *NH*, 76 (2006)

Chapman, S.D., 'William Elliott of Brewhouse Yard (1701-1792): Hosiery Entrepreneur', *NH*, 82 (2009)

Church, R.A., *Economic and Social Change in a Midland Town: Victorian Nottingham, 1815-1900*, London (1966)

Church, R.A. and Chapman, S.D., 'Gravener Henson and the Making of the English Working Class', in E.L. Jones and G.E. Mingay (eds), *Land, Labour and Population in the Industrial Revolution*, London (1966)

Cuthbert, N., *The Lace Makers' Society*, Nottingham (1960)

Cooke, Sheila M., *Nottingham between the Wars*, Nottingham (1992)

Davis, S., *Nottingham; City Beautiful*, Derby (2009)

Edwards, K.C. (ed.), *Nottingham and its Region*, Nottingham (1966)

Erickson, C., *British Industrialists: Steel and Hosiery 1850-1950*, Cambridge (1959)

Foulds, T., 'The siege of Nottingham castle in 1194', *TTS*, 95 (1991)

Foulds, T., Hughes, J. and Jones, M., 'The Nottingham borough court rolls: the reign of Henry VI (1422-55)', *TTS*, 87 (1993)

Fraser, D., 'The Nottingham Press, 1800-1850', *TTS*, 67 (1963)

Gray, D., *Nottingham: Settlement to City*, Nottingham (1953)

Gray, D., *Nottingham through 500 years* (2nd edition), Nottingham (1960)

Gurnham, R., *A History of the Trade Union Movement in the Hosiery and Knitwear Industry,* Leicester (1976)

Hardy, C. and Arthur, N., *Nottingham at War*, Bowden (1986)

Haslam, M.J., *The Chilwell Story*, Nottingham (1982)

Iliffe, R. and Baguely, W., *Victorian Nottingham: a story in pictures* (20 vols), Nottingham (1970-83)

Manning, Ian, *Images of Nottingham*, Derby (1994)

Oldfield, G., *The Illustrated History of Nottingham's Suburbs*, Derby (2003)

Pevsner, N. and Williamson, E., *The Buildings of England, Nottinghamshire* (2nd edition), London (1979)

Richards, C., *Nottingham Through Time*, Stroud (2008)

Seddon, P.R., 'Colonel Hutchinson and the disputes between the Nottinghamshire Parliamentarians, 1643-45: new evidence analysed', *TTS*, 98 (1994)

Stafford, P., *The East Midlands in the Early Middle Ages*, Leicester (1985)

Stapleton, A., *The Churches and Monasteries of Old and New Nottingham*, Nottingham (1903)

Thomis, M., *Old Nottingham*, Newton Abbot (1968)

Thomis, M., *Politics and Society in Nottingham, 1785-1835*, Oxford (1969)

Victoria County History, *Nottinghamshire*, I (1906), II (1910)

Wardle, D., *Education and Society in Nineteenth-Century Nottingham*, Cambridge (1971)

Weir, C., *Nottingham, A History*, Chichester (2002)

Wells, F.A., *The British Hosiery and Knitwear Industry; its History and Organisation* (2nd edition), Newton Abbot (1972)

Whitworth, D., *A Century of Nottingham*, Stroud (1999)

Wood, A.C., *A History of Nottinghamshire*, Nottingham (1937)

Wood, A.C., 'Nottingham 1835-1865', *TTS*, 59 (1955)

Wyncoll, P., *Nottingham Chartism*, Nottingham (1966)

Wynne-Thomas, P., *Trent Bridge, A History of the Ground to Commemorate the 150th Anniversary, 1838-1988,* Nottingham (1988)

Young, C.S.B., 'Excavations in Nottingham', *TTS*, 74 (1970)

Young, C.S.B., 'Excavations in Nottingham', *TTS*, 75 (1971)

Young, C.S.B., 'Excavations in Nottingham', *TTS*, 76 (1972)

Young, C.S.B., 'Excavations in Nottingham', *TTS*, 78 (1974)

INDEX

The index lists only principal subjects and selected persons and places. Pages which include illustrations are shown in *italic*.